Aniruddha Bose is an Associate Professor of History at Saint Francis University, Pennsylvania, USA. He is the author of *Class Conflict and Modernization in India: The Raj and the Calcutta Waterfront (1860-1910)* (Routledge, 2018). Originally from Calcutta and Mumbai, Aniruddha currently lives in the United States. With family links in the Indian railways, he strongly believes in writing histories of ordinary people who, working together, can change the world.

SHUNTING THE NATION

India's Railway Workers and the Most Tumultuous Decade in Modern Indian History (1939–1949)

Aniruddha Bose

SPEAKING
TIGER

SPEAKING TIGER BOOKS LLP
125A, Ground Floor, Shahpur Jat, near Asiad Village,
New Delhi 110049

First published by Speaking Tiger Books 2023

ISBN: 978-93-5447-529-0
eISBN: 978-93-5447-535-1

10 9 8 7 6 5 4 3 2 1

Typeset in Sabon Roman by SŪRYA, New Delhi
Printed at Shree Maitrey Printech Pvt. Ltd., Noida

Contents

Introduction

IN AUGUST 1947, India's leaders, with the support of the departing British, partitioned India into two countries: India and Pakistan. The motives of the Indian leadership and the departing British are well-documented though still disputed by historians. What is not in dispute, however, is that Partition resulted in a ghastly humanitarian catastrophe. The death toll is uncertain, but even the most conservative estimates place it in the hundreds of thousands. It was the single most lethal political disaster in the region's history. The estimates of the numbers displaced are similarly unclear but likely exceed 10 million. This makes Partition the biggest refugee crisis, not only in the region's history but also in terms of world history, rivaling in scale the refugee crisis precipitated by the Second World War. While the historical archive of the complex high-level politics that brought on this crisis is extensive, documentary evidence of the experiences of ordinary participants, survivors and perpetrators are relatively fewer. A combination of factors, including the deliberate suppression of memory, has resulted in a deafening silence of how ordinary Indians experienced Partition. The two following anecdotes are among these.

Around the time of Partition, the date is unknown, a train from Moradabad, United Provinces (UP), pulled into New Delhi railway station. The city was in the throes of sectarian religious riots. A vast refugee camp had come up in the Purana Quila neighborhood, temporarily providing many of the city's Muslim residents a last resort. Other, bigger camps were sprouting up, filled with refugees fleeing West Punjab, now in the new territory of Pakistan. The camps were getting crowded with traumatized Hindus and Sikhs, who brought harrowing tales of massacre and flight. Roving mobs of armed Hindus and Sikhs stormed the city's Muslim neighborhoods and hunted wandering Muslims in other parts of the city. As the train pulled into Delhi, the crew watched, with growing apprehension, signs of destruction everywhere. The crew had every reason to fear for their own safety. The engine driver was Muslim. The crew were well aware that lone Muslims were in grave danger. As the train approached the railway station, the engine crew decided to take no chances. The two Hindu firemen helped the Muslim train driver clamber into the train's water tank. It was a precarious hiding place. The tank was filled with water. If the train driver stood still, the water reached up to his neck. He had to remain silent.[1]

The precautions were entirely merited. As the two firemen waited on the railway station, an armed Hindu mob approached them. They were looking for the Muslim train driver. They had clearly been tipped off. Demonstrating an admirable presence of mind and courage, the two firemen elaborated a tall story. They claimed their Muslim train driver had abandoned the train and run away. The firemen even convinced the armed mob that they would report their comrade, and he was sure to lose his job. The firemen's subterfuge worked. The mob left them alone. The two firemen then drove their train out of the station. Once outside the city and clear of danger, they helped their engine driver out of the water tank. Showing amazing chutzpah, the driver was able to resume his duties and he safely drove the train back to Moradabad.[2]

This extraordinary narrative comes to us from the memoir of D.V. Reddy, who went on to serve as a high-ranking officer in the Indian Railways. At the time, Reddy held an important position at the Moradabad junction. In his memoir, Reddy claimed that he and other senior officers were fully aware of the dangerous situation in Delhi. In fact, they had taken steps to protect their staff and had worked out rosters to make sure that no Muslim crewmen operated any trains heading to the capital. This particular event was the result of a terrible lapse in the rostering process. Reddy's memoir makes clear his own relief that the Muslim driver had survived his ordeal relatively unscathed. His memoir was also complimentary towards the firemen who had so bravely and effectively protected their comrade.[3]

There are similar narratives that emerge from what became Pakistan. Here the roles were reversed. The country, especially in its West wing, had a significant Muslim majority. Even in East Pakistan, Muslims outnumbered Hindus in considerable numbers. These lopsided figures were exacerbated as Hindus and Sikhs fled with the approach of Partition, and Muslim refugees, from territories that were clearly going to remain in India. Many refugees left expecting to return, unaware that the scale and extent of bloodletting would make their return journey impossible. In any case, the bloodshed in Pakistan became no less intense than in India. Hindus and Sikhs found themselves in desperate circumstances with their lives on the line. For many, survival often came down to the support and solidarity of Muslim friends and colleagues. In 2017, the journalist Kabir Taneja chronicled his grandfather's harrowing experience while an employee of the North Western State Railway (NWR) company.[4]

Taneja's grandfather came from the Pashtun-dominated regions in territories that were to become Pakistan. From a small village called Kundal, on the banks of the Indus River, Taneja's grandfather, at the time of Partition, had gained a position with the NWR company as a trainee. He was working his way up to the position of Guard, usually stationed in the Break Van that brought up the rear of a train. Once again, the date is unknown, though most likely sometime in August of 1947. Taneja's grandfather was in training at the Mari Indus railway station, located in West Punjab. Taking no chances, his family had relocated to Mathura, in the United Provinces, a region certain to remain part of India. Taneja's grandfather still had his work to think about, and so was at his post on the morning of the incident, in the Brake Van of a passenger train headed for Ferozepur located in Central Punjab. Suddenly, a well-armed mob entered the railway station looking for Hindus and Sikhs.[5]

Once again, the solidarity of railway workers overcame the bigotry of religious sectarianism. Taneja's grandfather had a Muslim supervisor who helped keep him safe. While the mob rampaged through the passenger compartments, this Muslim supervisor got Taneja's grandfather a cap generally worn by Muslims, and a Muslim-sounding name to go with it. He then instructed Taneja's grandfather to keep his head down and pretend to be busy with some paperwork. When the mob approached the Brake Van and insisted that they had heard of a Hindu trainee on board the van, this supervisor fended them off. Keeping a cool head, the supervisor informed the mob that the Hindu trainee hadn't turned up that day and that his trainee for the day was, in fact, a Muslim. He even called out to Taneja's grandfather using his (made up) Muslim name, to which Taneja's grandfather responded with the Muslim greeting '*assalamalaikum*.' The supervisor even had the presence of mind to notice, much to his horror, that Taneja's grandfather's trunk was visible to the mob. The trunk had his real name painted on it. Discreetly, the supervisor shoved the trunk aside with his foot. Convinced by the performance, the mob left. A section was to return later, only to be stopped once again by the supervisor. They later found out that the mob killed many of the train's Hindu and Sikh passengers.[6]

This narrative survived in the form of memory. Narrated by Taneja, he had heard the story from his grandfather, a man who would go on to serve as a Brake Van guard for another 34 years. Taneja's grandfather, however, served those 34 years away from the Mari Indus railway station, and the Mari Indus-Ferozepur line. He served out his working years as a refugee in India, like over 100 thousand railway workers whose lives and careers had been turned upside down by the partition of British India.[7] There are gaps in the narrative, as there are in the memoirs of D.V. Reddy. Taneja's grandfather's supervisor remains anonymous, as do the crew on board the train in Delhi. But, more importantly, neither narrative gives the reader any insight into the competing motives of the actors involved.

Do the two incidents narrated above simply constitute normal behavior—good people doing good things? Or do they represent something else—class solidarity neutralizing religious conflict? The evidence is unambiguous. Indian (and Pakistani) railway workers transported millions of refugees across newly created borders with an efficiency unmatched in the history of public transportation. Their ability to transport such vast numbers was in fact not matched in scale by any public transportation system until perhaps 70 years later when the COVID-19 pandemic forced millions of laborers to leave India's cities for their homes. This time too, India's railway workers managed a herculean feat. But the feat of Partition remains unmatched for at least three reasons in addition to scale. First, the partition of India included the partition of the Indian Railways. Specifically, this meant the partition of the two most important railway systems necessary for the transportation of refugees, the Bengal and Assam Railway (BAR) company and the NWR company. The disruption was extensive but miraculously minimized through the extraordinary efforts of the workers of the two railway systems. Second, Partition was driven principally by the idea that Hindus and Muslims constituted separate nations and, therefore, could not coexist in a united, free India. The founders of Pakistan made clear their belief that Muslims could not survive as minorities in India. This, of course, created a dilemma for the tens of millions of Muslims who lived in what became India, including tens of thousands of Muslim railway workers. Indeed, many Muslim railway workers left India for Pakistan at this moment of crisis. The disruption of their departure was only exacerbated by the reverse flow of Hindu and Sikh railway workers from what became Pakistan. The number of railway workers-turned-refugees exceeded 100 thousand. Nevertheless, the laborers who stayed at their posts were able to keep the system functioning. Finally, Partition became a bloodbath in Bengal and Punjab, with the latter turning into a warzone. Trains carrying large numbers of desperate refugees became targets for attack by heavily armed mobs on both sides of the border. Nevertheless, Indian and Pakistani railway workers went on to transport 3 million refugees in less than three months. How was this possible?

This is not the only miracle of this era. Indian railway workers had performed another extraordinary task just a few years earlier. In 1939, the government of British India, without the consent of its subjects, declared war on Germany and Italy. Dragged into the Second World War, the Indian railway workers facilitated an initial buildup of the Indian military and its departure to fight Britain's wars on faraway shores. In the initial stages of the war, Indian railway workers sacrificed equipment and labor to build and support railway systems in British Iraq and elsewhere while carrying on their work in India. The challenge increased exponentially when the Japanese war machine smashed into the bloated British Empire in 1942. The Australian and Indian armies' heroic efforts faltered, and the much-vaunted British Navy came a cropper. By 1943, Japanese armies and their Asian allies, including Subhash Bose's rebel Indian *Azad Hind Fauj*, were on India's doorstep. Battered and beaten, the British Indian Army called on India's railway workers to facilitate the impossible and help mount a desperate defense of India's remote eastern borders. There is little doubt, notwithstanding the heroic fighting of the British Indian Army, this frontline would also have fallen without the support of the Indian railway workers. It is also important to note, in the period 1943–1944, eastern India witnessed two great human calamities. One, the flight of half-a-million Indian refugees from Burma, unaided by the British authorities, which led to the death of thousands. The second was the catastrophic carnage of the Bengal famine, deliberately fostered by Churchillian racism and compounded by British-Indian administrative incompetence; it killed 3 million Indians, a death toll far exceeding that of wartime Britain. Indian railway workers labored through all this, ensuring not just the defense of India but the rebuilding of India's war machine. The latter effort succeeded to such an extent that the Allies were able to launch a successful counter-offensive on the Burma front by 1944. This counter-offensive broke through the Japanese lines and pushed deep into Burma, quickening the collapse of Japanese defenses in Asia and helping bring the war to an end. None of this was possible without the extraordinary efforts of the Indian railway workers. This book also asks, how was this possible?

During these years, Indian railway workers were also at the forefront of India's freedom struggle. The decade 1939–1949 coincided with the culmination of this movement, resulting in independence from British rule. This struggle peaked in 1942 during the Quit India movement. The most violent and extensive uprising in almost a century, the movement posed special challenges for India's railway workers. In 1942, British India was at war with Fascist Germany and Italy, and its relationship with Japan was precarious. Indian railway workers were very much committed to the destruction of fascism, notwithstanding their unhappiness about the manner in which India's British masters had dragged the country into fighting the war. The Quit India movement, explicitly aimed at overthrowing British rule by any means, put Indian railway workers in a very difficult place. They were torn between conflicting objectives. On the one hand, they had to consider their role in fighting fascism, and on the other, in overthrowing British imperialism. The overwhelming majority of Indian railway workers resolved this conflict by prioritizing the fight against fascism. They continued to make great efforts to keep the railway system operational while extending moral support to the Quit India movement. This, however, created a new problem. The British Indian government began to use the Indian railway system to crush the Quit India movement using increasingly brutal methods, making the railway workforce complicit in the terror unleashed by the colonial state. As the movement escalated, it increasingly placed Indian railway workers in the crossfire. The second moment of political unrest came at the end of the Second World War. The decision of the British Indian government to try officers of the rebel Azad Hind Fauj on charges of treason led to popular protests on the streets and mutiny in the Royal Indian Navy (RIN). It was easier this time around. Indian railway workers didn't have to make difficult choices between fighting imperialism and fascism. Instead, they threw in their support with the uprising. Within months, the British government was negotiating its own exit plan. How did Indian railway workers make their choices so effectively? How did these get implemented? How was any of this possible?

Faiz Ahmed Faiz called Independence 'not the dawn hoped for.' He was lamenting Partition in particular, but the problems of newly post-colonial India and Pakistan were manifold. Two centuries of exploitative imperialism had left the region wretchedly poor. Virtually the entire population was severely undernourished, with the threat of famine looming large. Literacy rates were barely above the 10 per cent mark.

The healthcare system, like the education system, was all but non-existent. With the exception of some wartime industries, neither India nor Pakistan inherited much in terms of modern manufacturing. Their pools of skilled labor were constrained by the absence of training and opportunity. In addition, both countries had emerged in a precarious post-war world. The great powers, with the honorable exception of the USSR, were to a greater or lesser degree hostile to the idea of decolonization. American imperialism was at its peak, orchestrating coups and counter-revolutions across the globe, while European imperial powers scrambled to restore their lost or weakened empires. Internally, Partition had created terrible wounds that went beyond the partitioned provinces of Bengal and Punjab. The events of 1947 encouraged separatism based on region and language that threatened the balkanization of the entire region. Both countries risked falling into anarchy and chaos, with implications for the world. It was at this moment of crisis that Indian and Pakistani railway workers emerged as critical nation builders. The data from both countries is unambiguous. Despite all the disruption created by Partition, the railway systems in both countries emerged stronger in the years after Independence. Not only did the quality of service improve substantially, but the working conditions of the vast majority of railway workers also became more humane. At times, especially during moments of crisis, Indian and Pakistani railway workers went beyond their regular duties to help address national and regional emergencies. Strikingly, all this was achieved using financially sound methods; in fact, the finances of both railway systems emerged stronger after Independence. Their success was a clear repudiation of British management and the claims of an efficient British Empire. How was all this possible?

Finally, there was the problem of class conflict. The Indian railway system was a thoroughly modern enterprise. With the first railway lines laid down in the mid-nineteenth century, the entire railway system had emerged out of a capitalist-economic system fueled by finance capital and the exploitation of labor. There were vast variations in organizational systems and great changes that had transformed the Indian Railways since its origins in the mid-nineteenth century. Class conflict was endemic to the experience of the railway workers, particularly so in this decade. At a fundamental level, the interests of the management and labor were in contradiction, but several factors exacerbated and complicated tensions in the workplace. Indian social identity included hierarchical identities of caste, gender and religion. Railway managers sought to use these pre-existing forms of hierarchy to further the profit motive, creating new forms of control and fashioning new forms of conflict. In addition, the centrality of racial categories and racist ideologies to imperialism made race a critical feature of class conflict in twentieth-century India.

The decade 1939–1949 exacerbated these existing fault lines as war and political upheavals brought dramatic changes in the social landscape. The Second World War, bringing with it sharp increases in the cost of living, had an immediate effect on class conflict. The tensions of India's struggle for independence worsened race relations, and racist hierarchies became harder to maintain in light of Britain's fading grip on the country. The approach and eventual arrival of Independence energized the organized labor movement, creating opportunities for working people in India and, after partition in Pakistan, to more effectively fight for a fairer and more humane workplace. The decade ended with substantial improvements in working conditions and wages for the railway workers in India and Pakistan, with great promises of an even better future. All this was a far cry from the early part of the decade when incremental improvements were all that were on offer. This book asks, how was this possible?

There are many fine books on the history of Indian and

Pakistan Railways. The scale and importance of the railway system in the region's history has resulted in the writing of a substantial corpus of literature that dates back to the mid-nineteenth century.[8] The continuing importance of the railway system in India, and to a lesser extent in Bangladesh and Pakistan, has fostered a considerable interest in the field that has not faded with time. In fact, the importance of the railway system in India, as well as the general nostalgia that its history evokes in the region, has contributed in no small measure to a continued interest in the field. That nostalgia extends beyond the boundaries of South Asia and into the wider Anglophone world, where nostalgia for the British Raj, and the Indian Railways in particular, remains strong. Consequently, this is a field that has enjoyed considerable attention in the last twenty years, with several articles and books examining various aspects of the Indian railway history. In a 2016 review article, Ian Kerr noted that much of this historiography has been driven by a recognition of the 'multidimensional ways in which the railways were central to the making of modern India.'[9] Some of this literature has focused on the economic impact of the Indian Railways on the region. Bibek Debroy, Sanjay Chadha and Vidya Krishnamurthi's *Indian Railways: Weaving of a National Tapestry* is a recent example.[10] Debroy, Chadha and Krishnamurthi make a strong claim that Indian Railways have been central to the creation of an economically modern India. Others have examined the socio-cultural dimensions of this impact. Arup Chatterjee's *Purveyors of Destiny: A Cultural Biography of the Indian Railways* represents a recent intervention in this area.[11] Chatterjee chronicles the powerful and important place that Indian Railways holds in the national imagination. From films to fiction, Chatterjee underlines the centrality of India's railways to the country's cultural heritage.

There is less writing on railway labor. While the nostalgia-driven writing authored by British visitors remains enamored with cliches steeped in Orientalism and rose-tinted visions of the Empire, this gaze does not extend in any meaningful fashion to the railway labor force. There is some well-developed literature on the post-Independence period, especially covering railway labor in India, but the colonial period is relatively underdeveloped.[12] There are important exceptions. Ian Kerr's *Building the Railways of the Raj, 1850–1900* remains an inspiring text on Indian railway labor in the nineteenth century.[13] Underlining the monumental task of constructing and engineering India's railway system, the book is a comprehensive narrative of its subject. There is less writing covering events in the twentieth century, though the subject has begun receiving some interest. This book builds on some of that recent research on the impact of twentieth-century transformations on railway labor. In particular, Laura Bear's deeply psychological study of Anglo-Indians in *Lines of the Nation: Indian Railway Workers, Bureaucracy, and the Intimate Historical Self*, and Nitin Sinha's study of railway labor politics in 'The World of Workers' Politics: Some Issues of Railway Workers in Colonial India.' Both texts are sophisticated studies on Indian railway labor in twentieth-century British India, though neither author delves into the crucial 1940s period. Laura Bear's research highlights the role played by the railway bureaucracy in shaping Anglo-Indians as a distinctive caste group within the railway labor force. Her research is of relevance in particular because Anglo-Indians remained a significant force in the Indian Railways through the 1940s. The waning in their numbers notwithstanding, this book argues that Anglo-Indians played an important part in the survival of this workforce. Nitin Sinha's study, on the other hand, highlights the limits of race-based identities in shaping class conflict.[14] The data presented in this book indicates, like Sinha's, the limits of identity politics as a survival strategy.

This book argues that Indian railway workers deployed a vast variety of strategies to survive the challenges of the 1939–1949 decade. In order to survive the challenges of India's mobilization during the Second World War, the Indian railway workers labored to transport ever greater quantities of freight and people through punishing resource constraints. They demonstrated ingenuity and innovative thinking to achieve their astonishing results. When faced with the twin pressures of India's freedom struggle and the British Indian state, the Indian railway workers demonstrated caution and continued to serve at their posts while extending moral support to the Indian National Congress and the Indian struggle at large. During the crisis of India's partition, Indian railway workers demonstrated astonishing commitment by remaining at their posts and keeping the Indian railway service functioning through the worst moments of the crisis. In fact, they transported millions of refugees in a very short span of time, a feat unmatched by any other railway service in history. Indian railway workers used a variety of strategies to survive class conflict in this period. These ranged from acts of everyday resistance, such as theft, acts of disobedience, etc, to more dramatic instances of organized unrest. There were, in fact, several serious strikes in the period. Finally, railway workers survived the challenges of the early years of Independence in India and Pakistan by demonstrating ingenuity and fortitude, managing the fallout of Partition and the resource shortages that threatened to cripple the two newly created countries. The railway workers showed an extraordinary commitment to their work and service to their newly created countries. They took decisions that catapulted their role in nation-building to a place of crucial importance. Considering the vastness and diversity of the workforce, variations in demography, functions, etc, these differences in survival strategies are hardly surprising. The sheer diversity of challenges, ranging from famine to retrenchment, also goes some way in explaining why Indian railway workers used a variety of survival strategies. The evidence indicates that the workforce was capable of flexibility and adaptability, two attributes that turned out to be critical in this decade of uncertainty and upheaval.

This book makes a second argument. While the evidence indicates that the railway workers pursued multiple survival strategies in this decade, it also suggests that one strategy in particular turned out to be the most important of all. This was the survival strategy of collective action. Throughout the 1939–1949 era, the single most important survival strategy adopted by the railway workers was a strategy of working together through organization to overcome the challenges of the moment. During the Second World War, for instance, the crucial decision of the Indian railway trade unions to prioritize the fight against fascism made the astonishing contribution of railway workers to the war effort possible. Similarly, in the critical 1945–1946 period, the decisions of the railway trade unions to throw in their support for India's freedom struggle made a powerful contribution to the stunning political developments that led to India and Pakistan's independence in August 1947. During the blood-soaked carnage of Partition, collective action again played an important role. The humanitarian efforts of Indian and Pakistani railway workers helped mitigate the trauma and tragedy of the biggest refugee crisis in world history. In the workspaces, class-based solidarity, time and again, helped overcome religious barbarism. The high degree of organization and the rich tradition of collective action were central to these processes. In fact, all evidence on class conflict highlights the importance of collective action and organization. While individual acts of disobedience, theft and other forms of resistance were important, nothing achieved results quite like organized, collective action. The biggest victories of the railway workforce came through strikes and were negotiated through talks between railway administrators and trade unions. Finally, collective action again turned out to be crucial in the immediate aftermath of Independence. Most importantly, the critical victories on the negotiating table between the Railway Board of both independent India and Pakistan, and the work of implementing the new labor-friendly policies were made possible entirely by the strength of organized railway labor. This book argues that the single most important survival strategy turned out to be collective action.

The significance of Indian railway workers in this moment of history cannot be overstated. As stated above, it is difficult to imagine a successful defense of India's eastern frontier in the face of Japanese aggression without the heroic role played by the Indian railway workers. Without their support, the British Indian Army would undoubtedly have struggled to resupply and reinforce its frontlines. Building on such a counterfactual, it's even more striking to consider a scenario where Indian trade unions decided to throw in their support to the Quit India movement, and not prioritize the war against fascism. A hostile railway workforce might have caused havoc and would certainly have ensured the collapse of India's defenses. This might have extended the duration of the war by at least another year. Similarly, with Partition, the role of Indian and Pakistani railway workers might have been very different had the workforce not been able to overcome sectarian fragmentation. In fact, an alternative scenario, where the railway workforce fragmented like much of Indian society during Partition would have created a far greater holocaust than what actually occurred in 1947.

The role of the Indian railway workers was also important to the nation-building project of this era. Although railway trade unions sat out the Quit Indian movement, its leaders made their commitment to Indian independence clear in multiple statements. In fact, their statements also clarified that while the railway workers had to prioritize the war against fascism, they were very much in solidarity with comrades fighting for India's independence. Their support was also important in the critical 1945–1946 period. A loyalist reactionary railway workforce might have complicated India's bid for Independence substantially. Post-Independence, the world watched with bated breath, many expecting the imminent collapse of the two newly independent countries. Once again, the railway workers in India and Pakistan played a critical role in ensuring their survival and stability. Frustrating the expectations of reactionary imperialists, the countries survived the shock of Partition. They instead demonstrated that successful decolonization was possible.

Indian, Pakistani and now Bangladeshi railway workers remain significant. The Indian railway workforce remains over a million strong. With revenues exceeding $19 billion, the Indian railway workers play an important part in India's economy. During the fiscal year 2019–2020, they transported 8 billion passengers and 1.2 billion tons of freight. Indian railway workers operate 100 thousand passenger trains and 8,479 freight trains. The Indian railway system remains among the world's largest and busiest, rivaled only by railway systems in neighboring China, and in terms of freight, the United States. Pakistan Railways employs over 70,000 people. With revenues of $340 million, the Pakistani railway workers also play a significant role in the Pakistani economy. During the fiscal year 2018–2019, they transported some 70 million passengers and over 5 million tons of freight. Bangladesh Railways employs almost 28,000 workers. Annually, railway workers in this system transport some 65 million passengers and 2.5 million tons of freight. These are substantial numbers.

The significance of railway workers in South Asia becomes even more clear once their part in India's fight against COVID-19 is taken into consideration. Between 1 May and 26 June 2020, Indian Railways transported some 6 million laborers from the wealthier part of the country to their home districts. In addition to maintaining COVID-19 protocols, the Indian railway workers coordinated with volunteers and NGOs to ensure food and other comforts for what was certainly the biggest internal migration crisis in history. During the preceding days, the railway workers kept the country's supply chains functional by transporting 5.2 million tons of food grains across the country. During the catastrophic Delta variant wave, they played a crucial role in transporting oxygen from oxygen-surplus states in the south of the country to the deficit states in the north. Indian railway workers transported 35,000 MT of Liquid Medical Oxygen to asphyxiating hospitals across fifteen states.[15]

Organized labor in South Asia, like elsewhere, presents a mixed picture. According to the International Labor Organization, there are twelve major unions operating across the country. Recent data indicates that union membership hovers around the 100 million mark and may be rising.[16] The growth of informal labor and contract work is a reality in the country's labor markets. There are also significant concerns with the protection of migrant labor and women workers. The labor force in India still lacks meaningful social security and general safety and security. The situation may be worse in neighboring Pakistan. An insightful article published in the influential *Dawn* newspaper stated that 945 trade unions with a membership of 1.8 million workers were active in the country. The specter of contract labor is also a reality in Pakistan. As is the absence of protection for women workers. The general lack of safety and security is shared with India. Here too, though, the number of unionized workers appears to be increasing.[17] There is less data on organized labor in Bangladesh. But the ILO indicates the presence of substantial labor organizations, perhaps rising in strength. Though the Bangladeshi workforce faces many of the same problems as in India and Pakistan.

The reduction of organized labor that began in the last quarter of the twentieth century was intimately related to the loss of confidence in Socialism that occurred around the same time. The weakening of the Third World following the debt crisis of the 1970s and 1980s and the subsequent collapse of the

Soviet Union energized the Global North and its allies around the world. The loss of faith in the power of Socialism morphed into a belief in the power of free markets and individual consumerism. There was some echo of this loss of faith in collective action in South Asian academia, where the Subaltern Studies movement in the 1980s made studies of small, as opposed to large communities, central to historical research on the region.

The events of the past few years have however revealed the critical importance of collective action and labor organization. In 2016, an estimated 180 million laborers struck work, demonstrating that class struggle was alive and well in South Asia. In 2020, following the catastrophic response of the Indian government to the COVID-19 pandemic in the form of a strict and all-encompassing lockdown, an estimated 10 million workers fled cities across India for the relative safety of the countryside. The government responded with regressive labor legislation that substantially eroded safeguards that made the country's workplaces humane and safe. In Uttar Pradesh, the country's largest state, laborers saw even basic rights, such as the eight-hour workday, revoked. In response to this unprecedented assault on the working class, ten of the country's largest trade unions organized a two-day general strike. An estimated 250 million workers joined the strike, making it the largest in recorded history.

That November strike was also the start of a farmer's protest movement that lasted for almost a year. Taking advantage of its majority in parliament, the Government of India pushed through three laws empowering big agricultural businesses at the cost of small, medium and marginal farmers. A coalition of 30 farmer unions marched on the capital and began a protest that at times drew in hundreds of thousands. The protest lasted through the worst days of the COVID-19 pandemic, when the farmer unions were careful, to other times when the protests escalated into nationwide confrontations. Despite the best efforts of the Indian government, and its cheerleaders in global finance and the corporate media, the farmer unions succeeded. In December 2021, the government agreed to withdraw all three contentious laws and, in an abject surrender, consented to all the other major demands of the farmer unions. The message from these events is unambiguous. Collective action and organization are critical. This book seeks to inspire all working people who aspire to collective action and organization. Eighty-two years ago, India's railway workers faced a decade of uncertainty. Their collective action and organization ensured their survival.

There are a few definitional clarifications necessary. This book occasionally uses the term railwaymen to describe the Indian railway workforce. The use of the term is not meant to indicate that this workforce consisted solely of adult males. Documentary evidence, in fact, indicates that a substantial number of children worked for the Indian Railways in this period.[18] Similarly, the use of the term railwaymen is not to imply that women were not a part of the railway workforce. The 1951 Census of India, in fact, states that 14,459 women worked for the Indian Railways.[19] The use of the term railwaymen is largely driven by the ubiquity of the term in the historical record, as well as in popular usage. Similarly, this book sometimes discusses the experience of railway workers as a whole through many of the chapters. This is not meant to indicate that the experience of management and labor were interchangeable or without conflict. To the contrary, there is considerable evidence of class conflict in this period, but much of this is discussed in the chapter on the subject. Elsewhere, the experience of railway workers is taken and discussed collectively. For instance, when discussing how Indian railway workers rose to the challenge of the Second World War or the Partition crisis, the book often places the experiences and survival strategies of the railway workers as a collective whole rather than distinguishing between the survival strategies of management and labor. This has been done not to underplay class conflict but for narrative and organizational reasons only. Finally, the use of the term Indian railway worker is complicated by India's independence and partition. The text tries to maintain a distinction between British India and independent India, and relies on the chronology of events to maintain that distinction. Similarly, it is not always possible to clarify that Indian railway workers also include workers who became Pakistani after Independence. Any reference to these workers as Indian is not meant to deny the sovereignty of Pakistan.

ONE

Defeating 'Fascist Hordes'

IN SEPTEMBER 1939, the British Indian Viceroy Linlithgow committed British India to war against Germany and Italy. The irony of waging war against fascism while running an authoritarian regime in India may not have occurred to the British Indian ruling class, but their decision led to the first of multiple crises that hit the world of Indian railway workers in the 1939–1949 decade. Indians paid a steep price for a war that might not have affected the country at all had it not been dragged into it without consent. The Bengal famine, entirely war-related and certainly exacerbated by the vindictiveness of British Prime Minister Winston Churchill, killed 3 million Indians. A figure that, as noted earlier, dwarfed the death toll suffered in Britain itself. This war constituted the first great crisis of the 1939–1949 era for the Indian railway workers.

The evidence from this period indicates that the workers used multiple strategies to survive the Second World War. The first of these was a strategy of innovative thinking and flexibility. A form of frugal innovation or *jugaad* as it is sometimes described in twenty-first-century economic jargon. The war reduced resources for railway workers while substantially increasing their workload.

Evidence indicates that railway workers used a form of jugaad to manage this change in circumstances. The second major survival strategy was the extensive use of collective action. Whether it was a case of surviving price increases or unreasonable demands related to the war, railway workers relied on collective responses to ensure that their workspaces remained humane and fair. The most important of these responses was a decision reached collectively in 1942, when faced with the threat of war approaching India's very borders, to prioritize the fight against fascism. The significance of this decision cannot be understated. It is probably the single most important explanation for the heroic and extraordinary effort that railway workers put into their work during this exceptionally challenging period in Indian history. Surviving the war and the catastrophic humanitarian disasters that accompanied it can only be explained by this commitment.

The War

The Second World War created many challenges for India's railway workers. In the early days of the war, the British who controlled Indian Railway Board, again, with no consultation with Indians, dispatched enormous resources to assist with the war effort in the British-occupied Middle East. At the same time, the Railway Board tasked the Indian railway workers with the mobilization and transportation of tens of thousands of soldiers from bases across the country to be shipped off to fight the British Empire's wars. During the second phase of the war, many of these challenges were exacerbated by the refugee crisis prompted by the British withdrawal from Burma and the abandonment of Britain's Indian subjects in the country. The arrival of Japanese armies there brought the war to India's borders, and the railway workers were tasked by the hopelessly beleaguered British Indian government to support the poorly led and utterly demoralized British Indian Army in its desperate defense of India's eastern frontlines. This second phase of the war also brought with it one of India's worst famines. While famines were all but endemic in British India, the Bengal famine stands out for its scale. It also unfolded in full public view, under the glare of mid-twentieth-century mass communication providing a much-documented piece of the horror of hunger in the British Raj. Finally, Indian railway workers were called upon to facilitate the buildup of Allied armies during the last year of war and support the eventual counterattack that helped bring Japan's war in Asia to an end.

Considering these challenges, the achievements of the Indian railway workers are astonishing. The statistical data indicates that over the course of the war, India's railway workers carried significantly greater numbers of passengers and greater quantities of freight. In the period 1938–1939, for instance, Indian railway workers transported 53,06,23,000 passengers. In the period 1945–1946, however, this number had risen to 104,43,44,000, almost a doubling of the railway system's passenger traffic. The increases in the quantity of freight, though less striking, were still substantial. In the period 1938–1939, the Indian railway workers transported 88,361,000 tons of freight. This rose to 10,06,30,000 tons in the period 1945–1946.[20]

The significance of the role played by the railway workers has been overlooked for too long. The evidence is unambiguous. The workers ensured the country's survival during the Second World War. There is little doubt that without the herculean effort of this workforce, India's defenses along its Eastern borders would have collapsed. The 1944 Japanese assault on positions along India's borders, in particular, could very well have succeeded. This in turn would have left the plains of Assam with its substantial resources open to Japanese armies. A successful assault there might have even left Bengal and Calcutta vulnerable. This was the most industrialized part of British India.

The situation was particularly fraught because of the presence of Netaji Subhash Chandra Bose and his Azad Hind Fauj. The rebel Indian army of liberation, allied with Japan. Their presence, in substantial numbers, in the Indian subcontinent would have had a major impact on the National Liberation struggle in India. It is very possible that the trajectory of India's march towards freedom would have been entirely different.

The significance of the role played by the Indian railway workers in many ways goes beyond the fate of British India. Considering the importance of the Indian subcontinent to the Allied war efforts, a collapse of India's eastern defenses would have had a devastating effect on the Allies as a whole. For instance, it is quite inconceivable that British India would have been able to provide substantial resources, both in terms of fighting units as well as equipment and assets necessary for the war effort. It is also, similarly, more than likely that a land-based counterattack on Japanese Asia might never have occurred. While none of this is to suggest that the overall course of the war might have changed or that a Japanese victory on India's borders might have swung the war in Asia in its entirety, the important role of the Indian railway workers in the shaping of the Second World War simply cannot be denied. It is in this context, therefore, that a clear understanding of their survival strategies becomes crucial. There is simply no way that this workforce could have performed its extraordinary role without developing a clear strategy to survive the war.

The war created many challenges for India's railway workers. During the initial stages of the war, this came in the form of a colossal loss of equipment. The British Indian government focused their efforts on supporting combat operations in Africa and Europe. The Indian railway workers supported this objective by exporting almost a tenth of its equipment to shore up British imperial defenses in the Middle East and North Africa.[21] This amounted to several crores of rupees. Between September 1939 and December 1941, the Indian railway workers lost some 1,500 miles of track, 206 locomotives and 8,000 wagons. They supplied railway turnouts, crossings, turntables and other kinds of specialized railway stores. In addition, the Indian Railways lost large quantities of rails, sleepers and rolling stock. All this equipment played an important role in the Allied defense of the Middle East and North Africa, eventually contributing to Allied victories in those theaters. The lines were crucial to the transportation of substantial cargoes of jute, tea and other goods to the embattled Soviet Union during the second half of the war. The lines also facilitated the movement of several trainloads of Polish refugees who settled in India for the duration of the war.[22]

In addition, the British Indian government also handed over railway workshops to the military for the production of munitions. Railway workers employed at these workshops quickly transitioned from peacetime to war production. They machined shells from bars and manufactured fuse bodies, detonator plugs, gun carriage components and several 100 thousand bayonets. Indian railway workers were the first to manufacture armor-piercing shots in India. Experts regarded these munitions of a quality that could easily match the best produced in Britain. In addition to ordnance, railway workers manufactured thousands of other items. These included motor lorry bodies, stirrups, tent poles and steel sleepers. They even manufactured miniature items consisting of electrical targets for the training of dive bombers, natural lighting effects for training fighting vehicle gunners and small valves for blow lamp oil cookers. Railway workers also made ammunition boxes, and machined grenade casts. As the war progressed, they expanded their production lines to include armored cars and field artillery tractors.[23]

The first phase of the war also forced many railway workers into the military. From the autumn of 1939, high-ranking officers left their railway jobs to take up military duties. These ranged from recruitment work to positions in ordnance factories by officers with technical skills. Many Indian railway officers were also reservists and left their jobs to take up positions in the army and navy. Finally, all members of the Royal Engineering Corp working for the Indian Railways below the rank of Lt. Col. left to take up active military duties. Among subordinate staff, many skilled workers and supervisory staff transferred, on a temporary basis, out of their railway jobs to take up work on munitions production.[24] As the war accelerated, larger numbers of senior officers left the Indian Railways to take up positions in theaters overseas as part of specialized Railway Military Units. These included jobs in construction, maintenance and operations. By the end of 1941, over 100 Class I officers were serving the Defense Department and another 25 were at work in the government's Supply Department.[25] By 1942, some 230 Class I officers had taken up active military duties. Many subordinate officers were working on emergency commissions in Railway Transportation Units, and 16,000 railway workers were now busy in the production of munitions in what had formerly been railway workshops. These laborers included workmen trained as fitters, copper and tin smiths, turners, machinists, blacksmiths, electricians and electroplaters.[26] Large numbers of men and supervisors were training in the Railway Military Units for service overseas. The commencement of Japan's war with the British Empire, however, constituted a turning point for Indian railway personnel. The increased demand for services halted the hemorrhage of personnel.[27]

That increased demand is clearly captured in overall statistics. Before the start of the war, 45 million passengers traveled 1.5 billion miles a month. During the war, this number jumped to 80 million passengers traveling 3 billion miles. Taken on an annual basis, this was a staggering increase. The number of passenger miles (total number of miles traveled by each passenger) rose from 18.7 million miles per annum prior to the war to 32.5 million in the period 1943–1944. During the period 1944–1945, passengers made 156 million more trips aggregating 6.3 billion more passenger miles. This was the equivalent of an additional 600 trainloads of people per day. The passenger traffic load often included refugees. In 1942, the Japanese invasion of Burma created one of the greatest refugee crises of the war as half a million British Indian subjects fled to India. Between February and June of that year, Indian railway workers ran 132 special trains to transport these refugees. During the most intense period of the crisis, Indian railway workers were moving between 3,000 and 6,000 refugees every day. [28]

The expansion was even more dramatic when it came to military traffic. Prior to the start of the war, the armed forces required an average of 29 special trains each month, traveling 8,000 miles. During the war, the number soared to 920 trains, running a million miles. At times, this translated into an extraordinary 5,50,000 military personnel a month. The transportation of military personnel was more demanding than civilian traffic. Troops generally traveled greater distances, and divisions expected to be transported together with their equipment. Each division required 20 passenger trains and a further 48 for their stores. Railway personnel also had to ensure that troops were able to maintain regular contact with their headquarters and replenish rations and water at predetermined intervals. Railway workers were tasked with a massive coordination effort as they raced to ensure that soldiers boarded their trains and arrived at their destinations at expected times. On average, each division required 20 trains. Complicating all such maneuvers was the secrecy necessary for military operations. All too often, railway workers found out about such movement plans only at the last possible moment. During the Japanese offensive of 1944, Indian railway personnel assisted in the transportation of three divisions over a two-

and-a-half-week period. This required the movement of 80 additional trains across what was already a very congested railway system.[29]

Military stores came with added complications. The provision of military supplies from overseas meant pressure at the ports, and dockworkers tried to load and unload ships as quickly as possible. This meant that railway workers had a special responsibility to transport goods in and out of ports on time. Inward and outward movement of military freight often ran into several 100 thousand tons a month. The workers operated about 30 special trains every day, some making exceptionally long trips, including between Karachi and Ledo, a distance of 2,760 miles. On average, every division was accompanied by 48 trains of equipment, including vehicles, guns and stores. Military equipment was often heavier and bulkier than regular goods, and these ranged from 'fractious mules to 25-pounder guns, from the Jeep to 16-wheeler trucks, from bulldozers to 10-ton cranes.' And with constrained supplies of cranes, Indian railway workers had to devise new methods of loading and unloading.[30]

Changes in traffic patterns often meant that railway workers were transporting the heaviest loads over routes not designed for such a purpose. They had to make arrangements for special ramps and sidings and at railway stations, for special cranes. They also had to provide for specialized rolling stock, or even adapt existing stock when specialized cars were unavailable. Train operators had to take care that their awkward cargoes had sufficient clearance when passing through bridges and tunnels. They had to ensure that their loads were not too heavy, especially when crossing bridges. To keep the Allied armies supplied, both in Burma and China, Indian railway workers transported stores 1,800 miles across the Indian subcontinent. This journey required transfers from broad to narrow gauge lines, from rail to river transport, and again onto rail before their final disembarkation. The maintenance of this system required 15 million wagon miles every month. During the peak periods of the war, railway workers were moving almost 1.2 million tons of essential military supplies every month. They were also transporting these goods over vast distances. Resupplying troops on India's northeast borders meant that railway workers were moving goods 800 miles on average.[31]

The increase in freight traffic was more modest, though still significant. Before the war, Indian railway workers transported 10 million tons of freight each month over 1.9 billion miles. During the war, this rose to 11.5 million tons carried over 2.5 billion miles. Two sets of commodities in particular required attention from the railway workers. The first was coal. Mined in the country's east, specifically in two provinces, Bengal and Bihar, the railway workers had to transport the commodity to all corners of the country. Most locomotives used coal. In order to supply the firebox of a NWR company locomotive, Indian railway workers had to transport coal well over 1,000 miles. The closure of sea lanes during the second half of the war only increased pressure on the railway workers. The second commodity was food grains, which had to be transported from surplus to deficit provinces across the country. This meant that during the period 1942–1943, Indian railway workers were transporting 2.5 million tons between Punjab in the north and Madras in the south, a distance of 1,700 miles or between the Central Provinces and the Malabar coast, a distance of 1,400 miles.[32]

Although Indian soil avoided active warfare, Indian railway workers suffered from Japanese air raids. On 5 December 1943, for instance, 250 Japanese airplanes carried out an air raid on the city of Calcutta. In addition to bombing the city port, the pilots targeted a Bengal Nagpur Railway (BNR) company depot. Among the munitions used by the Japanese were anti-personnel bombs. These exploded into high-velocity fragments of steel and shrapnel. The bombs pierced steel rails, effectively destroying the main line running through the depot. The bombing destroyed 50 railway wagons and a locomotive. The bombing badly damaged the goods yard and residences of railway staff, in particular those housing janitorial workers. Several workers were killed at the BNR company yard as they sought cover under corrugated iron sheds, wagons and latrines. These were unfortunately inadequate as bomb shelters. Anti-personnel bombs ripped through the structures, killing those sheltering under them. After the bombing ceased, railway workers assisted in the grim task of removing corpses. The Air Raid Precaution Controller for the Railways memorandum to the Home Department of the provincial government listed Sikh, Hindu and Christian volunteers of the BNR company sanitary staff as having assisted in the subsequent disposal of corpses.[33] Calcutta, in fact, suffered multiple air raids throughout the war, and the railway workers had to bear the brunt if not of the attacks themselves, then their consequences. On the night of 22–23 December 1942, a Japanese aircraft bombed Calcutta. Three separate raids left 25 civilians dead and over 100 wounded.[34] Many of the city's residents, fearing an imminent Japanese invasion, left. Railway workers operating trains out of Howrah, the city's main railway station, suddenly had to transport an extra 150 thousand passengers who had packed into the station overnight and wanted to leave the city.[35]

Through the war period, Indian railway workers evacuated no less than a million passengers out of Calcutta and elsewhere. There had been similar scenes of chaos in Madras, at the Central and Egmore stations, in April that year. On hearing reports of advancing Japanese troops, the Madras Presidency Governor ordered the evacuation of all non-essential residents in the city. On 8 April, panicked residents paid colossal sums for tickets out of the city (though probably not Rs 50,000, several times the annual average income of the province, as reported by a credulous American intelligence officer). Eventually, railway authorities announced that the services were free after all. During this period of panic, the government of India ordered the industrialist Hirachand Walchand to close his massive shipyard in Visakhapatnam on India's east coast and relocate its material to Bombay on India's west coast. The Indian railway workers transported substantial material and labor for this relocation.[36]

Imperialism

While many of these problems were the direct result of the war, other issues emerged out of India's position in the British imperial system. Among the most pressing of these was a sharp rise in food prices. While disruptions in war often lead to volatility in food prices, the situation in India was exacerbated by the imperialist nature of the British rule. For instance, while the British government instituted an elaborate and strict system of rationing in Britain to control food prices, the British Indian government took much longer to implement similar restrictions in India, with rationing introduced only in the last year of the war.[37] Consequently, high prices emerged as a significant problem. During the first months of the war, retail prices across the country rose sharply. By December 1939, the cost-of-living indices in the 15 towns and cities for which such figures were available indicated that prices had increased by 10 per cent since August that year. [38] These prices continued to rise. By the second year of the war, prices had risen by over a third in real terms.[39] Much of this increase was the result of expanded government spending. Over the course of the war, government money supply rose from Rs 3.17 billion in 1939 to Rs 21.9 billion in 1945. While this expansion did increase purchasing power, the expansion of war material production meant that the availability of consumer goods actually contracted. The cost-of-living index rose from a base of 100 in 1939 to 168 and 231, respectively, for the periods 1942–1943 and 1945–1946. The cost of essential commodities such as rice, wheat, cotton and kerosene rose even more sharply. The price of rice, for instance, rose nine-fold between 1939 and 1943. By 1944, the price of wheat stood almost four times its price in 1939. In 1943, the price of cotton was five times its cost in 1939. The price of kerosene, widely used for lighting, doubled between 1939 and 1943.[40]

Indian railway workers were also much affected by floods during the war years. In July 1941, for instance, floods on the Bombay, Baroda and Central India Railway (BBCI) dislocated traffic on the main line between Bombay and Delhi for a full three weeks. In the following year, floods breached a vital section of the increasingly crucial BAR company, disrupting traffic for four months. On the other end of the country, the Indus River breached its banks, resulting in considerable damage to the NWR system. The important city of Quetta was completely cut off for several months during this crisis. In November, a severe cyclone emerging from the Bay of Bengal brought all traffic between Calcutta and Madras to a grinding halt. The cyclone damaged the BNR system as well as the East Indian Railway (EIR) system. The worst of these storms, however, came in the year 1943. In July that year, floodwaters from the Damodar River in Bengal breached the tracks of the EIR system at multiple points. The disaster occurred at a particularly difficult moment for the Indian railway workers who were stretched thin by the demands of the war and the catastrophic Bengal famine. In 1944, railway lines across the Bombay, Baroda and Central India Railway were affected when both the Tapti and Narmada rivers in west-central India breached their banks. These floods were severe. The Narmada floods were in fact the highest on record since 1876.[41] There was nothing natural about these disasters. The British Indian ruling class had pursued, from the nineteenth century, a catastrophic flood control policy characterized by massive engineering projects driven by blind faith in prevailing scientific wisdom. In reality, these projects, most often in the form of embankments, resulted in the destruction of drainage systems painstakingly built up over generations. The new embankments, many of which the British Indian state constructed along railway lines, exacerbated floods across the Indian subcontinent.[42]

The worst of these crises of imperialism, however, was the Bengal famine. In 1943, an estimated 3 million Indians died in the eastern Indian province of Bengal from hunger and disease. There had been a fall in the availability of rice. A cyclone in October 1942, followed by torrential rain and a fungal disease, affected the autumn and winter crops that year. The Japanese occupation of Burma further disrupted rice supplies to the region. The wholesale price of rice rose sharply. From Rs 13–14 per *maund* (82.3 lbs.) in December 1942 to Rs 30 by May 1943. By October 1943, rice was being sold in the port city of Chittagong at Rs 80 and in December, the same year, it had reached a staggering Rs 105 per maund in Dacca. Deaths from starvation peaked in the late summer and autumn of 1943. Mortality rates rose till December and remained high subsequently as an enfeebled populace succumbed to famine-induced epidemics of cholera, malaria and smallpox. Rural districts across the province bore the brunt of the famine. The provincial capital Calcutta remained an exception. Its position as an important center of imperial commerce and war production ensured the city's workforce remained reasonably well fed. The city also housed a substantial Allied Army. Concerns about their morale also informed the decisions of the state to ensure that the city did not starve. The availability of food in the city attracted tens of thousands of hungry and starving destitute. A totally inadequate relief service ensured that thousands died in the city's streets.

Like flooding in British India, there was nothing natural about this disaster. The sharp increase in prices was the direct result of an expanded public expenditure leading to inflation. Military and civilian infrastructure expanded in Bengal in particular, contributing to the sharp rise in prices. The role of comprador capitalists was also substantial. Hoarding and speculation contributed to the price increase, and with the state playing its traditional role of protecting the interests of India's moneyed class, relief was nowhere on the agenda. The refusal of the British Indian government to carry out any kind of intervention provided the final lethal blow.[43]

Indian railway workers faced another great crisis in the form of a sharp contraction in coal production during the Second World War. This occurred in the year 1943, just when a hapless British Indian government had promised a record 25.5 million tons of coal to the Allied war effort, 'a larger quantity than has ever been made available before.' By December that year, the same administration looked at a 6-million-ton shortfall. The reasons were not difficult to identify. Coal mining was a hard job and was very poorly paid. Rising wages elsewhere, especially in the fast-expanding manufacturing sector, began attracting coal miners. There were also lucrative and easier jobs available on military construction projects. Furthermore, there was some evidence to suggest that mine owners, both British and Indian, were colluding in reducing coal production. The British Indian government had imposed duties on excess profits. India's mining millionaires had their own incentives to limit production.[44]

The consequences of this shortfall in production were substantial. India's jute mills, producing the single most important packaging material of the era, relied on coal for production. Jute had widespread use in military production, necessary for the manufacture of parachutes, fuel drums and even temporary aerodrome runways. All these ground to a halt when jute mills across eastern India suspended production for an entire fortnight. Every major industry faced cuts in coal supplies, with steel manufacturers particularly hit badly with a 20 per cent supply cut. Ordnance factories also faced shortages, with disruptions in the manufacturing of trucks in Lahore, and Howitzer guns in Ishapore. The Indian Railways was singularly affected. Its coal stocks fell to 15.7 days, almost half the industry standard minimum of 30 days. The shortages were so extreme that railway workers had trouble even transporting coal to distant parts of the railway network.[45] The pressure was heightened with the closure of sea lanes on India's east coast.[46]

Finally, the imperialist nature of the British Indian railway system ended up creating an additional challenge for Indian railway workers in this period. The system was hopelessly inefficient by design. There were many elements to this inefficiency, but one that turned out to be particularly problematic during the war was the deliberate creation of an imports-dependent railway system. In 1862, shortly after the commencement of the first railway systems in the country, Indian Railways companies established workshops at Jamalpur in Bengal and Ajmer in Rajputana. The workmen at these workshops initially maintained the growing railway fleet, but later developed sufficient expertise and skill to start designing and even building their own locomotives. By the early twentieth century, Indian-made locomotives were comparable to British locomotives and much cheaper. Under pressure from British manufacturers, the British imperial government passed legislation to stop Indians from designing and manufacturing their own locomotives. From this point onwards, Indians were forced to rely on British- or Canadian-made models. Their role was limited to that of maintenance only.[47] The arrangement suited the metropolitan elite in Britain and Canada, and, to some extent, other parts of the industrialized world (Germany and the United States), but created a substantial problem for Indian railway workers when demand for their services rose sharply during the war and suppliers in Britain and Canada were no longer able to provide because of production constraints in their own countries. This arrangement extended to operations as well. Railway workers needed over 40,000 separate items of stores to operate the railway system, from pins to entire boilers. Much of this came, by design, from overseas. During the war, this supply came to an abrupt halt.[48]

This problem also extended to personnel. From the nineteenth century, the British Indian government had tried to restrict Indian engineers from working in the railway system. Moreover, merit-based promotion policies were systematically undermined by racial considerations. Consequently, on the eve of the war, of the 1,780 gazetted officers in British-administered railway companies, 849 were European.[49] During the war, Indian railway workers had to cope with the reality that suddenly, the supply of British railway officers had stopped entirely.

Rising to the Occasion

Indian railway workers rose to the occasion magnificently. The statistical data indicates that over the course of the war, India's railway workers carried significantly greater numbers of passengers and greater quantities of freight. As stated earlier, Indian railway workers were transporting twice as many passengers at the end of the war as they had been at the start of the war. The evidence also indicates that railway workers were transporting these passengers across a greater distance. The number of miles traveled by the average passenger rose from 33.53 miles in the period 1938–1939 to 37.8 miles in the 1945–1946 duration. The increases in the quantity of freight, though less striking, were also substantial, and as in the case with passenger traffic, Indian railway workers transported these goods over greater distances. In the period 1938–1939, Indian railway workers transported an average ton up to 182.8 miles. By 1945–1946, they were transporting the average ton across a distance of 206.4 miles. The increases in freight traffic were particularly striking when it came to military stores.[50] These rose from 3,25,500 tons in the period 1938–1939 to 38,37,600 tons in the 1945–1946 duration, a staggering 1,079 per cent increase. There were substantial increases in the transportation of agricultural products (2,42,69,600 to 2,59,62,000 tons), minerals (3,02,94,900 to 3,43,11,400 tons) and manufactured goods (22,16,600 to 25,63,900 tons) over the same time period.[51] These astonishing results were made possible by the enormous effort the Indian railway workers put into augmenting the Indian railway system.

Among the most important of these was the expansion in the capacity of railway lines in the war period. During that time, Indian railway workers constructed 35 miles of new single lines and doubled or quadrupled 405 miles of track. Indian railway workers built 204 crossing stations and 201 loops at railway stations. They also lengthened loops at 180 stations and remodeled 30 large railway station yards. In all, they arranged no less than 3,500 miles of track material, the equivalent of a good-sized railway system. Railway workers built watering stations and coaling arrangements for locomotives. In order to improve communication, the Indian railway workers extended telephone and telegraph services and introduced radio services. All of these substantially improved train control systems in the country. By the end of the war, no less than 20,000 new trunk telephone, train control and telegraph circuits were under construction or serviceable. Railway workers had put in place the first circuits for an operational teleprinter network, and wireless stations were in the works connecting railway headquarters and divisions with principal junctions. These had provided the beginnings of a flexible and direct method of communication for the railway system. Railway workers had also begun using mobile wireless communication systems, providing network with unprecedented abilities of communication during natural disasters.[52]

One particularly impressive piece of augmentation occurred along the 63.5 miles Midnapore-Bankura section in Bengal. Railway workers working on this section of the railways increased the line's capacity by no less than 180 per cent by doubling its tracks. The work involved the removal of 35 million cubic feet of earth, the provision of 10,000 cubic feet of reinforced concrete and the installation of 76 girders. Railway workers remodeled ten railway stations on the line and laid or shifted no less than 100 sets of points and crossings. They transported and laid down 1,200,000 cubic feet of stone ballast for cuttings, and 2.5 million cubic feet of ash and moorum soil for banks. The speed at which the railway workers completed these massive engineering projects was staggering. The first section was completed six months after the commencement of work. The second and third sections were wrapped up two and a half months later. Another striking example of engineering brilliance was the augmentation of the Asansol Khanna line on the East Indian Railway. In this case, railway workers constructed a fourth track, quadrupling the line. This involved laying down 52.25 miles of track, 15 million cubic feet of earthworks and the construction of 281 bridges and culverts. Railway workers working on the project completed it in just under a year.[53]

There was a significant increase in performance as railway workers made considerable improvements in the efficiency with which they used available locomotive power. They made this possible by developing successful new techniques of maintenance. These new techniques paid off handsomely. Prior to the war, Indian railway workers brought freight train locomotives to their running sheds for minor repairs on an average every 120 miles. During the war, this increased to anywhere between 250 and 450 miles. Similarly, the railway workers extended the mileage between running shed visits for passenger train locomotives from an average of 250 miles to anywhere between 500 and 650 miles. The improvements helped the Indian Railways rival the United Kingdom and the United States in terms of the proportion of locomotives undergoing repairs at sheds and workshops. This was particularly impressive considering that unlike in the United Kingdom and the United States, materials and spares necessary for repairs were often unavailable. It was also impressive considering that Indian trains were carrying substantially greater loads than before. During the war, railway workers increased average loads on freight trains by 8.5 per cent, and in passenger trains by an even greater 32 per cent. The improvements were so impressive that an otherwise condescending British official was forced to concede that when it came to locomotive and wagon maintenance, the Indian Railways 'have nothing to be ashamed of.'[54]

The Indian railway workers responded to the severe shortage of coal in the war years by making a series of modifications to their locomotives. First, Indian railway engineers and mechanics modified several coal-burning locomotives to oil-burning engines. This provided railway workers with some alternatives when there were severe shortages of coal. Second, many railway mechanics and firemen began using alternative fuels that they found could work without major modifications. These included cinder (partly burnt wood or coal that no longer created flames but still had a combustible matter in it) and sometimes wood. While these alternative fuels could not be used on regular trains, firemen were able to use them to run small shunting engines and stationary boilers. Finally, railway engineers came up with calculations of minimum coal requirements for given trips and coordinated with the firemen in trying to run locomotives on these bare minimum estimations. This kind of trip fuel control helped firemen run their locomotives more efficiently. All these measures make the substantial expansion in the railway services all the more impressive. By the end of the war, Indian railway workers were setting world records in the movement of rolling stock. In one particularly successful company, the railway workers registered an average of 95.4 wagon miles per wagon day on its meter gauge section. Across India, railway workers raised the average load of a broad-gauge wagon from 52 to 74 per cent of a wagon's maximum capacity. These were figures that could rival the best-run railway systems anywhere.[55]

As the railway system was overwhelmed, the railway engineers, operators and management began diverting traffic off their trains. Some freight was put on coastal steamers and 'country craft' like barges and small cargo boats. Railway porters had to work with boatmen and steamer crew to arrange for the loading and unloading of these cargoes. When possible, freight was divested onto sea-going boats and ships as well. A significant amount of freight began moving on road transport. This required railway porters to work with local trucking and transportation companies, loading and unloading freight between rail and road transportation. Several railway companies actually began operating their own road transportation services. A particularly important one was located in India's northeastern region and transported 160 tons of coal every day to the various tea plantations located in the region. Many railway workers made this possible. It freed up railway lines and made a significant difference to the survival of India's Burma front.[56]

Finally, the Indian Railway Board set up a sprawling new bureaucracy called the Railway Priority Organization. Established in March 1942, large numbers of railway clerks and lower-ranking railway office workers coordinated with government bureaucracies and private traders to manage the movement of goods across the Indian subcontinent. The Organization had three main functions. The first was to ensure the speediest possible movement of essential commodities, both war-related as well as those determined by civil needs. The second was the elimination, as far as possible, of unnecessary traffic. The third was to ensure the coordination of rail traffic with the other forms of transportation that were increasingly in use. The Organization divided the entire Indian railway system into distinct groups, placing each under a regional controller. The controllers and their bureaucratic machinery had responsibility over the movement of freight in their section of the railway network. The regional controllers and their teams coordinated with central and provincial government officials through Priority Panels established for the purpose. Each Regional Controller was responsible for maintaining active lists of commodities that required priority in their given region. In addition, the Regional Controllers worked to ensure the elimination of cross movement (the outward movement of a given commodity coinciding with an inward shipment of the same) and, when necessary, bans on the movement of a given commodity in or out of a region. Through the second half of the war, the bureaucratic machine of the Priority Panels worked with the Food Department to manage the transportation of essential food grains from surplus to deficit parts of the country, especially the movement of food grains, albeit over-late, as a relief to the Bengal famine.[57]

In India's Defense

As stated earlier, Indian railway workers transported men and material out of the country to support the British Empire's wars in Africa and Europe. But in addition, they also played an important part in the country's defense at their workshops. The workers customized substantial portions of their existing rolling stock to support the war effort. They built new ambulance coaches and converted existing stock into hospital ward cars and kitchen cars. In one case, the railway workers repurposed a tourist car into a blood transfusion coach. This coach came to be operated by the Army Transfusion Service and was much used during blood donation drives across the country. Railway workers also repurposed several broad-gauge wagons into refrigerated trucks to transport frozen meat from ports to army units posted far inland.[58]

Indian railway engineers and workers carried out several projects for the British Indian Army during the war years. This included the construction of 1,400 miles of sidings (low-speed track sections) for the military. Railway workers constructed an additional 70 miles of permanent and 153 miles of temporary sidings for airfields. This required substantial engineering and transportation for survey work and for the construction and building of railway tracks, including large numbers of railway turnouts or points. The workers delivered no less than 13 million tons of material for the construction of airfields through the war period. Indian railway workers also played a crucial role in the construction of the Avadi military base. Built to facilitate the Allied buildup in southern India, Avadi quickly became the largest military base in British India, and among the largest in the entire British Empire. Indian railway workers built 125 miles of track and 70 million cubic feet of earthworks for this mammoth project. Once again, the railway workers completed the project fully in accordance with the timetables set by the British Indian Army.[59]

Indian railway workers demonstrated a high degree of voluntarism. In addition to the thousands of railway workers drafted into departments supporting the war effort, many officers and men joined active duty. Others volunteered with the Air Raid Precautions services, serving as wardens dedicated to protecting civilians from the danger of aerial bombardment. Many railway workers donated generously to war funds and charities. One estimate puts their contributions in the hundreds of thousands of rupees. Their contributions to the Viceroy's War Purposes Funds and subscriptions to Defense Loans financed the purchase of fighter aircraft and ambulances. The British Indian government advertised many of these purchases in the press. On 20 August 1942, for instance, *The Bombay Chronicle* carried one such advertisement. Railway workers and their families tended to refugees and evacuees. They ran hundreds of free canteens for soldiers passing through their railway stations.[60]

The All India Railwaymen's Federation

Through the war, an umbrella organization representing trade unions negotiated with the Railway Board on behalf of the railway workforce. Between 1939 and 1944, under the leadership of Jamnadas Mehta, the All India Railwaymen's Federation (AIRF) regularly met representatives of the Indian Railway Board to discuss multiple issues and lobby the Board to make the railways a fairer place of work. In 1944, Jamnadas Mehta resigned his office as President and was replaced first by S.C. Joshi, and after, by Varahagiri Venkata Giri, who later went on to serve as President of independent India. These negotiations had a considerable impact on the decisions of the Indian Railway Board and played a very important part in ensuring humane working conditions. Over the next two decades, the AIRF leadership supported the expansion of union membership and the consolidation of trade unions, mirroring the expansion of the Indian Railways and the consolidation of railway companies. By 1939, biannual meetings with the Railway Board had become an established practice, and the AIRF enjoyed substantial legitimacy as representatives of the railway workforce.

During the war years, more than any other issue, the AIRF found itself at loggerheads with the Railway Board on the issue of pay. There were many different disputes. Some of these were localized and affected sections of the railway's vast workforce. For instance, in their November 1939 meetings, the AIRF took up the cause of the Accounts Staff, specifically clerks who had been transferred to the Railway Clearing Accounts office and the grant of compensatory allowance to these clerks. They also discussed pay scales for journeymen (mechanics) on the NWR company.[61] In January 1941, the AIRF pressed the Board on behalf of railway workers employed in the erstwhile Bengal Dooars Railway that had been incorporated by the Indian Railway Board.[62] In 1942, the AIRF negotiated with the Board on behalf of specific groups of employees from the BAR, the NWR, and the East Indian Railway companies.[63] In 1943, the AIRF raised the issue of the pay of draftsmen working for the East Indian Railway company.[64] More broadly, in January 1941, the AIRF called on the Railway Board to rethink the working of existing disciplinary rules and the rights of appeal open to workers subject to such rules.[65] In a meeting held in August of the same year, the AIRF complained about unfair difficulties that were blocking promotions for low-wage employees. During the same meeting, the AIRF also urged the Board to ensure fair principles to secure the interests of staff when company-managed railway systems were brought under state management.[66]

In addition to such specific concerns, the AIRF lobbied the Railway Board to factor in the sharp increase in prices that were having a real effect on the wages and livelihoods of the railway workforce. During an informal meeting in February 1940, for instance, Jamnadas Mehta raised the issue with the Railway Board.[67] In April, the AIRF sent a special deputation to urge the Board to address the growing crisis. The lobbying forced the Railway Board to appoint a Court of Enquiry to investigate the subject. The court recommendations and subsequent lobbying by the AIRF resulted in the establishment of a special Dearness Allowance (DA) for railway employees. From 1940, depending on their existing pay and location (with higher increases in larger cities), railway workers began receiving increments to mitigate the effects of inflation. These remained in place reflecting the importance of this victory as well as the colossal increase in prices. In 1940, the highest DA of Rs 3 per month was allocated to workers living in Bombay and Calcutta with salaries less than Rs 40 per month.[68] In 1944, the DA allocated for workers living in Bombay and Calcutta (Cawnpore had been added to the list), with salaries less than Rs 40 per month, was Rs 16. In the meanwhile, DAs had been extended to the highest earning categories of employees. The upper limit stood at Rs 1,000, with DAs set at 10 per cent of their income.[69] Towards the end of the war, the AIRF began pressing the Railway Board on its pay scales. AIRF representatives raised the issue in meetings held in 1944 and again in 1945.[70]

In addition to a DA, the sharp increase in food prices required the creation of additional tools to ensure that railway employees and their families were able to feed themselves adequately. From the summer of 1941, the Indian Railway Board began seriously considering the creation of subsidized Grain Stores to ensure that their workforce did not go hungry. Towards that end, the East Indian and the Great Indian Peninsula Railway (GIPR) companies opened their first grain store that summer. These were quickly adopted across the Indian railway system over the following months. There were considerable difficulties maintaining and expanding the system, but railway workers running the expanding Grain Shop network were able to purchase sufficient grain in the open market and acquire additional supplies from provincial governments to keep 150 grain shops functioning. Many railway workers doubled up as van drivers to create mobile versions of these shops.

By 1943, these grain shops became a crucial lifeline for half a million workers and their families. In addition to food grains, these shops also offered low-wage employees lengths of cloth as textile prices began to outpace wages.[71] From May that year, at prices pegged to August 1942, the grain shops began offering 18 commodities, including cloth, soap, fuel and matches. From

December that year, railway workers could buy milk for their children and vegetables for their families. By 1944, 435 shops and 156 vans were providing over 800,000 workers and their families with a lifeline. The average relief of Rs 10 every month constituted a quarter or more of the incomes of the lowest-paid railway workers. In August 1943, the average savings was Rs 14. In addition to these estimated savings, the evidence indicates that these grain shops developed into places for many commodities that had become unavailable in the open market. In its Annual Report for the year 1943–1944, the Railway Board noted, 'the man with a large family, who was hardest pressed, received most relief; employees were free from anxiety in regard to rising prices.'[72] By the end of the war, the total number of grain shops had expanded to 729, with 869,000 employees and their families availing of their stocks. These now also included footwear and woolen goods available to the least paid employees of the railway workforce.[73] The records are not entirely clear on the role of the AIRF in the establishment of these grain shops. However, the data does demonstrate that from 1943 at least, grain store policies were under active discussion in meetings between the AIRF and the Indian Railway Board. The AIRF raised the issue again in 1944 and in 1945.[74]

In addition to Dearness Allowances and grain shops, the AIRF pushed the Railway Board to offer better retirement benefits and better working conditions for the railway workforce. In April 1940, with a goal of universal retirement benefits, the AIRF urged the Railway Board to extend its Provident Fund benefit to a wider section of the railway workforce.[75] In August 1941, the AIRF raised the issue of extending Provident Fund benefits with the Railway Board again.[76] The issue was again raised during two half-yearly meetings the AIRF representatives had with the Railway Board the following year.[77] The AIRF also negotiated on working conditions of the railway workers. This emerged as a significant issue during the second half of the war. During two half-yearly meetings in 1942, the AIRF raised two issues connected with deteriorating work conditions. First, they pointed out the severe problem of staff shortages and its effects on working conditions. Second, the AIRF raised concerns about the application of work-hour regulations for running staff (laborers who performed heavy work operating trains).[78] During negotiations held in December 1943, the AIRF demanded that railway maintenance staff be granted weekly rest days. They again raised the issue of long working hours for running staff.[79]

Finally, the AIRF lobbied on behalf of the railway workers over employment issues. In January 1941, the AIRF negotiated with the Railway Board on behalf of apprentices and railway workers who had been retrenched in recent years, seeking to ensure some fairness in the process. During a later meeting the same year, the AIRF pressed the Railway Board to raise the mandatory retirement age for lower-ranking workers.[80] In a meeting with the Railway Board in December 1943, the AIRF demanded that employees on a daily wage system need to be offered greater security in the form of a monthly wage. They also demanded that the Railway Board accept the principle of legacy hiring, under which some kind of priority be given to the children of current railway employees. The AIRF proposed the creation of a percentage of vacancies that could be reserved for such applicants.[81] It again lobbied the Railway Board to heed the difficulties faced by and complaints of temporary workers in their September 1944 meeting.[82] During the last meeting of the war, the AIRF urged the Railway Board to consider re-employing temporary workers.[83]

Unions and the Railway Board

Of all the measures that were made possible by the AIRF–Railway Board negotiations, the Dearness Allowance and grain store measures were the most crucial since they addressed the critical issue of hunger. Consequently, for any meaningful research into survival strategies, the success of these two measures has to be clearly understood. A close analysis of historical records makes it very clear that while the AIRF–Railway Board negotiations were important, a no less-significant set of struggles at local and regional levels were also critical to the making of these two policies. Among the more important of these struggles were those that occurred in western India during the crucial 1943 period. This was the most difficult of the years when prices rose to dizzying heights with the British Indian administration lacking courage and initiative. While things never got as bad in western India as in the province of Bengal, the experience of railway workers were nevertheless important as the west coast became critical for the landing of supplies in this period. The historical records indicate that regional trade unions active among workers on the GIPR and the Bombay, Baroda and Central India Railway company were critical to the establishment of the Dearness Allowances and grain shops. They suggest that collective action on the ground level played as important a role as negotiations at the high table.

In January 1943, for instance, the ever-increasing rise in prices forced the GIPR company workers to confront their employers. At this time, the Railway Board had already issued directives to provide all its employees making less than Rs 120 per month receive a DA of Rs 8–10 per month. Considering that the price of rice had risen nine-fold between 1939 and 1943, and that of cotton stood at five times its 1939 price, a DA less than 10 per cent for many employees, and none whatsoever for employees making more than Rs 120 meant a significant fall in real wages.[84] Consequently, on 10 January 1943, 20 representatives of local unions agreed to organize a mass demonstration at the Kamgar Maidan in the Parel neighborhood of Bombay, with demands for a more reasonable DA.[85] The march took place at 6 p.m. on the 20 January 1943, with veteran trade unionist Narayan Malhar Joshi presiding over the gathering.[86] The success of the GIPR company workers in organizing a march galvanized the railway workers of the Bombay, Baroda and Central India Railway company. On 22 January, two days after the GIPR workers' rally, BBCI workshops at Parel and Mahalaxmi in Bombay ground to a halt as workers struck demanding enhancements in their DAs. In addition to increases in DA, the workers also demanded more generous rations at the railway grain shops to keep up with the escalating price of living.[87] On 28 January, Jamnadas Mehta, President of the AIRF, issued a statement assuring the workers that the Railway Board had accepted their demands. In a press statement, Mehta stated that he had received assurances 'that immediate steps will be taken with regard to the demand for more grain and increased dearness allowance.'[88]

On 17 February 1943, railway workers affiliated with the GIPR and BBCI unions gathered united at the Kamgar Maidan once again. The workers passed a resolution demanding a DA of at least Rs 30.[89] When the Railway Board failed to respond, the GIPR workers union began making plans for a general strike. On 6 March, the GIPR union passed a resolution calling on the AIRF to give the Railway Board a 14-day strike notice.[90] It was only in the middle of March that railway workers in Bombay received notice of an enhanced DA, effective 1 February. The increase was measly and disappointing. While the Board made DAs available to all employees drawing less than Rs 200 per month, a substantial improvement over the Rs 120 limit, the DA itself was set at a mere Rs 16.[91] There were additional concerns. S.C. Joshi, General Secretary of the GIP Railwaymen's Union, took issue with the lower rates of increase in regions beyond Bombay and Calcutta. In a press release, he stated, 'There is no justification for this, as the rise in prices for the necessaries of life in the rural areas if not more is at least the same as in urban areas.' He also expressed dismay that the DA wasn't offered in a retrospective manner, as had been offered to other public servants.[92] On 21 March, the BBCI Railwaymen's Union issued a similar press release. K.S. Nadkarni, General Secretary of the BBCI Railwaymen's Union, stated, 'The increase in the amount of Dearness Allowance announced by the Government of India falls far short of the requirements of the Railwaymen and is very disappointing.' Noting that the increases were substantially less than what had been demanded, Nadkarni concluded, 'Thus the whole scheme which is announced only after agitations and pressure by the railway workers, is highly unsatisfactory, gives hardly any relief to the starving lakhs of Railway workers and is bound to create great discontent among Railwaymen, the responsibility for which is entirely that of the Railway Board and the Government of India.'[93]

In order to maintain pressure on the Railway Board, the BBCI and GIPR unions organized a 'giant rally' on 20 April. The railway workers demanded a higher DA of Rs 30 and an end to the zonal system under which railway workers posted in smaller towns and villages received lower DAs.[94] On 12 May, *The Bombay Chronicle* reported that the two unions had passed a resolution in support of the AIRF in its negotiations with the Railway Board. In particular, the resolution supported the AIRF's decision to seek arbitration to resolve its dispute with the Board on the question of DA. The demands were simple. A 30 DA for all subordinate staff, with no discrimination based on place of residence. The resolution was also addressed to the railway workers, almost girding them for a long and difficult fight. It called on railway workers to 'strengthen the Union to win their demand for dearness allowance and to face the serious situation that may arise as a result of Government's refusal to adjudicate the dispute.'[95]

The 1943–1944 Annual Report of the Railway Board indicates that the Indian government responded to union pressure by expanding the grain shop network. Between 1943 and 1944, the total number of stores almost quadrupled, from 160 to 600, including 156 mobile stores. The number of railway workers with access to these stores also increased sharply, from 5,00,000 to 8,05,000. During the period 1943–1944, railway workers purchased 10,255,400 maunds of commodities measured by weight (about 4,21,937 tons), an average of 1.23 maunds (101 lbs.) per ration card holder every month. The Railway Board estimated its total subsidy bill at Rs 7.9 crore, realized from the sale of Rs 17.7 crore.[96]

There is little doubt that the AIRF was constantly in touch with the GIP and BBCI railway unions. The resolutions passed by the two unions through the year were always addressed to and in support of the AIRF. There is also little doubt that the AIRF was aware of and in constant communication with its constituents at the local level. Certainly, the AIRF was engaged with railway workers in large cities, such as Bombay. The evidence also sheds some light on the relationship between the highest levels of union administration and the laborers the AIRF represented. In fact, on at least one occasion, workers on the ground took their struggle in a direction entirely outside the control of the AIRF. The strike of 22 January 1943, which brought railway workshops in Mahalakshmi and Parel to a grinding halt, as discussed earlier, was not authorized by the AIRF and had, in fact, been the work of laborers operating outside the formal union structure. The AIRF chairman Jamnadas Mehta issued a press release attacking the strike leaders, though not the striking workers. Mehta stated, 'The demands of the workers though very legitimate do not justify a strike at this critical time. The strike has been engineered by a few inserted self-imposed leaders and the workers have thus been misled.' The AIRF negotiated on behalf of the workers and played an important role in its resolution.[97] This was not an isolated incident. However, over time, as regional trade unions kept pushing more aggressively, the AIRF gained a reputation of failing to advocate strongly enough for railway workers, accepting agreements that gave railway workers a poorer bargain compared to other government employees. Jamnadas Mehta, in particular, came to be seen as too close to the British Indian ruling class.[98]

The unions were unambiguous in their support for the interest of the workers, but they were also fully committed to the fight against fascism. In April 1942, with Japanese forces in control of Singapore, having handed the British Indian Army defending British Malay a stunning defeat, the Railway Board meeting with the AIRF included talks on the role of Indian railway workers and the war. The Board, in particular, was keen on discussing the responsibilities of railway workers during wartime. The AIRF, on behalf of the workforce, assured the Board by offering 'the whole-hearted cooperation of all railway workers in maintaining the normal working of the railways.'[99] The AIRF's assurances were entirely consistent with the sentiments of regional trade unions. On 21 August 1942, B.R. Kalappa, President of the Bengal Nagpur Railway Labour Union issued a resolution clearly stating the union's support for the war effort. The resolution stated, 'The workers generally and more particularly railway workers have already resolved to stand at their posts in the event of Axis aggression and they have already striven hard to maintain the transport service, notwithstanding the strain due to other war conditions.'[100] On 15 October 1942, the Great Indian Peninsula Railway Workers Union issued a similar manifesto. It stated, 'We should make a united front against Japan and gather all forces against it...under all conditions we must increase the output of war material to keep intact communications and strengthen the armed forces.'[101]

***

This chapter asks how India's railway workers survived the great challenges of the Second World War. The evidence indicates that the railway workers deployed multiple survival strategies.

The first was the widespread use of frugal innovation. Indian railway workers demonstrated a striking ability to make the most of rapidly depleting resources in the face of escalating demand. This is particularly evident in the successful response of the railway workers to the challenges thrown up by the war. The substantial increase in the movement of passengers and freight despite increasing constraints demonstrates this. More specifically, the conversion of coal-powered locomotives into alternative fuels demonstrate an exceptional ability for innovation. This ability became crucial in overcoming the challenges of the war itself. The war required Indian railway workers to transport substantial equipment and troops. It also required them to support the rapid buildup of India's industrial base to construct, almost overnight, a large and sophisticated military-industrial complex. They managed this through what is now widely recognized as frugal innovation.

The more important survival strategy however was collective action and trade union organization. These two strategies helped Indian railway workers survive the challenge of imperialism. While wars generate their own challenges, imperialism creates an additional burden, sometimes much greater than what a war might. Distortions in imperial economics created a life-and-death crisis for much of the Indian population. For 3 million British Indian subjects in Bengal, it brought death. The million-strong railway workforce faced hunger and starvation. It is in this context that collective action became a central survival strategy. The evidence is quite unambiguous. A dearness allowance and a massive network of grain shops provided the railway workers with a lifeline. It ensured that their wages, falling in real terms, did not leave the workforce without sufficient means of sustenance. It is this ability that made the Indian railway workers' war effort possible. A workforce on the verge of starvation simply could not have managed the extraordinary buildup of India's defenses during the Second World War. A third survival strategy was the organization of trade unions. While there may have been instances of collective action outside the realm of organized labor, the evidence clearly suggests that the major gains made by railway workers all occurred through negotiations between the Railway Board and unions. Their role, whether advocating for workers or committing to winning the war, was in all likelihood decisive.

TWO

The Freedom Struggle

THE YEARS 1942 to 1947 constituted a high-water mark in India's freedom struggle. In August 1942, Mahatma Gandhi called on his countrymen to 'Do or Die' in a final attempt to force the British to 'Quit India.' The movement was to become the biggest anti-colonial uprising since the great revolt of 1857. With Gandhi and much of the senior Congress party leadership behind bars, the movement turned violent and deadly. The unrest lasted for over a year and was crushed by the British Indian state only through the application of substantial and brutal military force. While the Quit India movement failed to bring British rule to an end, a second round of unrest proved more decisive in India's march towards freedom. In December 1945, the British Indian government charged three officers of the Indian National Army (INA) with treason. Emerging from the ranks of Indian Prisoners of War captured by the Japanese in Singapore and Malaya and bolstered through substantial recruitment from the Indian diaspora in Southeast Asia, the INA formed the kernel of the provisional government of free India and the most significant Indian military challenge to British India since the revolutionary army of 1857. The trial, however, galvanized anti-colonial nationalism in India. Mass protests quickly escalated into serious armed confrontations around the country, including a mutiny in the Royal Indian Navy. It was all too much for Clement Attlee's Labour Party government. The British Indian government ceased the prosecution of INA officers and soldiers, and the following year, India became independent.

This culmination of India's freedom struggle created two sets of challenges for India's railway workers. The first came in the form of pressure from the British Indian government, including the Indian Railway Board. Indian railway workers, with substantial sympathies for the freedom struggle, had to choose between their commitment towards the independence of their country and keeping the railway system functional. This choice was forced upon them, as the British Indian state and the Railway Board were entirely opposed to Indian Independence, especially during the Quit India movement. In fact, during the Quit India movement, the British Indian government and much of the Railway Board were quite hostile to Indian nationalism because of the pressures of war. Indian railway workers, consequently, were under great pressure to deliver increased services at a time when the state unleashed a brutal crackdown on their own countrymen. The situation worsened when the state began using the railways as part of its policing machinery, making Indian railway workers, in particular the Railway Police, active agents in the suppression of India's freedom struggle. An increased Indian component in the Railway Board tipped the balance in favor of Independence during the unrest of 1945–1946 period. However, Indian railway workers were still faced with the balancing act of maintaining services and supporting the freedom struggle.

There were other challenges. The approach of India's Independence raised difficult questions of race and religion. The Indian railway system had long privileged British and mixed-race Anglo-Indians. The acceleration of India's freedom struggle increased conflict between British and Indian employees. The mixed-race Anglo Indians remained ambivalent, with a significant section choosing indifference but an increasing number supporting and even joining the freedom struggle. Similarly, there is evidence of some ambivalence from the Dalit workforce. Comprising Indians from underprivileged castes, many had found work with the Indian Railways. The proportion of Dalits, or Scheduled Castes as the community was identified in this period, was rising, in part, due to aggressive affirmative action policies implemented by the Indian Railway Board. As the Independence struggle culminated, Indian railway workers had to navigate these challenges.

Indian railway workers responded to these challenges, as they did during the Second World War, by using multiple survival strategies. During the unrest of the Quit India movement, Indian railway workers extended moral support to the struggle but prioritized the fight against fascism and kept the Indian railway system functional. In fact, as discussed in the earlier chapter, Indian railway performance expanded dramatically, despite the war-related constraints of the Second World War. During the INA trials, Indian railway workers supported the freedom struggle with a greater degree of action. British employees, Anglo-Indians, Dalits, all made distinct choices and took appropriate measures to survive the challenges of the decade. Indians from more privileged caste and economic backgrounds sought to build on opportunities opened by the changing circumstances in the country to ensure that their new gains were protected as Independence drew nearer.

As with the Second World War, the centrality of collective action and trade union organization emerged as the most important of the survival strategies. The significance of trade unions was especially great during the difficult years of the Quit India movement. When Indian railway workers were faced with difficult choices of supporting India's freedom struggle against a brutal state bent on using their services against their own people and catering to the escalating demands of a war against fascism, the clarity offered by railway unions gave the workers a pathway out of what was undoubtedly a critical dilemma. While the choice placed the Indian railway workers in the path of Indian nationalists and even made them targets, this strategy ensured, to a significant extent, the safety and stability necessary at that moment of crisis. Even during the years immediately prior to Independence, during the crisis of the INA trials, the trade unions had played an important role by demonstrating unanimous support for Independence over continued imperialism. The power of collective action came to the fore during the unrest surrounding the INA trials unrest. During this period of uncertainty and escalating conflict between the British Empire and the Indian people, the solidarity of the Indian railway workers played its part. While this book does not claim that railway strikes informed Attlee's decision, there is no denying the power of their solidarity. The determination of soldiers, sailors and students fighting imperialism was undoubtedly strengthened by the awareness that their bravery had the support of the million-strong railway workers of India. And their struggle had support in the class struggles raging in the railway system.

Challenge I: British Demands

In August of 1942, when Mahatma Gandhi launched the Quit India movement, Indian railway workers were under great pressure. The Annual Report of the Railway Board for that year gives us some indication of that pressure. The war had come to India's borders. The Japanese had overrun much of the British Empire in Southeast Asia, and their armies had reached India. 'The growing tempo of the war and its near approach to India brought in their train numerous staff problems,' the report claimed. Indian railway workers, especially those from or posted in eastern India faced a very real threat of invasion. Railway workers with families in the especially northeastern region, bordering Burma, were the most vulnerable. But railway workers from or posted in Calcutta also had good reasons to be concerned. Cities along India's eastern seaboard were widely understood as vulnerable to naval landings of the kind that had overrun defenses in British Malay, Dutch Indochina and the American Philippines. Railway work was also becoming more dangerous. Japanese aircraft began bombing cities in India, and railway workers close to the fighting in the Northeast were vulnerable. The vastly expanded demand for railway transport also took a toll on railway workers in the form of workplace accidents. In addition, railway workers were called upon by the Railway Board to provide skilled labor for the country's defense. Many railway workers saw their workshops transformed into munitions production units, and more than 20,000 railway workers had been instructed to make munitions of all kinds for the British Indian military. Indian railway workers were anticipating and already experiencing the severe economic disruptions created by the rapid increase in the Government's war-related spending. A sharp increase in food prices and the prospect of greater increases in the future were adversely impacting the railway works with declining real wages, especially those at the bottom of the pay scales who were struggling to feed and clothe their families. It was also in this period that the catastrophic Bengal famine hit eastern India.[102]

During the especially violent phases of the Quit India movement, the British Indian government and the Railway Board turned to the Indian railway workers for assistance in crushing the uprising. The police and the British Indian military made regular use of the railway system to mobilize and deploy armed forces against activists of the Congress party. For instance, on 24 August 1942, *The Bombay Chronicle* reported that Indian railway workers had transported a contingent of troops to Muzaffarpur in Bihar to confront activists in the city.[103] Sources indicate that Indian railway workers in the state were, in this period, in fact, being asked to operate 'patrol trains' to terrorize the regional populace. Three days earlier, in the same region of British India, trigger-happy troops on board one such patrol train opened fire on activists in two small towns, Sadisopur and Bihta.[104]

The pressure was most acute on the Railway Police. Its officers became part of the government machinery the British Indian state deployed to break the will of the Indian people. This required brutality and cruelty of a kind unseen in the long history of the British Indian railway system. The work was also very dangerous. It placed Railway Police officers at risk of significant harm. On 27 October, for instance, a month and a half into the Quit India movement, cleaners on board the Sind Express at Karachi railway station discovered an unexploded bomb in an intermediate class compartment. The train had just arrived from Peshawar. The cleaners found the device, the size of a 'cricket ball,' located under a seat. The task of safely removing the bomb fell on the Railway Police.[105] They were tasked with the safety of all railway assets including trains and railway stations. This meant that Railway Police officers were often the first to be called on when railway authorities confronted or sought to intimidate Congress Party activists or their sympathizers. In another instance, on 6 December 1942, the Railway Police at Sylhet, Bengal, arrested an activist under stringent Defense of India rules. These rules had been introduced by the British Indian government as a special wartime act. Punishments included transportation for life, and even the death penalty. The Railway Police arrested the activist on the grounds that he was 'loitering in suspicious circumstances and making enquiries about locomotives.' They placed the activist with the city magistrate, who remanded him to police custody.[106] To prevent attacks on railway property, in self-defense or otherwise, the Railway Police were also under pressure to make arrests whenever any such attack did take place. On 17 December 1942, for instance, *The Bombay Chronicle* reported that the Railway Police in what is now the state of Gujarat had arrested twelve civilians 'in connection with' the derailment of a freight train between the Wadhwan and Bale Road stations.[107]

None of this, however, meant that railway workers could expect fair treatment from the British Indian government. Nor did it mean any kind of protection from the brutality and barbarism unleashed by the British Indian armed forces. On the contrary, the evidence indicates that railway workers, by virtue of the vital nature of their occupation, often became targets of the state's repressive machinery. One incident demonstrating this twisted state of affairs comes from the pages of *The Bombay Chronicle*. On 5 October 1942, an aircraft from the Royal Indian Air Force opened fire on railway workers laboring on lines near the Ranaghat railway station. The Bengal Premier, Abdul Kasim Fazlul Haq, stated that the pilots had 'mistaken' the railway workers for saboteurs. With little interest in ascertaining the veracity of their suspicions, the pilots had proceeded to try and machine gun the unarmed workmen. The only thing that seems to have prevented a bloody massacre was the incompetence of the pilots whose wild firing missed their targets entirely. The *Chronicle* operating under wartime censorship regulations was forced to conclude its report with a mild 'It was a miraculous escape, indeed,' and a demand for particulars 'with regard to the steps taken to prevent the recurrence of such errors.'[108]

At a macro level, during the period 1942–1943, the Indian Railway Board called on the Indian railway workers to transport over 622 million passengers. The total was only slightly less than the number of passengers carried the previous year. The Railway Board, however, called on its workforce to transport these passengers an even greater distance. Indian railway workers had to transport the average passenger 37.3 miles, exceeding the 33.79 miles of the previous year. Considering the vast number of passengers, this totaled an excess of 24 billion passenger miles for the year. It constituted a substantial 2 billion passenger mile increase over the previous year. The data is similar for freight transport. During the period 1942–1943, Indian railway workers had to transport 95 million tons of freight, marginally less than the 97 million tons the previous year. The railway workers did, however, transport the freight greater distances. The average ton traveled 211 miles, more than the 207 transported the year before. Once again, considering the colossal scale of freight under transportation, this translated into a staggering distance of 28-million-ton miles. Indian railway workers transported significant cargoes of military stores. During the period 1942–1943, they transported just under 13 million tons of military equipment. This constituted more than a doubling of military freight carried the previous year.[109]

In contrast to the violence of the 1942–1943 period, the British Indian state and the Railway Board placed less pressure on Indian railway workers during the 1945–1946 unrest. There were many reasons for this. Not least because the unrest was on a significantly smaller scale than during the Quit India movement. The unrest was also much less violent. Moreover, the war had ended, and the British Indian government no longer enjoyed the legal leeway afforded by the war to exercise brutality in quite the same way as during the war years. There was, however, an important exception.

The Royal Indian Naval Mutiny of February 1946 brought the barbarism of the British Indian state and its armed forces in its full, unmitigated form. The RIN Mutiny was an armed insurrection against British rule by naval ratings across the British Indian Empire. It was supported by sections of the British Indian Army and the Royal Indian Air Force. The uprising enjoyed widespread popular support, including from organized labor. The mutiny constituted a serious threat to the British Indian government. At its peak, some 20,000 sailors were in rebellion. They were spread across 78 ships and shore-based establishments. The unrest was driven in part over concerns with living and working conditions exacerbated by poor British leadership, but more importantly the INA trials and the general unrest against continuing British rule. The British Indian government used the services of Indian railway workers in seeking to crush the mutiny.

In Bombay, the most significant center of the mutiny, troops of the Royal Marines and 5th Maratha Light Infantry were reinforced by battalions of the Essex Regiment, the Queen's Regiment, and the Border Regiment. The troops also received armored support from the Royal Armored Corps. All these military assets were transported from their base in Poona to the city of Bombay by Indian Railway workers. An anti-tank battery of the Field Regiment of the Royal Battery was also transported to Bombay by rail from Jubbulpore. These military units then went on the rampage in the city, killing 236 people including unarmed civilians. They confronted naval ratings and exchanged fire on multiple occasions, while the British Indian admiralty and the Indian National Congress leadership tried to negotiate a peaceful settlement. Ultimately, a combination of active diplomacy and military force brought the mutiny to an end. The military force, was facilitated by Indian railway workers, who perhaps unaware or unwillingly, and reluctantly assisted in the mobilization and deployment of the soldiers and their equipment.[110]

Challenge II: Nationalist Ire

On the other hand, Indian railway workers were also under great pressure from Indian nationalists. This was particularly true during the 1942–1943 Quit India movement. The Quit

India movement began with Gandhi's proclamation on 8 August 1942. In contrast to his earlier campaigns, the Non-Cooperation movement of 1920 and the Civil Disobedience movement of 1930, Gandhi did not insist on non-violence in this campaign. The British Indian government arrested the Congress Party leadership, including Gandhi, depriving the movement of a national organization. However, new leaders emerged quickly and organized the struggle at regional and local levels. Without Gandhi's restraint and amid great government brutality, the movement turned violent. According to the government's own records, between August 1942 and December 1943, the police opened fire on no less than 601 occasions and the British Indian military on 68 occasions, including five when the colonial state made use of aircraft. It is entirely possible that this is an undercount. Moreover, these statistics fail to capture the horror of these punitive measures. In response, the Indian nationalists, with limited arms and armaments, set off 664 bombs and unsuccessfully attempted a further 1,319 bomb attacks. They sabotaged roads 474 times and destroyed or damaged 208 police stations and outposts. Government records claim that nationalist activists damaged 749 other government buildings, 525 public buildings and 273 private buildings. They also destroyed or severely damaged 945 post and telegraph offices. The official records indicate that the police killed 763, while the military were responsible for killing 297 people. Indian nationalists killed 63 policemen and 10 other government employees. Estimated losses to government property exceeded Rs 27,35,125, and Rs 30,07,274 to private businesses.[111] At the peak of the struggle, Indian nationalists had seized control over parts of the country, establishing liberated zones that the British Indian state was able to recover only after much effort.

The Quit India movement constituted a substantial challenge for the Indian railway workforce. Indian nationalists clearly identified the Indian railway network as a legitimate target of destruction. The Andhra Provincial Committee (APC) of the Indian National Congress party, for instance, issued instructions to all its district-level Congress Committees to disrupt the smooth functioning of the Indian Railways. The APC called on activists to travel by the Indian Railways but refuse to purchase tickets. The APC also called on activists engaged in a higher level of resistance to stop the movement of trains by pulling on the emergency brakes.[112] The final issue of Gandhi's widely read newspaper *Harijan* for the year 1942 claimed that 'Dislocation of traffic communications is permissible.' This included, according to the newspaper, 'Cutting wires, removing rails, destroying small bridges.' The newspaper argued that these acts 'cannot be objected to in a struggle like this.'[113] Nationalist activists across the country relied on underground radio stations and printing presses to develop a program of action. Many of these circulars carried specific instructions on the necessity of disrupting the railway system. One pamphlet in Bihar stated, 'The Government has not built Railways or roads for their [the people's] benefit. It builds Railways or roads for the transport of Government officials and troops from one place to the other. Where are Railways and roads to be found in villages?' Justifying the costs of disrupting the railway system, the pamphlet claimed, 'crores of Indians have always remained half fed. Even before the beginning of the movement, there were many persons who could not get grain, salt, fuel and other such things. They will, therefore, be able to anyhow bear these difficulties for a couple of months, but how will Government officials and troops carry on who consume eggs, butter and loaf only? They will have to face ruin in a couple of months.'[114]

Government data on the subject indicate that Indian nationalists followed these instructions. Between August 1942 and December 1943, the Quit India movement activists destroyed or severely damaged no less than 332 railway stations. The railways also recorded 268 cases of serious damage to rolling stock. In the immediate aftermath of Gandhi's proclamation, damage through sabotage of railway tracks was so great that its extent was impossible for the railway authorities to properly estimate. In the period between 8 August and 1 October, nationalist activists inflicted damages of approximately Rs 9 lakh. Between 1 October and 31 December 1943, the Indian Railways documented 411 cases of serious damage to railway tracks.[115] The Bihar pamphlet quoted earlier had provided a clear moral justification for such attacks. It stated, 'You are perfectly within your right to put out of action the system of communication, whether roads or railways or postal and telegraphic services...through which the police and the military and civil officials maintain their stranglehold on you.'[116] The Quit India movement activists had clearly taken the message to heart.

All this, however, left the railway workforce vulnerable. On 12 August 1942, at Dadar railway station in Bombay, Congress activists attacked railway workers who tried to defy a general strike. Local authorities were forced to position a military picket at the site to bring the situation under control.[117]At Lucknow, about 200 activists attacked a railway booking office. The activists not only 'destroyed records and broke window glasses,' according to *The Bombay Chronicle*, but also stoned the guard of a passing goods train.[118] On 17 August, the crew of a freight train running between Guntakal and Mandikarj stations in southern India sustained injuries when their engine derailed after Congress activists removed a portion of the rails.[119] In other cases, railway workers were able to maintain services only under exceedingly difficult circumstances. On 20 August 1942, for instance, operators running trains between the Konnagar and Rishra stations in Bengal began using hand signals as Congress activists had snapped telegraph lines in the area.[120] On 31 October, the guard on a moving Madras and Southern Mahratta Railway train was injured. The incident occurred between Dhodaj and Jejuri railway stations when nationalist activists stoned the passing train.[121]

Tasked with defending railway property, Railway Police officers in particular sustained injuries in the line of duty. On 29 August, for instance, *The Bombay Chronicle* reported that a Railway Police superintendent was injured during a confrontation at the Bolepur railway station in Bengal.[122] In another particularly tragic incident, a railway gatekeeper lost his ten-year-old son to a bomb explosion on 1 December 1942. The activists had planted a device hoping to damage the Saptapur railway station at Dharwar. The police suspected that the child had inadvertently picked the device up, perhaps mistaking it for a toy, when the bomb exploded. The child suffered serious injuries and died in the hospital.[123] On 3 October 1942, the brakeman on board the GIPR Peshawar Express died when his train derailed on the Igatpuri-Bhusawal line. The Quit India activists had removed a rail from the tracks, resulting in the derailment. The accident led to the derailment of the engine, one first-class compartment, two second-class compartments and one lower-class compartment. Another first class compartment derailed partially. The accident killed 13 passengers. It wounded an additional 29 passengers and the train's guard.[124]

During the 1945–1946 unrest similarly, Indian railway workers had to deal with the general breakdown in law and order and the sabotage of railway equipment. On 10 November 1945, for instance, a railway track inspector discovered missing fishplates and cut telegraph wires between the Hardattpur and Rajatalab stations in the United Provinces.[125] On 23 November 1945, some 2,000 activists blocked trains between Liluah and Belur in Bengal.[126] As the INA veterans returned to India, activists organized welcome receptions at train stations. On 14 December 1945, activists affiliated with the Madras Nationalist Youth Federation staged a mass demonstration at Egmore station, Madras.[127] When mass demonstrations in Bombay turned violent in January 1946, railway workers operating between Charni Road and Marine Lines stations on the Bombay, Baroda and Central India Railway line had to drive through activists pelting stones on the passing trains. Another group broke into a railway booking office at Ramwadi, Matunga, and removed its furnishing, setting them ablaze on the street outside.[128] On 13 February 1946, several hundred jute mill workers at the Kankinara railway station, outside Calcutta, held up railway workers operating the 99-Up Santipur train. When the police opened fire, the jute millworkers retaliated by setting the railway station and rakes from three different trains on fire.[129]

Survival Strategies

During the Quit India movement, many railway workers joined the struggle in an individual capacity as a survival strategy. In fact, there is evidence to indicate that the support of the Indian railway workers was entirely anticipated by activists of the Congress Party. During the movement, a pamphlet, 'A.B.C. of Dislocation' began circulating in the province of Punjab. The pamphlet contained elaborate plans for the building and operation of a nationwide guerrilla movement. The movement was to be organized around cells known as *Azad Dastas* (Free Units). The pamphlet contained detailed plans and proposals for the Azad Dastas. Many of these plans revolved around the disruption of India's railway system. Specifically, the pamphlet contained instructions on the removal of railway tracks and fishplates and the sabotage of overhead electric lines. The most pertinent instructions, however, relate to the disabling of locomotives. Here, the authors of the pamphlet clearly expected many individual railway workers to be sympathetic to their cause. The pamphlet stated that railway locomotives could best be damaged 'with the cooperation of railway workers. Special attention should be paid to it and our Labour Department should be asked to help.' During the early days of the Quit India movement, this anticipation seemed entirely justified. On 14 August 1941, a train pulled into Ballia railway station in the United Provinces. The train was filled with activist students from the city of Benares. The train itself proudly flew the flag of the Indian National Congress, by then a banned institution.[130]

There were many other instances of individual railway workers joining the struggle independently. One such worker was the stationmaster of the Hajipur railway station in Bihar. The railway station and town had been the site of considerable unrest immediately after Gandhi's Quit India declaration and had seen several violent incidents during the second and third weeks of August. These had culminated in a significant riot at the station during which two wagons were burned down completely. For his role in the riots, the police arrested the stationmaster later that month.[131] At the other end of the country, several railway workshop employees in Bombay were getting embroiled in the struggle as well. On 31 August 1942, the Bombay police arrested eight employees of the Matunga and Parel railway workshops under the Defense of India rules.[132] In the southern Indian district of Chittoor, a railway worker got involved with a group of activists working to disrupt rail traffic. On 23 August, the gangman and his comrades removed the fishplates from a section of the railway line between the railway stations of Panakappam and Chandragiri. It led to the derailment of a train. On 3 October, a special judge at Chittoor sentenced the worker along with seven of his associates to prison for five years.[133] On 11 October, the police at Dehradun, northern India, arrested five men on the grounds that they had been involved in the derailment of a goods train. The five included a railway watchman.[134]

The evidence is scanty from this point on. Not least because British press censorship laws dampened reporting of railway workers participating in the Quit India movement in an individual capacity. In fact, the movement was serious enough for the government to clamp down on reporting even on the state of the movement itself, leading to a striking silence in public sources outside the official archive. There is, however, additional evidence to indicate that many Indian railway workers supported the Quit India movement in particular, and the Independence struggle in general, and were likely prepared to join in the struggle. Inder Malhotra, journalist and author, was born into a railway family. The son of a stationmaster at Kalka, Punjab, Malhotra recalled how at the age of 12, in 1942, he and his friends had demanded that their school be closed in observance of a general strike, especially after news of a police shooting in Bombay reached them.[135]

Many railway workers adopted a second individual-level survival strategy. Faced with a choice between supporting the Indian freedom movement and the British Indian government, many railway workers chose loyalty to the Raj. While some of their colleagues joined activists seeking to overthrow the British rule in 1942, and again in 1945–1946, many railway workers decided to support the British Empire in its struggle for survival. There were several reasons why this survival strategy appealed to many railway workers. The British Indian railway workforce was exceptionally diverse. Some of this diversity had much to do with the complexity of the railway system itself; for instance, running a railway system required the operation of a staggering variety of mechanisms. Some of this diversity was exacerbated by the recruitment system in place. The official records of the Indian Railway Board indicate that in this period, the Indian railway system was tracking recruitment based on caste, race and religion. The tracking was part of a broader effort at altering the demographics of the railway workforce, particularly its upper ranks. There were two initiatives. Indianization, which was meant to reduce the European component of the workforce. And ensuring that the Indianization extended beyond the more privileged caste Hindus to include underprivileged castes and followers of other religions. Sections of the railway workforce believed that continued British rule suited their interests better. These especially included the European component of the railway workforce. To a lesser extent, there is evidence to suggest that many Anglo-Indian railway workers felt their futures more secure under the British rule. There is also some evidence to indicate that railway workers from underprivileged castes, especially Christian converts, may have been concerned with the upper caste dominance of the Indian freedom struggle. That many railway workers served the British Empire loyally in the face of the rising of Indian independence is made clear in the records of the Indian Railway Board. For their loyalty during the Quit India movement, the Railway Board awarded one George Medal, three other decorations and 32 commendations for individual bravery.[136]

In the year 1939, British railway workers made up just under half of all gazette officers in Class I Indian railway companies (849 of 1,765 or 48 per cent). Hindus constituted 30 per cent (533), Muslims, just under 7 per cent (123), Anglo-Indians and Domiciled Europeans (the latter constituting a rather vague category of Indians of European descent) 9 per cent (162). There were small numbers of Sikhs (34), Indian Christians (35) and Parsis (28). There were no Hindu Indians from the underprivileged castes. There were 7,602 highly skilled workers (subordinate staff). Of these, 962 were British (under 13 per cent). Hindus constituted 30 per cent (2,326), including 8 from the 'Depressed Classes' (Dalits). Anglo-Indians and Domiciled Europeans held 42 per cent of all such positions (3,227), constituting the most important demographic. Muslims made up 6 per cent (457). As in the case of gazette officers, there were smaller numbers of Sikhs (179), Indian Christians (220), and Parsis (163).[137] By 1946, the British proportion had fallen sharply among both gazette officers and subordinate staff (29 per cent and 7 per cent, respectively). The proportion of Hindus had risen among gazette officers (39 per cent) and subordinate staff (40 per cent). The number of Dalits had also increased in the ranks of subordinate staff (21), and there was at least one Dalit gazette officer. Anglo-Indians and Domiciled Europeans had risen in proportion among gazette officers (11 per cent) but declined among subordinate staff (34 per cent).[138]

The Railways' European staff and officers were loyal to the Empire. A small minority may have felt sympathetic to India's freedom struggle, and an even smaller number may have actively supported the struggle in this period, but most British railway workers stood firmly against the struggle.[139] F.E. Sharp, deputy inspector general of the Railway Police, directed operations when the Government of India turned to the Railways to transport the most significant political prisoners from Bombay to Ahmednagar for incarceration on 9 August 1942. Sharp ran into trouble in Poona where the train unexpectedly stopped. To his horror, passengers and other residents of the city, some anticipating their arrival, recognized his prisoners. Sharp later recalled,

> Hardly had I alighted on the platform when to my surprise I saw Nehru with remarkable agility climbing through the corridor window onto the platform. He was about ten yards from me and rushed straight towards the crowd. I got in his way and asked him to stop, but he made no attempt to do so and hence I was constrained to stop him with outstretched arms. He struggled violently with me screaming at the top of his voice that the Police were making a lathi charge and that he would not have it. I said that I knew nothing of this, and my orders were that he should not communicate with the public and he must please resume his seat in the train...He shouted to me..."I don't care about your bloody orders." He is a big man and was having a fair share of the struggle with me. At this moment, a sub-inspector caught him around the waist and with [the] help of two other constables...he was then overpowered.[140]

Sharp's survival strategy of loyalty to the British Empire in the face of nationalist unrest was typical of the British section of the railway workforce.

The Anglo-Indian and Domiciled European railway workers had mixed feelings about India's freedom struggle. While much of the community identified themselves with both Britain and India, the Anglo-Indian leadership gradually moved ever closer towards Indian nationalists as the twentieth century progressed. Henry Gidney, the most significant leader of the community till his death in 1942, advocated for a future India that was firmly within the British Empire. Frank Anthony, whose voice became the most important in Anglo-Indian politics from that point on, pushed the community leadership more decisively into the Independence movement. Correctly pointing out that the Anglo-Indian community's long loyalty to Britain had been betrayed by the British Indian state, Anthony urged Anglo-Indians to unambiguously support the freedom struggle. Nevertheless, many Anglo-Indians and Domiciled Europeans who worked in Indian Railways remained cautious. Roy Edward King Nissen, who spent much of his working life in the Indian Railways, later recalled that the Quit India movement enjoyed little currency in his social circles. Nissen himself, despite strong feelings on racial prejudice and discrimination that Anglo-Indians faced vis-a-vis British-born Europeans, did not recall any interest in joining the movement during these culminating years of the Indian freedom struggle.[141]

India's Dalit community, then referred to as 'Depressed Classes', constituted a substantial and underprivileged minority in the country. Their enumeration was and continues to be difficult, not least because many Dalits converted to other religions in the twentieth and twenty-first centuries. While Indian census enumerators did not count these converts, conversion did not offer full protection from the exploitation or oppression of the more privileged sections of Indian society, irrespective of religion. By the middle of the twentieth century, however, Dalits had acquired substantial political power through organization, collective action and the exceptional leadership skills of B.R. Ambedkar. In the years leading up to India's independence, it was difficult for any political movement in India to ignore Dalit political agency. In the context of the freedom struggle, Gandhi had tried a form of outreach himself, and while this outreach had yielded some dividends, substantial sections of Dalits were skeptical of his leadership. Ambedkar himself had reservations about Gandhi's ambitions and even on the question of India's independence. Ambedkar was concerned that an independent India could very well create a country that merely replicated the oppressive caste and class structures present in British India. Moreover, like much of the labor movement in India, Ambedkar believed that fascism constituted a far more dangerous threat to the world than British imperialism. During the Quit India movement, Ambedkar chose to focus on supporting the war effort rather than join in Gandhi's struggle. It is entirely possible that many Dalit railway workers felt the same way and remained cautious about India's freedom struggle during the Quit India movement. In her book *Ants Among Elephants*, Dalit author Sujata Gidla wrote about her grandfather who worked on the railways as a linesman. Gidla claimed that her grandfather, a Christian convert, strongly believed that his interests were more likely to be protected by India's British-Christian rulers than by an upper-caste Hindu-dominated Congress party.[142]

As India's independence grew nearer, relations between loyalists and nationalists frayed. In particular, relations between British railway workers and the more privileged sections of Indians working in the railway system began to worsen. The problem was particularly acute as both sides were keenly aware that each had the most to gain or lose with Independence. British railway workers anticipated the loss of their privileges and perhaps even their jobs with Independence, while their more privileged Indian counterparts anticipated replacing their British colleagues in a free India. Some of these mounting tensions are recalled in Abdul Kalam's autobiography *Recollections of a Railwayman.* Kalam began his career in the Indian Railways during the early days of the Second World War and was a trainee officer at Jamalpur during the Quit India movement. Kalam wrote about the resentment of British foremen at Jamalpur as more and more Indian trainee officers completed their graduation at the training institute. Kalam was quite clear; the foremen feared and resented a future where they would be subordinated to Indian officers. It was a future that was approaching fast. During the Second World War, the Indian Railways stopped recruiting British officers, dramatically increasing the proportion of Indians. Kalam also recounted one encounter with Rolf Emerson, a British railway officer. Kalam had just narrowly escaped a fight with departing British soldiers at the Bombay harbor, and Emerson, instead of backing up a fellow railway officer, let his racism get the better of himself. In addition to racist abuse ('Go back to your dirty Indian villages, you measly brutes who refuse to share accommodation with British soldiers'), Rolf ordered Kalam's suspension from the railway service. The incident, however, came on the eve of India's independence. The Chair of the Indian Railway Board, for the first time in its history, was an Indian. Kalam's suspension order was revoked.[143]

Collective Action as a Survival Strategy

Aware of their vulnerable position, the British-dominated Indian Railway Board reached out to Indian railway unions for support. During the difficult days of 1942, under pressure from India's faltering war effort, the Railway Board asked the AIRF for its support. The request was crucial. Gandhi launched his Quit India movement later that year. The AIRF–Railway Board meeting, held in April 1942, resulted in reassurances from the AIRF. The Railway Board's Annual Report for the year stated, 'The responsibilities of railway workers during wartime were discussed...and the Federation offered the wholehearted co-operation of all railwaymen in maintaining the normal working of the railways.'[144]

On several subsequent occasions, albeit with some reservations, individual trade unions did not waver from this commitment. On 21 August, B.R. Kalappa, President of the BNR Labor Union, issued a resolution that was supportive of the Quit India movement. He stated, 'The workers realize that their future is bound up with the political emancipation of the country...The workers urge [the] Government to release all national leaders... Only then can a better and lasting understanding be brought about between Britain and India.' Kalappa's proclamation specifically demanded the release of Maulana Abul Kalam Azad and Mahatma Gandhi on the grounds that they 'alone can control the situation and resume negotiations for a political settlement.' Nonetheless, Kalappa refrained from calling on his union members to wholeheartedly embrace the movement. His resolution clarified that railway workers affiliated with his union were staying at their posts in the interests of the war effort. Kalappa's above proclamation therefore also stated, 'The workers generally and more particularly railway workers have already resolved to stand at their posts in the event of Axis aggression and they have already striven hard to maintain the transport service, notwithstanding the strain due to other war conditions.'[145]

Similarly, on 15 October, the GIPR Workers Union issued a manifesto that tried to accommodate the war effort as well as the Quit India movement. Like Kalappa's proclamation, the manifesto was clearly supportive of the freedom struggle. It stated, 'We should attempt for Congress–Muslim League unity, on the basis of right for self-determination to minorities, the release of political prisoners, the establishment of a National Government, and the defeat of Fascist hordes.' Nonetheless, like the Kalappa resolution, the manifesto did not ask union members to join the struggle. Instead, referring to the importance of their work in the context of the war, the manifesto urged its members to remain at their posts. It stated, 'We should make a united front against Japan and gather all forces against it...under all conditions we must increase the output of war material to keep intact communications and strengthen the armed forces.'[146]

In contrast to this stated position during the Quit India movement, Indian railway unions refused to offer the Railway Board similar assurances during the 1945–1946 unrest. On the contrary, the evidence indicates that railway unions unambiguously came out in support of the freedom struggle. The months following the end of the war were characterized by a substantial expansion in union activity and labor unrest. While much of this unrest was concerned with issues of class conflict, the movements were also strikingly politicized. Labor movements in India demonstrated a consistent commitment to anti-imperialism. Indian trade unions, for instance, denounced the Allied Wars of imperialism in Dutch Indochina, and dockworkers refused to load Dutch ships carrying armaments. The start of the INA trials, however, unleashed a wave of labor unrest, perhaps unprecedented in Modern Indian history. In November 1945, public transportation in many cities ground to a halt as bus and tram workers, rickshaw pullers and taxi drivers, all went on strike. By February 1946, strikes had spread to the industrial sector, with cotton and jute mills, as well as heavy industrial units, shutting down because of labor unrest.[147]

The Royal Indian Navy mutiny escalated the movement even further. The RIN strike began in Bombay on 18 February 1946. That morning, naval ratings at the *HMIS Talwar* seized control of the base and expelled all senior officers. The mutiny then spread to a dozen other shore-based installations in the city, as well as 22 ships, anchored at the Bombay harbor. The mutineers established contact with sailors as far away as Karachi and Aden to coordinate a mass uprising. They also issued a charter of demands that included demands for the release of all political prisoners, the withdrawal of Indian troops from Indonesia and a speeding up of the demobilization process. The mutiny, over the next two days, spread to virtually every naval vessel in the vicinity of Bombay. Ten thousand sailors, commandeering 45 warships as well as additional smaller vessels, were soon in open rebellion. The rebel flotilla included two destroyers, the *HMIS Clive* and *HMIS Lawrence*, a frigate and four corvettes, in addition to other armed vessels. The shore-based installations included training centers, communication centers and residences for naval staff. The mutineers lowered British flags and insignia, replacing them with flags of the Indian National Congress party, the Indian Muslim League and the Communist Party of India.

On 20 February, confrontations broke out between the ratings and incoming Indian Army personnel. The ratings were armed with small arms and automatic weapons, while several warships pointed their heavy guns and other weapons towards the shore. On 21 February, the ratings clashed with units from the Royal Marines and the 5th Maratha Light Infantry. After exchanging fire, the ratings withdrew from the *HMIS Talwar*. In the meantime, hectic negotiations between the mutineers, the Royal Indian Navy leadership and the Indian political leadership resulted in a breakthrough. While the British Indian government refused to accede to any of the mutineers' major demands, negotiators were able to secure guarantees that the mutineers would not face prosecution and would be discharged at the earliest. On 23 February, the mutineers raised black flags on their ships to confirm their surrender.

The mutineers received considerable support from the civilian population in Bombay. On 20 February, industrial workers from the city's textile mills went on strike in solidarity with the ratings. They were joined by railway workers from the Great Indian Peninsula, and the Bombay, Baroda and Central India Railway company workshops. Mass transit workers of the Bombay Electric Supply and Transport company brought tram and bus services to a halt as well. The laborers marched on the streets and gathered in mass meetings in the city's parks and open spaces. Flying flags of their unions, the Communist Party, the Congress Party and the Muslim League, the workers urged others to join them with the slogan '*Izzatwala Bahar Ho!*' (Let the honorable march with us).[148]

Although peaceful in its initial stages, the increased military presence in the city raised tensions. On 22 February, with the police force and military under orders to curb the movement, laborers were pushed into violent confrontations. There were clashes at Lalbaug and Delisle Road, both in the city's industrial belt. The police and military also attacked laborers in their tenements. The military and police used armed force, including 'rifles, revolvers, and Bren guns.' By the evening, there were over 850 casualties with bullet wounds in the city's hospitals. *The Bombay Chronicle* estimated the death toll to be anywhere between 60 and 100. The dead included women and a ten-year-old child whose corpse journalists discovered in the city morgue. Reportage from the *Chronicle* sheds light on the ability of organized laborers to resist the attacks. Journalists from the affected neighborhoods reported that laborers fought back with barricades and a signaling system using whistles to warn comrades of approaching police and military patrols. These appeared at random, driving through crowded streets at high speeds, during which they knocked down pedestrians, stopping at other times and opening fire into crowds indiscriminately. Sections of the police and the military also actively prevented ambulance drivers from taking away wounded laborers. The armed forces even fired into the windows of J.J. Hospital in a bid to terrorize the population.[149] By 24 February, when the mutiny had ended, 270 were dead and over 1,700 wounded. There had been fierce fighting in the city. Some 75 policemen, including 15 officers, had been wounded. Over 300 cars, vans and trucks had been burned.[150]

The Royal Indian Navy mutiny, though centered in Bombay, also involved ratings in Calcutta. On 19 February 1946, some 300 sailors seized control of the *HMIS Hooghly*, a shore-based naval installation at the port.[151] They were soon joined by an additional 200 sailors at the Kidderpore Docks.[152] The strike was remarkably peaceful with ratings restricting their activism to a sit-down action only. On 21 February however, the situation turned ugly with at least one confrontation between naval ratings and armed soldiers of the Mahratta regiment. In the meantime, warships on the Hooghly began raising steam, a sure sign that their crew members were preparing to hoist ammunition onto their four-inch guns. By the afternoon, there were reports of sporadic gunfire across the area.[153] When ratings in Bombay negotiated an end to their strike on 23 February, the ratings in Calcutta refused to follow suit. The ratings held out for two more days before agreeing to resume work.[154] In the meantime, as reports of the brutality in Bombay reached the city, labor unions across Calcutta struck work. On 23 February, the public transit system ground to a halt as bus and tram workers went on strike. Large crowds stopped the movement of trains at the city's two main railway stations. Employees of the BAR at Sealdah terminus joined the strike. Consequently, even after the police cleared the crowds off the tracks, no trains departed the station. Meanwhile, 1,00,000 laborers from factories and workshops across the city gathered at Wellington Square in downtown Calcutta. The protestors condemned police and military repression in Bombay and expressed solidarity with the mutineers.[155] Services did not resume until the next day.[156]

Railway workers and parts of the working-class population went on strike in Madras as well. The strike broke out on

25 February in protest against the brutal suppression of the RIN strikes in Bombay and Madras. Like in Calcutta, tram and bus workers brought mass transit systems in the city to a halt. They were joined by workers from the city's printing presses and other workshops. Upon calls from trade unions, laborers at the city's locomotive sheds walked away from their jobs. In solidarity, railway workers operating the city's commuter rail system temporarily brought the services to a halt in the form of a one-hour strike. Clerical staff at the Madras and Southern Mahratta railway offices joined the strike in the afternoon. The staff members met in their office compound and passed a resolution condemning the police atrocities in Bombay.[157] Meanwhile, the strike spread to the nearby city of Madurai. There, locomotive shed staff, firemen, parcel office porters, pointsmen, gatemen and refreshment room staff, all walked off their jobs on the morning of 27 February. Their strike disrupted rail services, and in the evening, the workers joined a mammoth rally in solidarity with the RIN ratings.[158]

While the RIN strike has rightly enjoyed substantial attention in the post-colonial memories of independent India and Pakistan, a far bigger strike on the part of Indian railway workers has been largely forgotten. In August 1946, forty thousand employees of the South Indian Railway (SIR) company struck work. Like the RIN workers, the strike was the result of grossly unfair management practices made possible by the racism and disdain for the working poor, shared by the British managerial class across India. Like the RIN mutiny, the SIR strike affected a vast area, extending to both coasts of Peninsular India. The strike, in fact, extended beyond the territories of British India, affecting rail transport in the autonomous Princely States of Travancore and Cochin. It also gained the support and solidarity of working people across the Indian subcontinent, with sympathy strike waves affecting cities and regions as far as Allahabad, and companies like the NWR company, located over a thousand miles away. The strike also lasted much longer. While its psychological impact on India's British rulers may have been less, considering the smaller security threat railway workers posed, its impact on the morale of India's working class is undeniable.

The origins of the SIR strike lay in a series of decisions made by the British Indian government in its post-war hubris. Emboldened by the success of the British Indian Army in defeating the Japanese in Southeast Asia and buoyed by the exultation in Britain following its successful war against Germany, the British Indian leadership felt little need to reward the Indian railway workers for their efforts and sacrifices during the war. Instead of fulfilling previously made promises of improved pay, job security and working conditions, the Railway Board announced reductions in wages and the retrenchment of over 30,000 employees. In response, the AIRF gave the government a 'strike notice.' Nine lakh railway employees were to walk off their jobs beginning 27 June. The AIRF's demands were unambiguous; a rollback of the Board's retrenchment plans, increases in wages and dearness allowances and a three-month pay bonus. All demands were in line with promises made by the Railway Board at various times during the war and recommendations made by a special committee report led by Justice B.N. Rao. The AIRF issued a strike ballot, which received overwhelming support from the railway workforce.[159]

In the meantime, regional trade unions were already going on strike. In April, railway workers at Hubli, in southern India, struck work demanding compensatory allowances in lieu of cuts in their grain shop rations. On 1 May, 70,000 railway workers of the NWR company staged a four-hour strike. They demanded higher wages, improved rations and a rollback of the retrenchment process. The railway workers also protested the corrupt and repressive management practices of what was still a largely British managerial class. During these months, every major railway system experienced labor unrest in the form of public protests and preparations for strike actions.[160] In the face of this concerted action on the part of the railway workforce, the Indian Railway Board made a tactical retreat. It offered the workforce an interim relief package of Rs 4/8 for all railway workers earning less than Rs 250 per month, totaling a substantial Rs 9 crore. The Board also established a high-powered Indian Railways Enquiry Committee to investigate the demands of the Indian railway workforce. The Indian Railway Board also agreed to temporarily suspend the retrenchment of railway workers.[161] In return, the AIRF called off its strike.

In September, a largely Indian Interim Government replaced the British-dominated Viceroy's Executive Council. This accounted for a significant break from the past, constituting the first government in modern India that could even remotely claim to be representative of the Indian people. The members of this interim government were considerably more sympathetic to the demands of the Indian railway workers. In fact, it was under the watch of Railway Minister Asaf Ali that the Indian Railway Board got its first Indian members. Nevertheless, with the immediate threat of strike action receding, the then still British-dominated Railway Board and upper management decided on a program to systematically undermine the power of organized labor in the railway system. The SIR management was the most aggressive in this campaign. Through the summer of 1946, the SIR locked out much of the labor force at the Golden Rock Railway workshop in Tiruchirapalli. The railway managers dismissed scores of important SIR Labor Union members, demoted hundreds more and penalized over a thousand. The managers, in their campaign, ordered punitive transfers of large numbers of even low-paid employees and made changes in service rules to block appeals against such transfers. A statement condemning such policies by the AIRF made no difference.[162]

At midnight, 24 August 1946, 30,000 railway workers

on the SIR system went on strike. The men included clerical staff, engine drivers, fitters, gatemen, pointsmen, shunters and stationmasters. Railway stations and workshops stood silent. Two trade unions, the SIR labour union and the All India Station Masters' Association (AISMA), had given the call, and the response was sufficient to cripple services in the region. It was the biggest strike in Indian railway history. The SIR system covered railway lines that extended from Madras to the southern tip of India, extending onto the Princely States of Travancore, Cochin and the Malabar Coast in southwestern India, some 40,000 miles of track. Three hundred of the 650 railway stations on the system closed down. Capturing the immediate effects of the strike, *The Bombay Chronicle* reported 'Egmore station [Madras] which used to be most lively and crowded in the evening, looks desolate with only a number of steel helmeted railway police on bandobust [patrol] duty.'[163]

The SIR management responded with several initiatives to break the strike. J.F.C. Reynolds, general manager of SIR, announced substantial wage increases for strikebreakers. He doubled wages for all laborers earning less than Rs 30 per month, offered a 66.66 per cent increase for all railway workers earning between Rs 31 and Rs 100, a 33.33 per cent increase for all railway workers earning between Rs 101 and Rs 250, and a 20 per cent increase for all other employees 'who work under arduous circumstances until the position is again reviewed.'[164] The Indian Railway Board, meanwhile, sanctioned Rs 30,000 for Reynolds to hire blacklegs to help break the strike.[165] The SIR management received unexpected help when the largely Congress Party-controlled Madras provincial government came out in opposition to the strike. With important levers of the provincial government machinery on its side, the SIR management was also able to deploy brute force against the strike. On 26 August, for instance, the police used tear gas against women railway workers at the Madurai station.[166] The police also began arresting strike leaders. On 27 August, they arrested E.M.S. Namboodiripad, later chief minister of Kerala, and A.K. Gopalan, a future parliamentarian in independent India.[167]

In response to this, striking workers resorted to sabotage. They placed a large stone near the Meenambakkam and concrete slabs near Saidapet, both railway stations in the vicinity of Madras. Elsewhere, railway workers removed fishplates on the Pondicherry-Villupuram section to hold up traffic there. At some locations, railway workers threw stones at passing trains. In at least one place, striking railway workers assaulted a strikebreaker. These tactics forced the SIR management to deploy special patrol trains and place restrictive prohibitory orders near railway lines.[168]

Meanwhile, strikes of solidarity broke out across the Indian railway system and even across the Indian working class. In addition to strikes in solidarity with the BAR, Bombay and Nagpur, Great Indian Peninsula, and NWR companies, laborers from many other industries across southern India also struck work. These included 70,000 laborers in Travancore and a further 40,000 in Coimbatore. Four thousand tannery workers in Dindigul struck work in solidarity, as did laborers in a variety of other industries, from hotels to sanitation. In far off Allahabad, over a thousand miles from Madras, textile workers struck in sympathy. In addition to industrial labor, there is also evidence indicating support from agricultural workers. Many railway workers supplemented meager incomes with farm work, often living and maintaining homes in rural areas. These rural communities provided support in the form of fundraising and shelter when union members sought protection from the police.[169]

The most serious confrontations were however at the Golden Rock Railway workshop. A massive workshop with state-of-the-art facilities, it became the site of a horrific clash between armed policemen and railway workers. On the morning of 5 September, a large contingent of policemen arrived at the workshop to arrest two important union leaders, one of whom was K. Ananda Nambiar, later a parliamentarian in Independent India. The police then confronted a thousand-strong workforce who tried to prevent them from taking away the union leaders. In response, the police attacked the workers, leaving over a hundred injured. They also opened fire on the crowd using live ammunition.[170] The firing killed four workmen, all young men in their twenties.[171]

The strike came to an end on 22 September. Following a meeting of the joint strike committee representing the SIR labor union and the AISMA, S. Guruswamy, general secretary of the AIRF, issued the following statement, 'In deference to the advice given by the Railway Member to the strikers and his personal assurances to me, the Joint Strike Committee has today unanimously decided to call off the strike forthwith and at the same time request the General Manager of the Railway to allow adequate time for the strikers to resume duty as it will take some time for this decision to reach the strikers.'[172] There were many reasons for the withdrawal. First, the brutality of the railway authorities and the willingness of the Madras provincial government to look the other way at best, at worst, aid the persecution of the movement, weakened the ability of the railway workers to sustain their strike. There is also evidence to indicate a systematic campaign of disinformation on the part of the railway authorities, which played a role in the resolution. From the earliest days of the strike, the SIR's media communiqués emphasized the limits of the strike. The communiqués systematically undermined the scale of the strike by emphasizing not the significant number of workers on strike but the percentage. This indicated that the strike was not total and, therefore, a failed enterprise. The communiqués also emphasized just how much of the system was still functional, minimizing the effects of the strike. Even these were dismissed by pointing out how they were inconveniencing passengers and freight.[173] On the other hand, larger changes were afoot that gave Indian railway workers hope. In early September, Asaf Ali had become India's first railway member of the interim government. A sympathetic and friendly figure in the country's most powerful institution of government raised new possibilities for railway workers. Indeed, it was assurances from Asaf Ali's office that made a decisive impact on negotiations leading to a withdrawal of the strike.[174]

***

The evidence indicates that Indian railway workers deployed a variety of survival strategies during the culmination of India's freedom struggle. Buffeted by pressure from the British Indian government determined to use the railway system to crush the nationalist movement, Indian railway workers had to find creative means to support the freedom struggle that held the possibilities of a better future for the majority of them. There were variations and even contradictions in these strategies. Nonetheless, several identifiable patterns are present in this story. There were two major challenges in the form of pressure from the British Indian state. The first challenge was demands from the British Indian government that Indian railway workers do their part to ensure the failure of the Quit India movement. This was particularly difficult as it was often clearly against the interests of the railway workers concerned. The second was the pressure from Indian nationalists who expected support from Indian railway workers and identified the railway system as a part of their adversary, the government's repressive machinery. Indian railway workers responded individually in two ways. Several of them, on their own initiative, joined the struggle for freedom. On the other hand, British railway workers largely stayed loyal to the colonial state. Important sections of the railway workforce, such as Anglo-Indians and Dalits, were cautious. The most important survival strategies however came in the form of collective action. In 1942, during the Quit India movement, Indian railway unions unanimously expressed their solidarity with the freedom struggle but also refused to bring their services to a halt, arguing that there could be no letup in the war against fascism. This decision allowed individual railway workers to resist the competing pressures effectively and survive the challenge of that difficult moment. However, during the 1945–1946 unrest, Indian railway unions came out fully in support of the freedom struggle, allowing the workers to play their part. This the workers did with substantial effect through collective action, especially in the form of strikes during those two years.

The significance of this course of action and survival strategy lies in the role played by the Indian railway workers in India's freedom struggle. There is consensus amongst historians that the unrest of 1945–1946 was critical to India's independence. While much of the British ruling class foresaw Indian independence as inevitable at the end of the Second World War, there was little indication that this was coming anytime soon, especially not as soon as 1947. That Clement Attlee made his declaration of Britain's intent to depart had much to do with that unrest. The British ruling class were rattled by the popular unrest generated by the INA trials. The climb down of the British establishment from accusing INA troops of treason to releasing them without any real punishment is indicative of this. There is also sufficient evidence suggesting that the naval mutiny played an important part in Attlee's decision. Here, the Indian railway workers certainly had a small but significant role. Railway workers in Bombay stood with the naval ratings in confronting the military forces unleashed by the British Indian government. The Indian National Congress party was the biggest beneficiary of the unrest. The party won an overwhelming majority of the vote in the 1946 elections and formed the interim government. But the Congress Party was not the only victor. Loyalist parties across the country performed badly, sending out an unambiguous message to the British ruling class that the propertied class among the most loyal set of Indians, with the right to vote, had become an insignificant minority. This played its own part in Attlee's decision. Certainly, there would be no going back. The South Indian Railway strike was about class-based issues but also intrinsically tied to the nationalist project. The railway strike targeted unfair and cruel management practices facilitated by imperialism. The strike occurred and continued because of the imperialist nature of the British Indian state and the Indian Railway Board. It came to an end because this form of government and public institutions was coming to an end. The emergence of a free India made possibilities for a fairer workplace a far more realistic prospect. This was understood by the railway workforce and supported in its entirety.

THREE

'West Bound Refugee Train Passes Amritsar Safely'

IN 1947, AS British rule in India drew to a close, India's rulers decided to partition the country. Forged through a series of short but intense negotiations, the departing British, leading lights of the Indian National Congress party and the Muslim League party agreed that this was the best possible solution to a long-running political question that had turned tragically violent in the run-up to Independence. The partition process affected Indian and now Pakistani railway workers profoundly. The division of British India into two countries required the partition of the Indian railway system. Two railway companies, the NWR and the BAR, were particularly affected. The NWR tracks fell on both sides of newly created boundaries in the western portion of what was formerly British India. The BAR tracks fell on both sides of newly created boundaries in the east. The effects of Partition however were felt across much larger portions of the railway system.

Partition, in fact, turned into a humanitarian catastrophe. Perhaps the worst in the region's history. It precipitated a bloodbath unprecedented in scale and horror and a refugee crisis that remains unmatched to this present day. Partition was premised on the idea of a separate nationhood for British India's Muslim population, the world's largest but constituting a minority in the country. It was also precipitated by repeated rounds of religiously inspired violence organized and orchestrated by Hindu and Muslim extremists and the Muslim League whose leadership, at least on occasion, identified violence as a legitimate tool necessary to achieve the party's political aims.[175] The decision to partition the country, however, exacerbated the problem substantially as many people in the two religiously mixed provinces, Bengal and Punjab, concluded that a form of religious ethnic cleansing was the most effective way to ensure the provinces or at least a section of them ended up in Hindu-majority India or Muslim-majority Pakistan. It is now estimated that Partition killed more than half a million people and displaced a further 10 million.

Indian and Pakistani railway workers deployed multiple survival strategies to overcome the challenge of Partition. Many of these were taken at an institutional level. Railway operators at all levels of the railway bureaucracy made changes in procedures and protocols, took quick decisions and thought in innovative ways to ensure that the railway system continued to function and passengers and staff remained safe through the crisis. After Partition, the railway systems of both countries demonstrated a willingness to collaborate in order to minimize the disruptive effects of the process. At an individual level, many railway workers displayed bravery and courage, keeping their passengers and each other safe. Others showed prudence, seeking security through migration or simply avoiding danger. At times, a few railway workers turned to active collaboration with thugs, criminals and murderers, participating in bloodshed and profiting from the looting. Finally, some railway workers turned to collective action, organized on the basis of religion, community or occupation within the railway system. These railway workers sought to secure their interests in this turbulent moment through collective bargaining.

Indian railway workers played a very important role in the partition of the country. It is now estimated that railway workers in India and Pakistan transported 3 million refugees through the Partition crisis. This is a staggering figure unmatched in the history of railway transportation. The figure is even more impressive considering that this feat of transportation was undertaken by a railway system that was undergoing a major administrative partition of its own. More importantly, railway workers transporting these refugees were doing it not from the safety of a distance from the location of the crisis (as European railway workers have through the recent refugee crises precipitated by wars in Ukraine and Syria). Rather, in many cases, Indian and Pakistani railway workers transported these refugees through what had effectively become warzones. Thousands of Indian and Pakistani railway workers carried out their work at great personal risk to themselves and their families.

The evidence is quite unambiguous. When faced with a crisis of unmatched proportions, Indian and Pakistani railway workers rose to the occasion with great courage and determination. There is little doubt that their heroism saved hundreds of thousands of lives. In fact, it is fair to state that without a functioning railway system, Partition could have been much more catastrophic. Such a situation is hardly inconceivable. The railway system might easily have cracked under pressure. No reasonable authority could blame engine crews for refusing to operate in Punjab where law and order had collapsed, and the worst forms of human butchery had become everyday affairs. While the violence was relatively muted in Bengal, rail transportation in this region too had become hazardous. Indian and Pakistani railway unions would have been well within reason had they refused to operate trains under such dangerous and trying working conditions. As a matter of fact, Indian and

Pakistani railway authorities suspended significant portions of their regular services in response to the crisis. Alternatively, the railway workers on both sides could easily have turned on each other. Hindus, Muslims and Sikhs were engaged in a brutal communal war in Punjab, Bengal and to some extent in Sindh. In fact, there is every indication to suggest that some railway workers did participate in communal violence.

The question then becomes, why did these things not come to pass? How did the railway system continue to function when much of the remaining state machinery collapsed? During the peak of the crisis, even the military, the most well-resourced branch of the British Indian state, found itself floundering in the Punjab countryside. Why did so many railway workers demonstrate bravery and decency rather than slip into barbarism? How did so many railway workers demonstrate solidarity with their comrades that transcended religious differences at a moment when the country's ruling class accepted religion as the primary basis for Pakistani nationhood? This chapter examines survival strategies to answer these questions.

The humanitarian crisis began in the summer of 1947. On 3 June, British India's last Viceroy, Louis Mountbatten, announced his 'Partition Plan.' Less a plan and more a recipe for disaster, Mountbatten announced that the territories of British India were to be divided into two new dominions, India and Pakistan. The religiously mixed provinces of Bengal and Punjab had to be divided between the two countries. Most importantly, the plan stated that British suzerainty over British India was to end on 15 August 1947, significantly earlier than the anticipated date of June 1948 announced by British Prime Minister Clement Attlee. The much-shortened timeline might have given the British the opportunity to escape responsibility for whatever went wrong during Partition, but it made the administrative process much more difficult. This was, in fact, central to the humanitarian catastrophe that followed. A final

British disaster capping two centuries of catastrophic British rule.

Two particularly onerous challenges that resulted from Partition were the division of territories in Bengal and Punjab and the division of national assets between the two dominions. All this was unfolding as communal violence between Hindus, Muslims and Sikhs was escalating. In March, communal riots in Rawalpindi resulted in over 2,000 fatalities. The riots spread to Amritsar, Attock, Jhelum, Multan and Lahore, signaling the start of not only the violence and bloodbath that followed Partition but also the refugee crisis. A crisis where the railways quickly emerged as an important mode of escape. In 1967, an official Government of India report described this early movement of refugees making this very point: 'Overnight he has packed up, rushed to the nearest railhead, thence to flee eastward to safety in India.'[176]

Communal violence continued through the summer, engulfing especially the towns of Lahore and Gurdaspur. Both cities were religiously mixed and located in Central Punjab. For many residents of the two cities, ethnic cleansing through religiously inspired violence seemed the best means of ensuring their homes ended up on the right side of the border. The British Indian government's mishandling of the partition of the country continued till Pakistan's and India's Independence on 14 and 15 August respectively. The specially created Boundary Commission released its maps only that day, keeping the populations of Bengal and Punjab unsure of where their respective provinces were to be partitioned until the very last minute. By then, the world was beginning to wake up to the reality of a massive refugee crisis. The national press accompanied its giddying articles on Independence and the establishment of free India and Pakistan's first governments with sober stories on the growing movement of people. While Mountbatten exalted with his head in the clouds, even the senior-most members of the departing British administration began sounding the alarm. On 18 August, Francis Muddie, governor of West Punjab, wrote that in two border districts alone, refugees numbering between 100 and 150 thousand needed immediate evacuation. Of course, he correctly envisaged the central role railways would play in such an evacuation. 'It will take 45 trains to move them, even at 4000 people per train,' he wrote.[177]

The bureaucracies of independent India and Pakistan finally responded to the crisis by establishing Military Evacuation Organizations (MEOs) on 1 September 1947. Working together, the two MEOs tried to coordinate the biggest refugee evacuation program in history. On 20 October, the two MEOs finalized their plans to move about 10 million refugees. The planners noted that over 2 million had already moved between the two dominions. The plan made specific mention of trains: 'Railway trains will be used to move urban populations, rural people who have no bullock carts or cattle or who are unfit to walk. Each train will carry at least 2,500 people…'[178] To put this plan into operation, the MEOs established a Refugee Rail control center in Lahore. The plan required the contribution of 20 trains from India and 12 from Pakistan with five to six trains running between the two dominions daily. The trains came to be known as India and Pakistan 'Specials' and were free of cost to users. The plan also included provisions for water, food and sanitation, as well as plans for safety and measures to prevent overcrowding.[179]

The plans were overoptimistic, with the MEOs unable to provide adequate water, food and sanitation or prevent overcrowding or even guarantee the safety of its passengers. Nevertheless, the system ran 643 refugee Specials, successfully transporting over a million Hindus and Sikhs from Pakistan to India and over a million Muslims from India to Pakistan between 27 August and the end of November 1947.[180] Railway companies in eastern India and Pakistan transported additional passengers. Here, the pressure was less due to the more muted violence and staggered migration. The traffic was also largely one-way because the flow of Muslims from eastern India into East Pakistan remained negligible. In his speech to India's Constituent Assembly in February of 1948, free India's first railway minister, John Mathai, stated with justified pride, '...altogether during a period of two and a half months the Railways were called upon to move as many as 3 million refugees, which represents the capacity of a thousand passenger trains.'[181]

There are no comprehensive accounts of Partition-related attacks on railway stations and trains. However, newspaper reports indicate a clear escalation over the autumn of 1947. The violence began in railway stations, with several attacks in the first two weeks of August leading up to Partition. There were also at least two occasions when mobs brought trains to a halt. The attacks occurred in two provinces in western India: Punjab and Sindh, and one province in eastern India: Bengal. On 3 August 1947, for instance, unknown attackers threw bombs on the Majitha and Fatehgarh Churian railway stations, both located north of Amritsar, Eastern Punjab. There had been terrible riots that day all across that city. Six stabbing incidents and an explosion in a factory had forced local authorities to put in place a curfew in the town. The bomb at the Majitha railway station killed four and injured three. The bomb thrown at the Fatehgarh Churian station killed one and wounded six others.[182] Four days later, on 7 August, riots broke out in Calcutta, over 1,200 miles east of Amritsar. In addition to substantial rioting across the city, there was a clash at the Ballygunge railway station. The station serviced commuter trains. The riot spilled out of the station itself and onto the railway tracks. A mob forced a commuter train to stop. The attackers killed a passenger and kidnapped two others.[183] The violence in Calcutta did not stop there and continued to affect the railway system.

The following day, an even larger mob, several hundred strong this time, stopped a passenger train just outside the city. The attackers hacked 11 passengers to death.[184] The violence in Calcutta continued unabated though the railway system was spared for a few days. On 11 August, however, a pitched battle between Hindus and Muslims at Sealdah railway station left five people dead.[185] Finally, there were riots in the province of Sindh, a Muslim-majority province slated for Pakistan but with a significant Hindu minority. The province had seen less violence compared to Punjab. On 9 August, however, clashes broke out at two railway stations in the city of Hyderabad. Members of the Hindu Sabha and Congress Party volunteers clashed at the Shahdapur and Tando Adams railway stations leading to several injuries.[186]

Independence Day, 14 August in Pakistan and 15 August in India, provided railway workers in both dominions a respite from the violence. The very next day, however, serious riots broke out in Punjab and continued over the following weekend. There was a perceptible increase in the scale and ferocity of the violence. Its effects on the railway system also increased in tandem. In contrast to the first part of August, mobs seemed emboldened enough to stop trains and disrupt traffic. On 16 August, barely a day after Independence celebrations, there were riots at the Amritsar station and on the line running to the new border post at Wagah. The disturbances were serious enough to disrupt rail transportation between Delhi and Lahore. Operators on the Eastern Punjab railway halted all services on the Amritsar line. On Friday, 16 August, the Down Frontier Mail departed Delhi for Lahore, and was rerouted through Bhatinda.[187] The services remained disrupted until 19 August, when the violence briefly receded again.[188] The situation continued to remain stable for the next few days, though with the violence never fully abating. For instance, on 23 August, there was an altercation between a military non-commissioned officer serving as a military escort for a refugee train and an assailant who stabbed him. The NCO was able to fire back, wounding his attacker.[189]

The last week of August saw a significant escalation. Incidents of violence on the railway system began clearly spilling over from clashes at railway stations to lethal attacks on trains. Ominously, the violence also began spreading to the regions around free India's capital, Delhi. On 24 August, a riot at the Badami Bagh railway station in Lahore left three passengers dead, stabbed by a mob while waiting for their train. Later that afternoon, rioters forced a train to stop nearby. The attackers killed three of the train's passengers. The unrest that day, in fact, disrupted rail traffic throughout Punjab. The Punjab Mail heading towards Lahore was forced to stop twice. A mob forced the train to stop near Faridkot, while another mob stopped the train farther along its journey. There were several casualties as both sets of attackers assaulted the passengers. A passenger train running between Pakpattan and Kasur also came under attack. A mob near the Khudian Khas railway station in Montgomery district, Central Punjab, attacked a train filled with refugees. The attackers murdered several passengers. The unrest forced Indian Railways operators to suspend all services on the Delhi–Bhatinda line.[190] On 27 August, government authorities reported that 13,000 railway freight trucks were stuck on either side of the India-Pakistan boundary as a direct result of the disturbances.[191] On 31 August, a mob attacked the Frontier Mail at the Khanna railway station. Attackers murdered a passenger and burned down the first-class compartment.[192]

During the last three days of August, the violence was particularly bad in and around Delhi. On 28 August, a mob forced a refugee train from Gurgaon, Rajasthan, to stop 20 miles from the city. Seven people died in the ensuing violence.[193] On 31 August, a mob attacked a goods train at Bahadurgarh railway station on the outskirts of the city. It was a luggage train with the belongings of government employees who had opted to work for the Government of Pakistan. While troops were able to disperse the mob with minimal force, they were unable to stop the train from burning down. There was also an altercation at the New Delhi railway station. Baloch soldiers of the new Pakistan Army clashed with Indian Railways personnel. The soldiers had arrived to escort government employees who had chosen to relocate to Pakistan and assaulted a clerk of the railway mail service attached to the Ahmedabad Mail. The soldiers were scheduled to take the train in two special compartments. The passengers on board, however, refused to let the train leave with the soldiers. Eventually, the railway personnel decoupled the two compartments.[194]

The terrors of August were, however, soon overshadowed by events in September 1947. Armed mobs began attacking trains filled with refugees on a regular basis. There were at least 25 instances when railway personnel operating refugee and passenger trains came under attack in this month alone. On 1 September, mobs attacked two trains on the outskirts of Delhi. The first was a commuter train packed with local passengers between the Narela and Badli railway stations, about 10 miles to the northwest of the city. *The Bombay Chronicle* reported that 'it is feared, some persons were killed.' A second attack occurred at Patel Nagar station.[195]

On 2 September, there was a well-planned and coordinated attack on a refugee train near Shafiabad on the Jodhpur railway system. The attackers began their operation by first removing a rail from the tracks, ensuring a derailment. When the train arrived, the locomotive pulling the compartments and wagons toppled over. Two other wagons also went off the rails. An armed mob then attacked the train. The passengers included several Sikh refugees. The attackers, clearly informed about their presence, targeted them. The attackers killed 11 men and four women. They also wounded 17 others. The targeting became evident when the attackers chose to leave the many other passengers on the train unharmed. The railway workers operating the train were also left well alone. There was little that the railway staff on the line could do. Once word reached the Jodhpur railway bureaucracy, officials arranged for the dispatch of a relief train. The attack had occurred around noon, and the relief train left at half past four. The train reached the site only after midnight. The passengers, including the wounded, had waited almost 12 hours. It took another 10 hours before the train reached the nearest major railway station, by which time another passenger died from inflicted injuries.[196]

There were two lethal attacks on trains over the following two days. The death toll from the two attacks exceeded any recorded till then. On 4 September, a murderous mob held up the Delhi Express at the Shekendrapura station near Khurja, west of the capital. The attackers massacred 30 passengers on board. A second attack resulted in 200 fatalities. A fearful clash at Amritsar railway station led to the bloodbath. The attack occurred when two trains arrived at the station at the same time. One headed east, filled with refugees from Pakistan. The other headed west, filled with Pakistan Army soldiers. The two trains passed each other while crossing the Beas River when passengers on one of the trains opened fire on the other.[197] On 8 September, vicious rioting ripped through Delhi, forcing train services to a complete halt. The fighting spilled into New Delhi railway station where mobs pulled passengers out of trains and killed them.[198] On 9 September, a porter at the Victoria Terminus railway station in Bombay, 900 miles south of Delhi, stumbled upon a bomb on board the Calcutta Mail. *The Bombay Chronicle* reported on the discovery: 'It was an insignificant card-board box which looked rather heavy for its puny size. Inside, from a slight opening, the coolie could see four roundish looking "fishy" objects. Intuitively he felt that it contained dangerous and inflammable substances and without touching the discarded parcel, he drew the attention of a Railway Police Constable to his find.'[199] While it remains unclear who planted the device, considering the violence of Partition, it was in all probability, related.

The attacks continued through mid-September. On 11 September, a mob attacked a refugee train at Badami Bagh, Srinagar. A soldier escorting the train died defending the passengers. The attackers wounded two other soldiers and 15 refugees. In New Delhi railway station, meanwhile, a guard used lethal force against a mob trying to attack a Pakistan-bound goods train. He killed three of the assailants.[200] Over the next two days, mobs held up three trains in West Punjab, near the city of Mianwali. Troops protecting the trains, however, successfully kept the refugees safe. On 13 September, there was another bloodbath involving armed soldiers firing on a refugee train. This time, the incident occurred at Sheikhpura and involved a train filled with Hindu and Sikh refugees headed for India and the armed escort of a train filled with Muslim refugees. At least 60 people were killed and an additional 70 wounded.[201] On 16 September, troops escorting a train opened fire at a mob of assailants at Bhatinda, East Punjab. The soldiers left two attackers wounded. Armed soldiers also inflicted several casualties while trying to disperse a mob at Asaoti railway station, also in east Punjab.[202]

The last two weeks of September saw the geographical spread of attacks expand across northern and central India. An armed gang stopped a train near Ludhiana, East Punjab, and engaged its armed escort in 'hand to hand' fighting. The battle raged for 45 minutes. Twelve passengers died, and 37 were wounded. An additional 40 were missing. The commanding officer and three of his men sustained injuries. There was also an attack on a refugee train at Lahore railway station. Gunmen opened fire on the passengers killing 21 and injuring 13. There were also several attacks in Sindh and the United Provinces. A mob stormed a moving train between Sukkur and Jacobabad, robbing its passengers. A mob threw out a couple from another moving train. Another mob shot and robbed a traffic inspector and threw out two passengers on board a third moving train. There was also an attack on a train in Mathura, in the United Provinces. Police opened fire to disperse a mob intent on looting the freight train.[203] On 20 September, a mob stabbed and then threw a male passenger off a moving train, while a woman passenger suffered a similar fate near Muzaffarnagar in the UP. Both passengers survived but sustained injuries. Attackers also threw a passenger off a train at Babina in the UP. Meanwhile, a mob at Gwalior, central India, threw some 18 passengers off the UP-Madras express.[204]

On 21 September, there were grisly scenes at Lahore railway station. The violence in the city had escalated after the arrival of a refugee train with 166 corpses on board, including those of 59 children and 29 women. There were another 106 wounded on board. Angry mobs tried to stop refugee trains filled with Hindus and Sikhs from departing for India. Mobs held up refugee trains at Mughalpura and Harbanspur, both located on the outskirts of the city. Their passengers were rescued only by the timely arrival of armed troops.[205] Meanwhile, another refugee train headed for Lahore from Delhi came under attack at Beas and then again at Amritsar. While the train's escort was able to protect the passengers during the first assault, the second attack led to a fearful massacre. When the train finally pulled into Lahore railway station, 400 of the 600 refugees still alive were wounded. The director of Public Relations, Pakistan, stated that the survivors had escaped by pretending to be dead.[206] This particular attack may have been the worst of the Partition. A press communique from the Cabinet Press Secretariat placed the death toll at a staggering 3,000.[207] On 22 September, a mob attacked a refugee train at Amritsar.[208]

On 25 September, *The Bombay Chronicle* reported on no

fewer than eight separate attacks on trains between 18 and 22 September. The report was based on military sources and lists military casualties only. On 18 September, a mob attacked the No. 1 Special train at Ludhiana, East Punjab. The train, very likely carrying refugees to Pakistan, was defended by an armed escort. A major and three soldiers sustained injuries. On 19 September, the No. 2 Special train from Delhi came under fire twice, at Rajpura and Sirhind, both in East Punjab. The train's armed escort was able to beat off the attackers without sustaining casualties. On 19 September, the No. 3 Special from Delhi came under attack on the Beas River. The train was particularly vulnerable at the time of the attack. Its crew had detached the train's locomotive to water its engine, leaving the passenger compartments waiting on a bridge. The attack left a soldier dead and two of his comrades wounded. On 20 September, a mob attacked the No. 5 Special from Delhi at Sirhind, again while the engine crew had removed the train's locomotive for watering. The train's escort opened fire to defend the passengers. On 21 September, mobs attacked a refugee train headed to India three times. First at Pind Daddan Khan, then at Mughalpura, and finally at Harbanspura, all in West Punjab. The same day, the armed escort of another refugee train successfully fought off an attack between the Lahore city and Cantonment stations. On 22 September, there was another attack on a refugee train at Sanahwal near Ludhiana in East Punjab. Chillingly, this entire report was based on a statement from a military spokesman. It did not include details on civilian casualties. The *Chronicle*, in reference to the 21 September attack, stated, 'There were no casualties among the refugees in this attack,' leaving readers in little doubt that there were dead refugees from all the other attacks.[209]

On 26 September, *The Bombay Chronicle* carried a headline that captured the scale of the catastrophe—'West Bound Refugee Train Passes Amritsar Safely.' Things were so bad that the normal passage of a train became headline news and an occasion for celebration. Below the headline, however, the newspaper reported that three trainloads of refugees, under armed protection, still waited for safe passage. In the Gujranwala district of East Punjab, meanwhile, just a day earlier, a mob had attacked a refugee train at Kemoke railway station. The mob massacred 300 passengers despite the train's armed escort's attempts to defend them. The mob also kidnapped the survivors, leaving behind only about 30 survivors.[210] On 28 September, two bombs ripped through Shimla railway station, leaving two wounded. The railway station was packed with refugees, and a police search of the area led to the discovery of several weapons.[211] It was hardly surprising. Considering the scale of violence and the futility of the armed escorts, many refugees chose to be prepared for the worst.

On 23 September, the journalist D.F. Karaka filed an eyewitness report from Punjab. Karaka had seen horrors before. He had covered Japan's war in China, been embedded with the British Indian Army in the run-up to the battles of Kohima and Imphal, and then reported through the final stages of the Second World War in Europe. He had been one of the first journalists to reach the Bergen-Belsen concentration camp.[212] Titled 'From One Living Hell to Another,' Karaka's report tried to capture the horror of Partition. He wrote specifically about refugee trains.

> On Sunday night or early Monday morning a train arrived at Amritsar station...The train was carrying refugees from West Punjab. The train had been stopped, attacked in Pakistan, and the people in it shot, killed, and wounded. The escorting guards could do but little. Judging from those who escaped death, it is reasonable to presume that round a thousand was the casualty figure.
>
> Later on Monday, another refugee train arrived in Amritsar from East Punjab and, in retaliation, this train was stopped,

> and the refugees attacked and many likewise butchered. Again the guards on the train could do but little and an English commissioned officer and several Indians paid with their lives. The fury of the murders made no distinction.
>
> I saw this train myself this morning. The stench was like the stench of Belsen the brutality is worse than that of the Nazis. The survivors are still on the platform, some dazed, some just weeping. There was a son caressing his dead, aged father. There was a woman sprawled naked. There were children just flung around the place. Compartment after compartment were filled with the dead.[213]

September was the worst of the crisis. Under normal circumstances, the violence that followed in October and November would have constituted horrifying extremes. But, in context, they represented a slow and steady de-escalation. There were no major attacks on trains through the first two weeks of October. On 15 October, however, a mob attacked five passengers on board the Bombay Mail at the Tando Alawar station in Sindh. The attackers then threw the passengers off the train. While the crew were able to stop the train and pull the passengers back on board, their condition was serious by the time they reached the hospital.[214] And it was only towards the end of the month that railway workers had to deal with a major attack on a moving train. On 28 October, a mob forced a refugee train to stop at Jwalapur, northwest of Delhi. The attackers killed four and injured a further 15. The train's armed escort opened fire to defend the passengers, wounding six attackers.[215] The last attacks occurred in November. Like October, they were terrible but muted after the trauma of September. On 4 November, police in Shimla discovered arms on board a Pakistan-bound train.[216] The very next day, inmates of a refugee camp at Ludhiana, East Punjab, placed stones on railway tracks in an attempt to derail a train.[217] On 9 November, two bombs ripped through Saharanpur railway station, northwest of Delhi. Subsequent investigation revealed that Hindu/Sikh extremists had placed the bombs inside the sheets and blankets meant for a refugee train preparing for departure. The bombs had exploded prematurely.[218]

There has been much writing on the nature of this violence. Historians have noted how the experience of violence varied by class, for instance. The rich and resourced suffered the least, while the poor and vulnerable suffered the most.[219] There has also been much written on the gendered experience of the violence. Women were the worst victims of Partition.[220] Children and the elderly also suffered disproportionately. The experience was similarly differentiated for railway workers. Engine crew members and railway station staff were exposed in ways quite different from clerks and bureaucrats ensconced in offices and gated communities far from scenes of violence. Railway workers also had very different perspectives on Partition depending on their religion, location and family situations. Nonetheless, the violence of Partition constituted the single most difficult challenge that Indian railway workers faced in this turbulent decade.

There were other challenges. The partition of India prompted many railway workers to migrate across the newly created boundaries. Many of these were railway workers who made carefully considered decisions, while others simply joined the stream of desperate refugees pouring across the borders. Their movement had been noticed early. On 3 August 1947, two weeks before Independence and Partition, *The Times of India* reported that Muslim railway workers were relocating to what was set to become Pakistan, while Hindu and Sikh railway workers were moving from the same to India. The numbers, even on that early date, were staggering. *The Times of India* estimated that no fewer than 25,000 Hindu and Sikh employees of the NWR had sought transfers to the new East Punjab Railways on India's side of the border. Meanwhile, some 52,000 Muslims from various railway companies across what was to become independent India were preparing to relocate to Pakistan.[221] The estimates were overoptimistic. Within days, *The Times of India* revised its figures to state that the number of Hindu and Sikh railway workers headed to India now exceeded 80,000.[222] The numbers kept climbing. The Annual Report of the Indian Railway Board published in 1948 put the number of Hindu and Sikh railway workers who had left what had become Pakistan for India at a staggering 1,26,000.[223] The Annual Report of the Pakistan Railway Board for the period 1947–1948 also indicated far higher figures for the movement of Muslim railway workers from India. The report stated that 30,000 railway workers had sought transfers to Eastern Bengal Railway alone. An additional 75,000 railway workers had arrived via Bombay and another 24,000 via Punjab. The total, just under 1,30,000.[224]

The movement of such large numbers of employees created enormous challenges for both Indian and Pakistan Railways. Many of these transfers occurred over a very short time span. John Mathai, India's railway minister in 1948, estimated it as a mere two and a half months.[225] Considering the very difficult circumstances of Partition, Muslim railway workers seeking transfers to Pakistan faced great difficulties in making it to their new jobs and homeland. With rail transportation disrupted in Punjab for much of August and September, many of these railway workers had to take a circuitous route via Bombay. This required stays at newly created refugee camps in Bombay before departing for Karachi by sea. The irony of railway workers being forced to make a sea voyage was, in all likelihood, not lost on anyone. Their situation, however, was probably far better than the 24,000 railway workers who made the journey through Punjab. Navigating refugee movements, jumpy policemen and soldiers, and an exceptionally dangerous Punjab countryside made for a harrowing and dangerous migration.[226] For Hindu and Sikh railway workers, the dangers lay behind. Life in West

Pakistan was so dangerous that very few felt safe. *The Times of India* estimated that less than 1 per cent of non-Muslim railway workers on the NWR system had chosen to remain.[227]

The rapid transfer of such large numbers created several problems for both Indian and Pakistan Railways. The problem was particularly acute as Muslims, Hindus and Sikhs had come to dominate separate spheres of work. For instance, the Indian Railways faced shortages of engine crew and workshop labor. On the other hand, the majority of railway workers migrating from Pakistan to India were clerical staff. This led to immediate problems. The overall shortage of engine crew members in the Indian Railways at its worst stood at 18 per cent of the pre-Partition strength. On certain railways, such as the East Indian Railway company, the shortages exceeded 45 per cent. There were comparable shortages at railway workshops.[228] In Pakistan, on the other hand, the railway system was crippled by shortages of stationmasters, signalers, doctors, and signal, mechanical, electrical and curl engineers.[229] While both Indian and Pakistani railway officials grappled with staff shortages, they also had to resolve problems of surpluses elsewhere.[230] In Pakistan, the problem was particularly acute, especially concerning workshop labor and running staff. Officials at the NWR company accounted for surplus of non-gazetted staff at 11,062, while Eastern Bengal Railway company officials estimated a surplus of 16,469 staff.[231] The problem in India, though less pressing, was also quite significant.[232]

In addition to the problems of migration, Indian and Pakistani railway workers also had to manage a number of administrative challenges. The first of these was the sudden appearance of international boundaries across what had until then been a single unified railway system. Indian and Pakistani railway workers had to, almost overnight, identify and set up border posts across their railway systems. Railway workers across seven different railway companies in India and Pakistan,

Assam Railway (AR), Eastern Bengal Railway, East Indian Railway, and the Oudh and Tirhut Railway (OTR) on the eastern India-Pakistan border, and Eastern Punjab Railway (EPR), Jodhpur Railway (JR) and NWR on the western India-Pakistan border, had to coordinate their efforts to establish customs and immigration checkpoints with set protocols for freight and passengers. As was to be expected, managing these new international transit points became an enormous challenge for railway workers who had never imagined taking on such duties. At an administrative level, railway workers had to develop an entirely new routing system to make sure that all passengers and freight crossing the newly created boundaries passed only along these newly designated border crossings. There was also the additional hassle of customs checks, which led to long delays, frustrating the crew and throwing off schedules.[233] The situation was particularly difficult for Pakistani railway workers at the border posts. The shortage of customs officers in that country forced stationmasters to double up as customs agents, assessing goods, collecting duties, etc.[234]

A second, more serious, problem became the maintenance of rolling stock. Two issues emerged during the Partition crisis that became particularly challenging for railway workers. First, the immense pressure on Indian and Pakistani railway workers to transport 3 million refugees as quickly and safely as possible left the railway systems on both sides of the border with limited room to schedule maintenance for their rolling stock. This problem was particularly acute on the western border. The second problem emerged out of the newly created boundaries, cutting off access to supplies and workshops on the other side of the border. For instance, the newly created Eastern Punjab Railway in India, whose employees had belonged formerly to the NWR, lost access to the NWR workshop at Mughalpura, which now fell across the border in Pakistan. Similarly, railway workers on two railway sections of the NWR in Pakistan faced significant challenges with maintenance after they lost access to the Kalka workshop that now fell across the border in India. In eastern India, railway workers with Assam Railway and Eastern Bengal Railway lost access to the Saidpur Railway workshop that fell in East Pakistan. On the other hand, Pakistani railway workers on the Eastern Bengal Railway were left without a single broad-gauge workshop as the Kanchrapara workshop lay across the newly created border in India.[235]

The challenge was particularly severe for Pakistani railway workers. The bulk of the British Indian railway systems remained in independent India. This allowed Indian railway workers to redistribute their requirements across the many railway workshops left behind in Indian territory. Pakistani railway workers did not have such an advantage. Laborers at the Mughalpura workshop in West Pakistan and the Saidpur workshop in East Pakistan were the sole workshops for their respective wings of Pakistan Railways. At the Mughalpura workshop, railway workers struggling with repairs and maintenance for rolling stock necessary for Partition evacuation efforts were also tasked with the conversion of the new country's entire stock of coal-burning locomotives to oil-burning engines. This became necessary due to disruptions in the supply of coal from coal mines now on India's side of the border. Laborers at the Mughalpura workshop also had to take over the maintenance of narrow-gauge stock from the Kalabagh-Bannu and Kohat-Thal Railways. These used to be repaired and maintained at the Kalka workshop, now across the border in India. Laborers at the Saidpur workshop in East Pakistan were also under considerable pressure. The workshop had facilities to maintain and repair narrow-gauge rolling stock, but with Partition, railway workers on the Eastern Bengal Railway had been left with no workshops that could maintain and repair its broad-gauge rolling stock. The Kanchrapara workshop, where such rolling stock maintenance and repair used to be carried out now lay across the border in India.[236]

At a more administrative level, Indian and Pakistani railway workers had faced the challenge of partitioning their railways. The partition of tracks was relatively simple since the boundaries were drawn up by a government Boundary Commission and then handed to railway officials as a *fait accompli*. There was little that railway workers could do to inform this aspect of decision-making. On the other hand, railway officials had to divide up railway assets in a fair and reasonable manner. This included financial decisions as well as the division of rolling stock and machinery. The division of rolling stock included considerations on locomotives, boilers, carriages, freight trucks and even ferries maintained by the railway systems. Railway workers had to take into account the age and condition of their stock before reaching agreements. There were also negotiations on rolling stock under construction or on order.[237] Furthermore, they had to make decisions on the fair division of mundane office supplies, including but not limited to duplicating machines, typewriters and engineering manuals.[238] The implementation of their decisions constituted a substantial challenge. A large number of passenger coaches meant for Pakistan remained in India as railway workers on both sides struggled to find locomotives to pull the coaches across the newly created borders. The failure added to the many challenges already facing the Pakistani railway workers who now were operating with fewer coaches than they were entitled to.[239]

To cope with these challenges, Indian and Pakistani railway workers came up with a number of survival strategies. These are best categorized as institutional, individual and collective. Of the three, institutional strategies are the best recorded, for these included the measures taken by the railway bureaucracy to cope with the challenges of Partition. They were also measures that enjoyed the support of the Indian and Pakistan Railway Boards and functioned well enough to merit a report in the official archives of the Railway Boards. Indian and Pakistani railway workers played their part in shaping these institutional survival strategies and, once in place, made effective use of them to keep the railway system functioning and their workplaces fair and, at least, relatively safe.

There were a number of institutional strategies that became significant in this crisis. The most important ones dealt with mitigating the threat of violence against railway passengers, their freight and their crew. When violence flared up in Punjab and refugee trains came under attack, Indian and Pakistani railway officials began regularly rerouting or suspending services. For instance, they suspended all regular passenger services on the old NWR system that linked East and West Punjab. These were never resumed despite efforts on the part of many railway workers. Freight traffic also never returned to pre-Partition levels.[240] During particularly difficult periods, especially during the bloody months of August and September, railway officials in both India and Pakistan regularly suspended and rerouted traffic across the border. For instance, in mid-February, Indian railway officials rerouted the Down Frontier Mail. Its regular route through Amritsar had become too dangerous, so traffic managers in India gave the train crew instructions to travel west via the still relatively safe Bhatinda line.[241] By late August, as violence spread to this region, traffic managers in India suspended traffic even along this line. There were other traffic management strategies. Simply waiting out unrest or awaiting armed protection ensured the safety of passengers and railway crew. As referred to earlier, on 26 September, *The Bombay Chronicle* reported that there were at least three refugee trains waiting outside Amritsar for safe passage.[242] Indian railway officials also came up with a rostering strategy to ensure that the religious composition of the train crew minimized the danger from communal mobs. In northern India, for instance, railway officials began instituting deployment strategies to prevent any Muslim crewmen from manning trains heading in the vicinity of the capital. As in the case narrated at the start of this book, a Muslim crewman who slipped through the cracks of the system and ended up driving his train into Delhi was in considerable danger.[243] Finally, Indian and Pakistani railway officials vastly expanded the security for their trains. Indian Railways recruited over 5,000 new policemen across its railway systems.[244]

Institutional survival strategies also became very important for railway workers seeking to move between India and Pakistan. As stated earlier, some 1,26,000 railway workers moved from the Pakistan territory to India, and another 1,29,000 moved in reverse. Institutional practices to securely move this significant workforce ensured the safe transportation of the railway workers and their families. Indian Railways responded to the crisis by setting up transfer offices in Lahore and Calcutta. After Partition, the Indian railway officials relocated their Lahore office to Amritsar and finally to Ambala, also in Eastern Punjab. A massive bureaucracy worked at these transfer offices to facilitate the safe migration of Hindu and Sikh railway workers and their families from Pakistan to India.[245] In many ways, though, the Indian side had it relatively easy. While it was losing a substantial portion of its railway system, the bulk of the railway administrative and technical machinery remained in India. The Pakistani railway system, on the other hand, had a much harder task. Since Delhi had been the capital of undivided India, independent Pakistan had to facilitate the movement of much of its top bureaucracy to the new capital in Karachi. This was true of the entire Pakistani government and the railway system. Pakistani officials had to establish a much more elaborate system to accommodate the transfer of its workforce.

To facilitate the movement of Muslim workers to Pakistan, the emerging Pakistani government worked with their Indian counterparts manning transfer offices at Lahore and Calcutta. After Partition, and especially from mid-October, Pakistani officials expanded the scale of operations to help Muslims seeking to emigrate to Pakistan. The decisions of the Indian Railway Board informed much of this process. In late August, the Indian Railway Board issued instructions to release all Muslims seeking transfers to Pakistan. This led to a substantial increase in the number of railway workers moving to Pakistan with their families. The Pakistani government expanded its transfer office machinery to Bombay as many railway workers and government officials expressed a preference to sail from Bombay to Karachi rather than risk taking a train through Punjab. The numbers that passed through Bombay grew very quickly, overwhelming the ability of the Pakistani state to manage their evacuation. For one, there was limited shipping available. This led to long delays for many families. The Pakistani transfer office set up relief camps in the city to temporarily house the migrants. At its peak, 20,000 public servants, including railway workers and their families, lived in these relief camps, awaiting transportation to Karachi. In order to ensure that the migrants were adequately fed and clothed, the transfer office opened a ration shop and banking facilities. It also ensured advance pay for many of the waiting migrants. In all, 75,000 government employees, including railway workers, passed through Bombay to their new lives in Pakistan.[246]

In addition, there was the question of what happened once railway workers got to their new countries. In India, and Pakistan, the government struggled to provide housing, care and, most importantly, new jobs for incoming migrants. Indians and Pakistani railway workers established several programs to help with the 'rehabilitation' of incoming railway workers and their families. These became important tools for survival. Indian railway officials worked to provide incoming migrants with new jobs. In order to accommodate the sudden influx of over a 100 thousand railway workers, Indian railway officials placed a temporary freeze on all hiring for the lowest two categories of staff, ensuring that refugee railway workers did not face competition in securing such positions. Others were absorbed as and when openings appeared. The efforts of the transfer office staff were very successful. Within a year, only 300 of the 1,26,000 incoming railway workers remained waiting for new jobs. Transfer office officials placed these 300 workers on special 'Supernumerary' posts to be absorbed into the workforce as soon as vacancies appeared.[247]

With more limited resources, the Pakistan Railways had to provide its incoming workforce with even greater support. In the absence of adequate housing in Karachi, railway authorities retrofitted railway carriages to house incoming migrants. Pakistan railway officials and workers labored heroically to identify and provide incoming refugees with documentation, especially ration cards, enabling them to use the grain shops of Pakistan Railways. The depleted workforce manning the grain shops rose to the occasion, working voluntarily well beyond the prescribed number of hours to complete the task. The railway staff were able to feed the destitute refugees even when provincial governments proved unable to keep up deliveries of grain. On one occasion, railway officials substituted rice rations when wheat supplies stopped in their entirety. To cope with surpluses in sections of its workforce, railway officials in Pakistan developed two strategies. The first involved retraining staff members for work, while the second specifically involved workshops, where workshop managers introduced double shifts, albeit this was possible only where there were no material constraints. Railway officials also coordinated their efforts with provincial governments, railway contractors and the private sector to secure jobs for the surplus workforce. Pakistani railway officials struggled to reabsorb this surplus workforce. At the end of the 1947–1948 period, the NWR still had a surplus workforce of 7,179 employees. Eastern Bengal Railway, much worse off, had 15,323 surplus workers.[248] The numbers for the Eastern Bengal Railway did not decline till the following year when these were reduced to 1,340.[249]

Finally, Indian and Pakistani railway workers entered into a number of agreements to manage the problem of maintaining their rolling stock. Specifically, railway officials at the Mughalpura workshop offered to carry out periodic and intermediate overhauls and repairs, the manufacturing/reconditioning of locomotives, carriages and wagons, machines, machine parts and machine tools for Eastern Punjab Railway. Pakistan Railways also committed to building coaches and machine timber for the Kalka workshop in India. Unfortunately, the overwhelmed staff at Mughalpura struggled to deliver on these commitments. There were similar problems in Eastern India. Railway officials from India had reached mutual aid agreements with officials in East Pakistan for the periodic overhaul and repair of carriages and wagons from Assam at the Saidpur workshop. East Pakistani railway officials had also committed to the transportation of meter gauge locomotives from Assam to the Kanchrapara workshop in West Bengal. Agreements that East Pakistani officials struggled to fulfill.[250] Things were, if possible, worse in East Pakistan. Barring a meter-gauge workshop at Saidpur, railway operators in East Pakistan had no workshops for their rolling stock. Officials reached an agreement with Indian Railways for maintenance and repair work for broad gauge rolling stock at the Kanchrapara workshop in India. Workmen and engineers at Saidpur had to rapidly improvise and begin manufacturing duplicate parts as per agreed-upon terms with Indian Railways. The officials quickly realized that the Kanchrapara workshop was overwhelmed. Many locomotives were stuck waiting in sheds, reducing availability.[251]

In addition to such institutional strategies, many railway workers fell back upon individual initiatives to survive the challenges of Partition. Three strategies helped Indian and Pakistani railway workers at this moment. The first of these were strategies of solidarity and humanism. Many Indian and

Pakistani railway workers demonstrated individual courage and kindness as a survival strategy. In addition to the two instances mentioned at the start of this book; when two Hindu firemen protected their Muslim comrade in northern India, and a Muslim guard protected his Hindu trainee in western Punjab, there are records of several other occasions when individual railway workers through acts of bravery and compassion kept their passengers and colleagues safe. In August of 1947, for instance, an assistant stationmaster posted at Khanewal railway station, West Punjab, agreed to see to the safe passage of a Sikh family trying to make their way to India. The family had secured passage on an express train and had made arrangements for a journey on the train's first-class compartment. The train was filled with refugees, and communal rioters were spilling into the station even as the train pulled onto its platform. One member of the family had been shot in the leg. The train passed through a Punjab countryside in flames. The family saw women, pursued by mobs of men, commit suicide by jumping into wells. Dead, dismembered bodies lay on the railway tracks. Fires burned down houses, crops, animals and carts. At each of the train's scheduled halts, the assistant stationmaster ushered the family into the bathroom. The precaution was entirely necessary. Mobs of armed men approached the compartment demanding to know if there were any Sikhs on board. The assistant stationmaster traveling with his wife and child assured the attackers that they, a Muslim family, were the sole passengers in the first-class compartment. He left only at the last Pakistani station at Kasur. The Sikh family got off at Ferozepur, across the border in India. Their train had been attacked. They were the sole survivors.[252]

Not all railway workers were heroic. In fact, for many, individual survival strategies may have pushed them in the opposite direction. There is disturbing evidence that several individual railway workers collaborated with the murderous mobs engaged in the attacks of this period. In addition to fictional accounts of such collaboration, there is reason to believe that individual conspiracies were at play during at least two attacks on trains in Punjab. On 19 September, a mob attacked Refugee Special No. 3 from Delhi close to the Amritsar railway station. The attack was timed precisely at a moment when the train was especially vulnerable. The train's crew had detached the locomotive to water the engine leaving the passenger compartments stranded with no possibility for escape. The very next day, 20 September, another mob attacked Refugee Special No. 5 from Delhi. Once again, the attack seemed timed to coincide with precisely the moment when the train's passengers were particularly vulnerable. The engine crew had detached the locomotive from the passengers' compartments, ostensibly to water the engine.[253] It is quite possible that both such attacks were random. Certainly, it is possible that the mobs knew that engine crew members needed to water their locomotives and were certain to detach their passenger compartments to do so, it is also quite likely that there was an element of collusion between them and the attackers. The memoirs of D.V. Reddy indicate that there was considerable suspicion among sections of the railway bureaucracy that individual railway workers were colluding with attackers. Indian Railways instituted protocols to deal with the problem. Every single refugee special or train that came under attack was immediately examined by a special committee. The committee members sought to establish the culpability of the train's crewmen.[254]

A third individual strategy for survival was dictated by prudence. Many railway workers, Indian and Pakistani, correctly identified the sheer danger of heading into the bloodbath of Partition. The great responsibility of manning slow-moving trains crammed with refugees and their belongings, with only a small contingent of armed soldiers for protection, must have been sufficient for many railway workers to ask just what their jobs were worth. The historical literature on Partition is substantial and clearly demonstrates that the dangers were real. Punjab, and to a lesser extent Bengal, was awash in weaponry. Leftovers from the just-concluded Second World War, much of this weaponry was lethal and no less sophisticated than what was carried by the Punjab Boundary Force of the Indian and Pakistani armed forces. The men yielding these weapons and attacking trains were also, often, veterans themselves. Trained and experienced in warfare, comfortable with the sophisticated weaponry available and capable of devising complex tactical maneuvers, the men of the Punjab Boundary Force often found themselves outmatched by their attackers. This was the situation in the best of circumstances. There were no guarantees, and it was all too much for many railway workers. On 27 August, days after fierce clashes in Punjab, railway crew began refusing services to drive their trains across the dangerous plains of Punjab. Just three days earlier, riots had ripped through Lahore, spilling onto the railway tracks. There had been violence at Lahore railway station. Mobs forced refugee trains to stop and assaulted their passengers. One refugee train from Delhi had been attacked no less than three times. Things were no better on the Indian side of the border. A mob had stopped and attacked a passenger train on the line between Pakpattan and Kasur. Finally, another mob had forced a refugee special to stop in Montgomery district. All attacks had left dead passengers behind and traumatized crew driving their corpse-laden trains across the border.[255] It was hardly surprising that many engine crews, especially in this case, transporting freight expressed reluctance to take the risk themselves.[256]

Finally, Indian and Pakistani railway workers also used individual strategies that were neither heroic nor evil nor even prudent. Instead, they can be described as taking the best possible opportunity available to them. The choice of Abdul Kalam, then a junior engineer with Indian Railways, is an excellent example of this kind of survival strategy. At the time of Independence, Kalam was in a difficult situation. As described in the previous chapter, he had had an unfortunate run-in with a very senior British Indian railway officer, Rolf Emerson. Emerson had tried to pull rank and have Kalam dismissed from the service immediately, but Kalam had been protected by the chairman of the Railway Board, a position which for the first time was occupied by an Indian. Emerson, however, had not let things go. Instead, Kalam found his professional life increasingly constrained by official harassment instigated by Emerson. Kalam fought back as best as he could, but as he described it, this was a fight between 'an ant and an elephant.' He was still a trainee, while Emerson held one of the most powerful offices in the Indian railway bureaucracy and was expected to take over as chief commissioner of the Indian Railway Board. Kalam was training in Britain for much of 1947 and then, in the weeks leading up to India's independence and Partition, in the United States. Unsure of what might remain of a career clouded by such a powerful enemy, Kalam decided to resign. This was weeks before Independence and Partition. Had he remained in service, Kalam might have been able to seek a transfer to Pakistan Railways like so many fellow Muslim officers. Alternatively, he could have remained in India without any trouble as Emerson lost his job soon after Independence and Partition. Kalam's family was in India, but he did what seemed reasonable. He applied for a position with the Pakistan Railways. His application was accepted, and Kalam took up his post in what had become East Pakistan. He went on to build a spectacularly successful career, rising to the very highest office in the Pakistan Railways—chairman of the Pakistan Railway Board.[257]

In addition to such individual survival strategies, Indian railway workers also pursued survival strategies of collective action. Historical records are filled with many examples of such strategies. One instance is described in detail in the memoirs of D.V. Reddy. At the time of Independence and Partition,

Reddy was superintendent of power at the Moradabad railway station in the then United Provinces. It was a very senior post, and Reddy supervised the station's workshop. Many employees reported to his office. As Partition drew close and religious conflict escalated across northern India, many of the workshop's Muslim employees began taking a serious view of migrating to the newly emerging Muslim homeland in Pakistan. In contrast to Kalam, who acted on his own, these employees chose to respond to the situation collectively. To Reddy's surprise, the workers approached him as a group and asked for a collective transfer to Pakistan. According to his own writings, Reddy pushed back, trying to persuade the workmen to remain. Reddy had his own reasons; the loss of so many skilled workmen would constitute a substantial blow to his workshop. To his despair, Reddy was unable to persuade his workers to remain. The negotiation went on overnight, but the workmen were adamant. Their argument was simple; it had become too unsafe for them and their families to choose India over Pakistan. Working together, the laborers held to their position, forcing Reddy to acquiesce. Reddy informed his superiors, facilitating the transfer of the workforce. Reddy's memoir makes clear his opposition to the workers' demands. He wrote that he actually went into a coma after the workers left. From the laborers' point of view, though, a survival strategy through collective action made a lot of sense. While Kalam came from a fairly privileged family with substantial resources of his own, the ability of Muslim workshop laborers was considerably less. Reddy might have been able to browbeat an individual worker or even a small number of workers into staying, but he was clearly helpless against a determined collective of laborers. Working together opened up possibilities for these workmen.[258]

There are other instances of collective action as a survival strategy. An article in *The Bombay Chronicle* reveals how the railway workers used this strategy during the worst phase of Partition violence. The incident occurred on the Jodhpur Railway system. A Princely State with its own railway company, railway workers on the Jodhpur system fell outside the ambit of the Indian Railway system and were integrated into the Indian and Pakistani railway system only after Independence. On 1 September, saboteurs removed a railway track to derail a refugee train and attacked the Sikh passengers on board. Following the incident, the *Chronicle* carried an official statement from the traffic manager of the Jodhpur Railway. The statement included grisly details of the attack and the sabotage that had preceded it. The statement also indicated that many railway workers had walked away from their jobs demanding better protection, 'All the traffic staff between Khadro and Nawabshah have left their stations and it will be impossible to operate this section until protection is assured to them.'[259]

It is impossible to tell if the action was justified. Khadro and Nawabshah were railway stations located in a sparsely populated part of northwestern British India. It was also south of Punjab where the Indian and Pakistani governments had deployed much of their military machinery. Moreover, as a Princely State, the primary responsibility for security lay with the authorities of Jodhpur rather than either of the two dominions. Either way, from the perspective of the traffic staff on the Khadro Nawabshah line, the security arrangements were insufficient. The railway workers also clearly understood that their best bet for an improvement in security lay in collective action. Individual walkouts or protests were unlikely to move their superiors or the Jodhpur authorities. The *Chronicle* provides no indication if the strike succeeded, but there are no references to the work stoppage in future editions of the newspaper. The strategy might have failed in this instance, or it might have succeeded leading to a quick but not newsworthy restoration of services.

The most important instance of collective action as a survival strategy, however, may have been the part played by

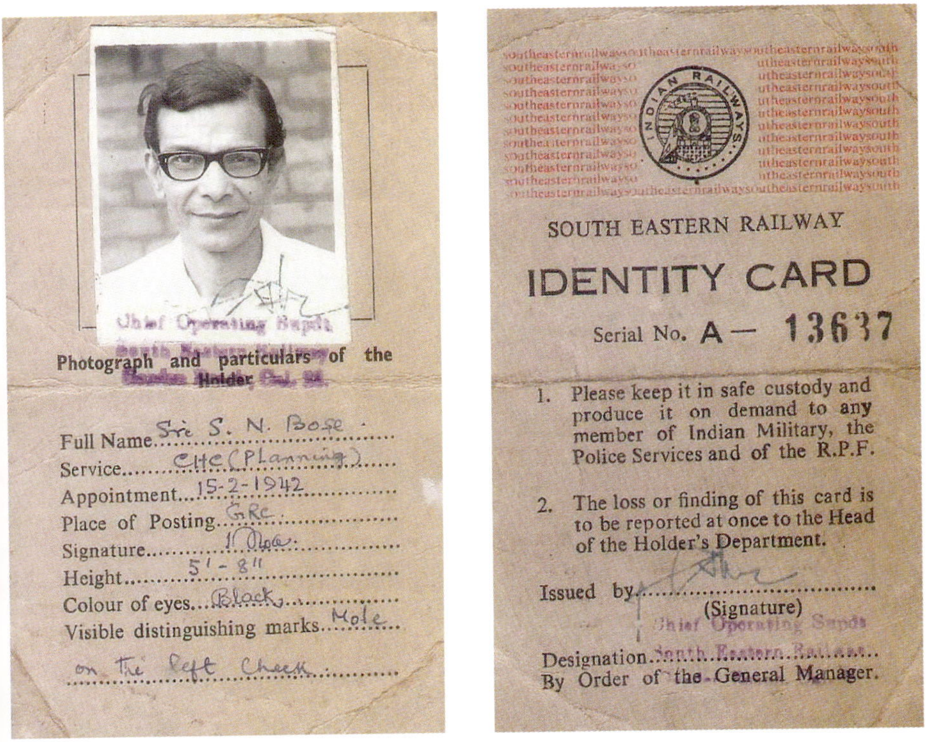

This World War II photo ID belonged to the author's great-uncle. Indian railway workers played a crucial, though overlooked, part in the eventual defeat of fascism.

Courtesy: Aditi Baidya

A view of the assembly shop of the BNR workshop at Kharagpur, West Bengal.

Courtsey: Wikimedia Commons

The BNR Hospital in Calcutta was inaugurated by former INA officer Shah Nawaz Khan and is a symbolic recognition of the important role of India's railway workers in the freedom struggle. The author was born in this hospital, one of the countless beneficiaries of the struggles waged and won by the Indian railway workers in the 1939–1949 era.

Courtesy: Aditi Baidya

An NWR train carrying displaced refugees after the partition of Punjab, 1947.
Courtsey: Wikimedia Commons

Young Indian railway engineers in free India, freed from the constraints of colonialism, prepare to build a new future for their country. The author's grandfather is second from the top, on the right hand side of the table.

Courtesy: Suvendra Dutta

The author's grandfather used a device like this to test railway tracks for safety based on the sounds made upon striking. For decades this device has kept passengers safe. (The device used by the author's grandfather has now been refashioned as a walking stick.)

Courtesy: Sakti Kunz

Sahayaks at Chattrapati Shivaji Terminus.
Indian railway workers in service of their countrymen.

Courtesy: Indra Nath Bose

The author's son pretending to be a Sahayak. Indian railway workers continue to inspire the future through their service.

Courtesy: Author's personal collection

railway trade unions. These were powerful institutions capable of mobilizing thousands of workers across the railway system. The unions could have done substantial damage to the Partition project, specifically the evacuation of refugees had they chosen to withhold their support to the project. Certainly, the railway unions would have been well within reason to refuse services considering the catastrophic security breakdown in the border areas and, in fact, even beyond, extending to the regions around the Indian capital. Instead, on at least two occasions, railway unions assured the Government of India of their commitment to evacuating refugees despite all the dangers posed by the project. One was on 21 September, when the central executive committee of the powerful South Indian Railway Labor Union passed a resolution assuring its support. The committee issued a statement assuring Prime Minister Jawaharlal Nehru that in 'this moment of national crisis' Indian railway workers were fully committed 'to man necessary troop, refugee and food trains.' Crucially, the statement specifically clarified that railway workers would form a unified and patriotic workforce. Echoing that statement, S. Guruswamy, AIRF general secretary, called upon railway workers to 'offer their maximum cooperation to the Government.' A week later, at its Annual General Council meeting, the AIRF passed a resolution pledging its full support to the two dominions of India and Pakistan. The federation called upon all railway workers 'to offer their services in whatever capacity they were called upon to serve to meet the present critical situation in the country.' It is important to keep in mind that these resolutions came at a time of considerable strife that went beyond the Partition crisis. Many railway unions were then engaged in difficult negotiations with the Railway Board over issues of working conditions and pay scales. Their statements of support were made in a context where the threat of strikes loomed in the air.[260]

***

The Partition constituted the greatest crisis of the twentieth century for Indian and Pakistani railway workers. It created the biggest refugee crisis in modern world history and railway workers were called on by the governments of India and Pakistan to transport 3 million refugees across newly created boundaries in a very short period of time. Challenging as it was, their work faced more difficulties due to the appalling bloodletting that accompanied the Partition project. The violence was horrific enough for eyewitnesses to compare it with the holocaust, but in many cases, railway workers and their families became victims and targets. Their trains became the object of the most vicious attacks. Finally, complicating their work, the old British Indian railway system was systematically partitioned into two separate railway systems along the newly created boundaries. Partition also uprooted over 200 thousand railway workers and their families, adding to the burden of this crisis.

As Indian and Pakistani railway workers had done before, during the Second World War and the culminating years of struggle for India's freedom, they responded with multiple strategies. Some of these were taken at an institutional level and made use of individually or collectively. Some others were taken at an exclusively individual level. Some were entirely generous and selfless, such as individual acts of bravery that saved the lives of comrades and passengers. Others were more pragmatic or cruel. However, the most important were once again, collective strategies. These were particularly effective, whether ensuring collective security or the continual movement of refugees despite the overwhelming challenges. It is the latter that is most important to history. The decisions of railway unions were critical. The railway union's support for the evacuation plan through the worst of the Partition crisis made the greatest difference. But perhaps, more importantly, unionization and collective action may have helped in ensuring that the railway system never collapsed. While some railway workers colluded with extremists, the overwhelming majority stayed true to their comrades and their passengers. The long years of collective class-based identities, forged through joint struggles throughout the Second World War and struggles for Independence, ensured that railway workers did not fall victim to the poison of communalism. There was no partitioning of the class called railway workers.

FOUR

'This Dawn is Not that Dawn'

ON 14 AND 15 August 1947, two new countries emerged onto the world stage, India and Pakistan. The two countries faced crippling problems inherited from their recent past. A lopsided economy that for long had served the interest of British capital rather than Indians. An underdeveloped industrial infrastructure historically deprived in favor of an over-developed military. A literacy rate lower than 16 per cent. Appalling mortality rates and average life expectancy, brought on by public medical policies that focused only on the healthcare of the tiny British expatriate population. Moreover, both countries had to deal with the trauma of Partition. India had lost a substantial portion of its territory, along with resources. Its infrastructure networks in the northwest and east had ruptured. The country was flooded with refugees and bitter communal violence. Pakistan was worse off. Not only was it facing the same problems as India, but the country had also inherited significantly less industrial and skilled human resources than its neighbor. Relations between the two countries, already poisoned by the violence of Partition, worsened over territorial disputes.

There were specific challenges facing Indian and Pakistani

railway workers. Both railway systems had to rehabilitate over 1 lakh railway workers who had crossed the border and sought sanctuary in either country. Railway workers in India and Pakistan had to ensure that all of them were able to find jobs and restart their lives. Next, Indian and Pakistani railway workers had to rebuild their railway systems, in the case of the latter, quite comprehensively. Partition had severely disrupted railway movement in both countries and railway workers had to accommodate the new needs of the two countries in its aftermath. More broadly, the makers of the British Indian railway system had designed it for the exploitation of India's resources for the British Empire's capitalist class; now Indian and Pakistani railway workers had been presented with the opportunity to remake this system to serve people's needs.

The evidence indicates that Indian and Pakistani railway workers responded to these challenges through a variety of survival strategies. The moment offered the Indian and Pakistan Railway Boards and Indian and Pakistani railway workers a rare opportunity for convergence. The ruling class in both countries, free from the constraints of imperialism, were now in a position to build countries for their citizenry. The people of India and Pakistan faced the possibility of a future without hunger, with free education, robust health care and an escape from crippling poverty. For Indian and Pakistani railway workers, Independence opened up additional possibilities. Life as a railway worker in British India had been characterized by racism and exploitation. Independence created the possibility of new terms of employment free from both.

Responding to the efforts of Indian and Pakistani railway unions and the Indian and Pakistan Railway Boards, the old racist recruitment and differentiated promotion and salary structures disappeared in this era, creating a fairer and more just railway system. The Indian and Pakistan Railway Boards also committed to ensuring that their workforce had adequate housing, access to the highest possible levels of healthcare and better educational facilities for their children. The two boards also ensured that the old existing forms of support did not disappear. On the contrary, they took several steps to ensure that these supplementary forms of income, crucial to the less-paid sections of the respective workforces, continued and, in some cases, expanded in this period. Of course, none of this came down solely to the goodwill of a new, more enlightened railway managerial class. They were the result of the persistent struggle of the million-strong railway workers of India and Pakistan. A struggle built on the gains made over the course of the previous decade, especially in the areas of solidarity and organization. The railway unions in India and Pakistan, deploying strategies of collective action, once again ensured the emergence of effective survival strategies in post-colonial India and Pakistan.

The evidence from the immediate aftermath of India's and Pakistan's independence demonstrates three developments. First, Indian and Pakistani railway workers substantially improved railway services after Independence. This served to belie the lie that institutions in India, such as the railways, could not function properly without British managerial control. On the contrary, the evidence clearly shows that Indian and Pakistani railway workers were much better at running the Indian and Pakistan Railways than the British. Second, working conditions and terms of employment improved substantially for railway workers in India and Pakistan. A fairer workplace in the form of better wages and shorter hours became a reality for a million men, women and children. Finally, the survival of Indian and Pakistani railway workers, and the ability of these railway workers to revitalize and indeed reinvent their respective railway systems had a significance that went beyond their economic role. The survival and stability of Indian and Pakistan Railways played a role in the survival and stability of both India and

Pakistan. In both countries, the railway systems played a very important role in ensuring the movement of basic commodities, such as food, as well as the resources needed for industrial and national development. Although the post-colonial governments in both countries fell well short of national aspirations on both counts, the railway systems and their railway workers played an important part in ensuring that life got substantially better in this part of the world.

The evidence from this period is also quite unambiguous. Collective action remained the single most important form of survival in the immediate post-colonial period. Organized labor in India and Pakistan was the most effective in getting their respective railway boards to make the necessary changes to ensure the survival of both railway systems as well as the welfare of their respective workforces. While decolonization did bring in a more sympathetic managerial class, this class had limited incentives to ensure that Indian and Pakistani railway workers operated in a fair and just workplace. On the contrary, the capitalist nature of the Indian and Pakistani states remained unchanged in fundamental ways. Under these circumstances, labor organizations remained important.

The Crisis in Indian Railways

In the years after Independence, Indian railway workers faced many challenges. The first and most immediate of these emerged in the aftermath of Partition and had to specifically do with staffing. During the crisis, a majority of the running staff and skilled workshop labor left India for Pakistan. While many Hindu and Sikh railway workers came to India from Pakistan, a majority of these were clerical staff. This created a twinned problem of staff shortages in some areas and surpluses in others. To manage the shortages, Indian Railways dramatically expanded recruitment, instituted intensive training programs, recalled retired staff members, reassigned skilled railway workers, posted railway workers on temporary assignments and finally, relaxed criteria for promotions. All these measures, however, created great challenges for the railway workers. For existing workers, it created new responsibilities as new recruits required guidance, especially when usual training schedules were no longer available. The challenges were also great for the new recruits who had to take on difficult jobs, often without sufficient training. A glimpse into the difficulties and challenges faced by Indian railway workers at this moment comes from the memoirs of D.V. Reddy. Reddy described the accelerated recruitment and training procedures he introduced at Moradabad in United Provinces when faced with an acute 60 per cent shortfall in running and maintenance staff. According to Reddy, in the immediate aftermath of Independence, 'bare minimum' running and maintenance staff kept the railway systems operational. In order to facilitate this expansion in responsibility, all running staff, at their own time, attended special training sessions. Reddy recalled that 700 cleaners took up new duties as firemen. Their appointments came after a single-day interview process that included literacy and medical examinations.[261]

Indian railway workers also faced great difficulties with absorbing the refugees who had arrived from Pakistan. Like their counterparts fleeing India, these refugees arrived in India facing destitution. The Annual Report of the Indian Railway Board stated 'a good number of them had to leave all their belongings in Pakistan.' To provide refugee families with some support, the Indian Railway Board authorized the release of a two-month advance pay for the incoming railway workers. In addition, refugee railway workers could also make use of a special 'Rehabilitation Advance' equivalent to three months' pay, repayable over 36 installments. Beyond such short-term measures, however, refugee railway workers had much difficulty finding jobs in the Indian railway system. Many of them discovered that thanks to a lack of organizational uniformity, their positions and ranks in the NWR company and the Eastern Bengal Railway company did not correspond to comparable positions in other Indian railway systems. There was also the additional problem of competition with railway workers in these companies. Refugee railway workers who were qualified for leadership roles risked facing resentment from colleagues with whom they were now in competition. Railway administrators had to compile seniority lists to accommodate such potential areas of conflict.[262]

There were other difficulties. Refugee railway workers arrived in India with their personal belongings only. It was unreasonable to expect otherwise, considering the seriousness of the Partition crisis. Yet, without their professional service records or information on pension contributions, refugee railway workers found themselves at the mercy of their colleagues who had to establish service records and similar details based on trust and affidavits. Such approaches could not be taken for pensions, and that created considerable hardship for retired railway workers or railway workers on the verge of retirement. As of 1948, a year after Partition, 14,000 refugees were still awaiting to establish their pension records.[263]

The second great crisis that emerged in this period was hunger. Shortly after Independence, the Government of India pursued a policy of gradual decontrol in the prices of several important agricultural products. Specifically, cereals, edible oils, pulses and sugar. The government also began lifting restrictions on the movement of major food grains. The policies not only increased the supply of these commodities in the free market but also resulted in a steep rise in prices. Under these circumstances, the extensive grain store network of the Indian Railways became a lifeline. During the period 1947–1948, the estimated average savings was calculated at a high Rs 30 a month in parts of the country. Indian railway workers relied on these grain stores to buy cereal, cooking oil, fuel, tea and coffee, pulses, sugar and soap. The importance of these grain shops increased even further the following year as a special Inquiry Committee recommended increasing the allotment of monthly wheat/rice rations to railway personnel. In the 1948–1949 period, the scale of rations increased to 16 ounce (oz) per railway worker, an increase over the existing 12 oz per railway worker. Considering the very heavy manual labor often involved in railway work, the rise made much sense. It was a recognition that adequate labor could not be achieved on empty stomachs. The 12 oz limit for all other adult family members, however, remained. That year, over 6,00,000 railway workers and their families turned to almost 600 grain shops spread across the country to stave off hunger. The following 1949–1950 period, the grain shops introduced sugar, further aiding railway workers in their struggle to stave off hunger.[264]

The third great crisis came in the form of changes in the management of traffic flows. Two big changes emerged in this period. The first of these came in the form of shifts in traffic patterns that resulted from the tragedy of Partition. These were felt most keenly by railway workers operating the systems adjacent to the territories that had now become East and West Pakistan, and those that had historical links with these territories. Railway workers of the Sealdah division in the western part of Bengal were particularly affected. This section once operated seamlessly with the railway system that had now ended up across the border in East Pakistan. All traffic between this railway system and the various railway stations in East Pakistan now went through two newly created international junctions, at Banpur-Darsana and Bongaon-Benaphul. On the western Indian border, Indian railway workers noticed a sharp drop in freight traffic, specifically the shipment of cotton from Punjab to the cotton mills of Kanpur, United Provinces. Pakistani cotton merchants had begun taking advantage of high rates in global markets, far exceeding the ceiling prices fixed in India. It was a minor problem, all things considered. But one the railway workers had to manage nonetheless.[265]

By the 1948–1949 period, railway workers in eastern India began reckoning with steep declines in freight traffic from East Pakistan. In particular, the volume of jute arriving at railway stations in and around Calcutta was falling. Railway workers at Ballygunge, Chitpur, Cossipore Road, Kalighat, the Kidderpore Docks and Ultadanga noted the fall in volumes. From under ten million maunds in 1946 to 6.4 million maunds in the period 1948--1949. It was an inexorable decline that over the following decades would doom the jute-based eastern industrial engine of the Indian economy. It was also during this year that railway workers on two smaller railway systems partitioned in 1947 found their work disrupted. Railway workers on the Oudh and Tirhut line had to make changes in their traffic management as authorities on both sides of the border insisted on the passage of freight and passenger trains through designated border crossings. On the western border, railway workers with the Jodhpur Railway system who had kept the last linkages in freight and passenger traffic between the two countries operational suddenly received word that all train services between the dominions of India and Pakistan on their system were to abruptly come to a halt 27 July 1948. With this decision, all railway communication between India and West Pakistan came to a standstill.[266]

The fourth challenge emerging in these years was maintaining the Indian railway rolling stock. During the Second World War, Indian railway workers had been forced to see a significant fall in the quality of their rolling stock as were unable to maintain their trains to the standards of the pre-war years. There were many reasons for this, as discussed in the first chapter of this book; among them, the heavy use to which Indian rolling stock was put as well as the sharp fall in the availability of spare parts in the country. The problem was particularly acute when it came to locomotives. By 1949 the rate of engine failures across the fleet had become quite significant. There were also serious problems with passenger coaches. Many were in a serious state of disrepair. Much of this was tied to the interruption in the normal replacement programs that had kept the railway rolling stock functional in the pre-war years. Older locomotives, wagons and coaches were harder to maintain, and the inability of the British Indian government to purchase or build replacement rolling stock during the war years made the maintenance challenges worse. The consequences of decline in the quality of rolling stock affected the ability of Indian railway workers to deliver services. In the immediate aftermath of Independence, the demand for freight and passenger traffic increased significantly. On the one hand, this was the result of the post-colonial Indian government's focus on developing the country's industrial capacity and, on the other, also of an increased interest in passenger comfort. All of this combined to add to the challenges of Indian railway workers.[267]

The Crisis in Pakistan Railways

Pakistani railway workers faced challenges of a magnitude substantially greater than those faced by their counterparts in India. Foremost among the challenges was the issue of staffing. Partition had affected Pakistani railway workers far more than their counterparts in India. At the end of the period 1947–1948, the total strength of the Pakistani railway workers stood at 168,541. Of these, at least 30,000 were refugees who had arrived in East Pakistan. An unknown number had made their way to West Pakistan, where the surplus staff numbered 11,000. This surplus, however, did not represent the total strength of incoming railway workers. In East Pakistan, the surplus represented only about half the incoming workforce. If the proportion was similar in West Pakistan, almost a third of the total strength of the railway workforce in the country was made up of refugees.[268]

Rehabilitating this often-traumatized workforce emerged as an early challenge for Pakistani railway workers. Many incoming workers found that their skills were not required in Pakistan. Many drivers, shunters and firemen on the NWR discovered that they were 'surplus staff' facing retrenchment. Others, such as railway workers with experience in engineering, discovered that they needed extensive training before they were qualified to operate the systems in Pakistan. On both railway systems, junior staff members with limited experience found themselves in positions of leadership and great responsibility.[269] On the other hand, the system had lost some 1,26,000 railway workers to India, creating great shortages of skilled workers in many areas. Even a year later, Pakistani railway workers found it difficult to find sufficient commercial clerks and stationmasters to man the railway system.[270]

Following the staffing challenges, Pakistani railway workers, especially those serving in the Eastern Bengal Railway, faced a serious challenge in staving off hunger. In the immediate aftermath of Partition, Pakistani railway workers came to rely on the railway system's network of subsidized grain stores more than ever. During the year 1947, railway workers in East Pakistan saved an average of Rs 35 per month from goods purchased through railway grain stores. Their counterparts in West Pakistan saved an average of Rs 22. These were substantial sums for employees at the lower end of wage scales. Under these circumstances, the unavailability of mustard oil, jaggery, dal, potatoes and onions on the Eastern Bengal Railway grain store network had an immediate impact on the diets of the workforce there. Several essential spices and herbs such as cumin, turmeric and cilantro leaves also disappeared from the shelves, as did supplies of ghee. Even staples such as sugar and rice became erratic in their availability through the autumn and winter of the 1947–1948 period. Railway workers in West Pakistan often faced shortages of wheat, for which grain stores substituted rice on multiple occasions. The grain stores also struggled to supply dal.[271] Many of these shortages continued into the next year. The supply of essential commodities such as wheat, rice and sugar remained erratic. Railway workers in East Pakistan continued to deal with shortages of mustard oil. During the 1948–1949 period, railway workers in East Pakistan saved an average of Rs 29 per month and Rs 18 per month in West Pakistan. On 1 April 1949, all subsidized grain stores were closed on the Pakistani Railway system.[272]

The third great crisis faced by Pakistani railway workers lay in the dramatic alterations in the flow of post-Partition traffic. In West Pakistan, export traffic now moved south to the port of Karachi instead of its old routes East, into the interiors of British India. The port of Karachi also became the sole point of entry for imports for the entire region. This also constituted a significant change as many ports across British India until then had served as entry points for imported goods, and there was much traffic shunting in from East Punjab before Partition.[273] Railway workers in East Pakistan also faced similar traffic problems, as the port of Calcutta, now in India suffered increasing disruptions. Instead, railway workers in this part of the country had to readjust to a sharp increase in traffic to and from Chittagong, now the sole entry and exit point for external trade. Abdul Kalam, then freshly arrived in East Pakistan wrote, 'A system wherein logistics originally designed exclusively for feeding the hinterland from Calcutta now had to be drastically reoriented—in fact reversed—because the Port of Chittagong in the extreme southeastern corner of East Pakistan had become the sole inlet for imports from the sea.'[274] In addition, railway workers in East Pakistan also had to accommodate the complex border arrangements with India that required Eastern Bengal Railway trains to enter Indian territory even when transporting goods and passengers on domestic routes. For instance, tracks between Haldibari and Siliguri fell in the Indian territory but were managed by Eastern Bengal Railway, while the section connecting Rohanpur-Godakari, though in Pakistani territory, was managed by the Oudh and Tirhut Railway company.[275]

A fourth crisis that hit Pakistani railway workers in this period was in the maintenance of their rolling stock. As noted in the previous chapter, both the Eastern Bengal Railway and NWR services were crippled with the Kanchrapara and Kalka workshops falling in Indian territory. But Pakistani railway workers had to face additional challenges. Like the Indian railway system, Pakistani railway workers had inherited a rolling stock worn down by years of overuse during the Second World War. This rolling stock then came under great strain as Pakistani railway workers transported millions of refugees across the newly created borders. Significant problems emerged in the immediate aftermath of Partition in East Pakistan. First, staff at the Saidpur workshop, till then used exclusively for meter gauge rolling stock, had to start maintaining broad-gauge rolling stock. This included the manufacture of spare parts as negotiations with counterparts in India for the maintenance of rolling stock and supply of spare parts fell through. The Annual Report of the Railway Division for the period 1947–1948 stated, 'A number of engines had to wait in sheds on the E.B. Railway for periodical overhauls in shops and this reduced the number of engines available for use.'[276] Chaos and confusion followed as the Eastern Bengal Railway managerial staff tried to arrange for spare parts through the port of Chittagong. In order to relieve pressure from Saidpur, Pakistani railway workers reopened an abandoned railway depot at Pahartali. However, as the Annual Report of the Railway Division for the period 1948–1949 stated, 'Great difficulties were experienced for want of efficient and experienced hands.' Exacerbating the crisis was the unexpected failure of a number of Calcutta-based firms to honor their contracts for the supply of stores to the Eastern Bengal Railway.[277] The problems were less acute on the NWR system. Railway workers here struggled with maintenance as stores ran low. Here too, however, railway workers found Indian companies failing to honor commitments to supply parts leading to shortages.[278]

The shortages in stores created multiple problems across the railway system. In the Annual Report of the Pakistan Railway Division for the period 1948–1949 for instance, the authors noted that shortages of spare parts had affected the running of engines and pumping plants at the Mirpur Khas electrical installations. There were also shortages of fixtures leading to problems with light fittings on trains. Even more alarming were shortages in the supply of locomotive headlights. A massive shortfall in the supply of roller bearings brought the manufacturing of headlight generators to a grinding halt. Erratic supplies also affected the running of NWR's Diesel Electric Locomotive fleet. Pakistani railway workers operated fourteen of these shunting locomotives at the Karachi port with much operational efficiency. But delays in replacing broken crankshafts, brake blocks, rubber hose pipes and other spares hampered their efforts. Pakistani railway workers also had much trouble with a fleet of Diesel Hungarian Ganz Rail Cars based out of Lahore. Shortages of spares and limited mileage hampered services in general. There was also much difficulty in track maintenance because of shortages in railway track materials, especially wooden sleepers. Pakistani railway workers were also hampered in their work by erratic electricity supplies. Finally, shortages of coal had plagued services frequently since 1947. Supplies had been disrupted during the Partition crisis, creating operational challenges. Pakistani railway workers had been forced to suspend passenger services and curtail freight traffic to ensure sufficient coal for the movement of refugees during the peak of the crisis. In the autumn of 1949, coal supplies from India came to a complete halt. The problem was particularly acute on the north NWR where workmen struggled to maintain services.[279]

Finally, Pakistani railway workers had to overcome the challenges created by natural disasters. During these first two years of Independence, services were interrupted along the Chittagong-Nazirhat and Kumira-Mir Sarai lines. Rain washed away a bridge on the Nazirhat branch. In many places, farmers breached embankments in order to save their fields, flooding railway lines in the process. Housing and other railway structures were also repeatedly washed away in the heavy Bengal rains. Railway workers in West Pakistan had to cope with severe flooding. In these years, floods interrupted traffic on the Kasur-Husainiwala, Kasur-Lodhran, Jassar-Dera Baba Nank, Lahore-Shahadarabagh and Shahadarabagh-Wazirabad sections. The floods also washed away several bridges.[280]

Nation Building: India

After Independence, Indian and Pakistani railway workers also faced several challenges related to the fragility of their newly independent countries. For Indian railway workers, the most pressing challenge lay in addressing widespread hunger across the country. Consequently, railway workers in independent India found themselves faced with the challenge of transporting far greater quantities of food than ever before. In part, they were moving significant quantities of imported food grains from ports to inland markets, as well as large quantities of food grains from food surplus to food deficit regions. There were many complications that emerged from this process. First, as noted earlier, Indian railway workers had to transport the increased freight of food grains in aging rolling stock. In March 1949, the Indian Railway Board estimated that about a third of all locomotives operating in its system were over-age.[281] Second, the transportation challenges worsened because of inefficiencies in the open market. Railway workers discovered a significant increase in cross-movement. Traders based on market rates booked and then rebooked consignments to various destinations to take advantage of price differentials. In other cases, traders seeking a price advantage purchased grain from markets far away rather than locally at higher prices. All this left railway workers exhausted and frustrated.[282]

The problem extended to supporting India's industrialization program. The post-colonial government was greatly invested in the rapid industrial development of the country. Seeking to reverse the colonial de-industrialization of India, Indian railway workers found themselves tasked with supporting a mammoth transformational project. During these years, the Government of India began work on no fewer than four massive hydroelectric and irrigation projects: the Damodar Valley, Bhakra, Tungabhadra and Hirakud Dam projects. These were, and remain, the largest dams in the country. In all, during these years, Indian railway workers were called upon to transport more freight and passengers than ever before with fewer trains and fewer tracks on which to do so.[283]

In addition to the increase in freight and passenger traffic, they had to construct two major train routes to accommodate disruptions created by Partition. The first of these was the Assam Rail Link, designed to provide a railway connection between the northeastern portion of the country that had now been sundered from the Indian railway network. Indian railway workers had to build a rail link covering a distance of 143 miles through thick malarial forests. Indian railway construction crew cleared the jungle, engineers surveyed the route, built bridges and laid down tracks before the first trains could pass through the route. In less than six months, construction workers moved 200 million cubic feet of earth, including heavy boulders up to six feet in diameter and buried tree trunks. They laid bridges across 368 channels and 22 rivers, including the Tista, Torsa and Sankosh, which were all major rivers. The construction crew also built railway stations, warehouses and accommodations totaling 5,50,000 square feet. By April 1949, the rail link had been completed, within a single working season, in a region that lay in the Himalayan foothills and where annual rainfall exceeded 250 inches a year.[284]

The second major project lay on the other end of the country. Construction work on the Mukerian Pathankot Line began in November 1949. A shorter route of just under 27 miles, the line reduced the traveling time between Delhi and Pathankot, which lay at the gateway of the Kashmir and Kulu valleys. The terrain was substantially easier, passing through largely flat agricultural lands, but with an important exception. The railway construction crew had to bridge an average of 132 feet of waterways per mile. These included two major rivers: the Beas and the Chakki. It required the construction of over 100 bridges, including a single-span bridge of 350 feet across the Chakki. The construction crew had to move a million cubic feet of earth. Construction required the use of 3,50,000 tons of cement, 12,000 tons of steel girders and railway track material and 1.5 million cubic feet of pitching stones. The railway construction crew also built buildings with a plinth area of 1,02,000 square feet.[285]

Indian railway workers found themselves playing a more direct role in the new country's industrialization project. In 1947, they began building what would become one of the most technologically sophisticated industrial units in the country. Manufacturing locomotives and spare boilers, the plant helped transform India from an importer of finished locomotives to self-sufficiency and later an exporter of cutting-edge locomotives. With a covered area of almost 9,00,000 square feet, the project was significant in its scale. An additional million square feet provided room for shops and offices. The assembly shop was

1,560 feet long and 200 feet wide, with a ceiling height of 75 feet. It was equipped with 985 different machines intended to manufacture 80 per cent of the 5000-odd components required for the manufacture of locomotives. A vast array of works was located in the plant. These ranged from pattern making, foundries, forges and smithies, die sinking, drop stamping, heat treatment of steels, welding, tool making, boiler making, etc. The factory was highly unusual. Few locomotive manufacturing plants housed so many components under the same roof. In India, with its severely underdeveloped industrial infrastructure, the railway workers had no choice but to create and house all the ancillary industries at once and on site.[286]

Indian railway workers also built a residential township around the plant to house the working population living nearby. Located in a remote and largely impoverished part of the country, the railway workers became part of the Indian government's early experiments with industrialization, locating large units in remote and poor parts of India in order to bring prosperity to those regions. This, however, added to the complications of the Chittaranjan project. Not only did railway workers build a factory, but they also had to introduce skilled labor to operate the plant. It made the construction of a brand-new city imperative. Skilled workers needed housing. Over malarial forests and fallow paddy fields, the construction crew built a city to accommodate over 5,000 families. The entire project required 11,000 tons of fabricated steel and 1.7 million cubic feet of cement. The plant went into operation in January 1950.[287]

Nation Building: Pakistan

Like their counterparts in India, Pakistani railway workers also faced challenges related to nation-building activities in this period. For them, the most important of these was in the management of the Chittagong port in East Pakistan. A port of limited significance in British India, Chittagong after Independence and Partition emerged as the single most important port in the eastern wing of the country. The work of Pakistani Railway workers, therefore, became of prime significance to the survival of the eastern wing and its people, over half the country's population. In addition, like their counterparts in India, Pakistani railway workers constituted an important organized form of labor directly under the control of the state. Consequently, Pakistani railway workers often found themselves faced with tasks that constituted civil emergencies that fell well outside their areas of expertise as well as other public services. All these added to the challenges of this period.

In 1947, the Chittagong port had the feel of an aging provincial outlet. Located about 10 miles from the mouth of the river Karnafuli, the port could berth four ships on jetties built in the 1800s. The jetties were in an advanced state of decay and disrepair. The port's warehouse capacity was a mere 300,000 square feet. This was despite the fact that India's British rulers had declared it a 'Major Port' in 1928, and it had played a fairly significant part in Britain's efforts during the Second World War. Its location, close to India's frontlines, however, had turned Allied commanders wary. Consequently, the port of Calcutta had developed rapidly, leaving Chittagong to decay. After Independence, the Government of Pakistan left the development and management of the port to the most powerful civilian institution in East Pakistan, the Eastern Bengal Railway company. Therefore, with all the challenges Pakistani railway workers were already facing, there was the added burden of civil construction projects that included the extension of warehousing at the port as well as landing facilities. The latter included the extension of two existing jetties and the construction of pontoon and lighterage jetties for the loading and unloading of ships in mooring.[288] The following year, the

Eastern Bengal Railway workers also began work on electrical work at the port, including electrification projects at the newly constructed pontoon jetties.[289]

In West Pakistan, railway workers in the service of the NWR company were called upon by the West Pakistan authorities to provide their expertise and workshops on the maintenance of public utility machinery. For instance, the Posts and Telegram Department in West Pakistan turned to staff at the Mughalpura Railway for the manufacture and maintenance of a wide range of articles necessary for its work. Similarly, the Public Works Department's Electricity Branch asked the railway workers at Mughalpura to recondition equipment for its Sialkot Power House. The Public Works Department also sent orders for the manufacture of spare parts for and repairs to many motors used at its Okara Power House. Orders also came in from the Military Engineering Services Department and the Supply and Development Department of the Government of Pakistan.[290] Later, the Meteorological, Public Health and Mining departments all turned to the Pakistan Railways for assistance.[291]

Abdul Kalam's memoirs are filled with glimpses of some of these challenges. As noted earlier, Kalam had been posted on the Eastern Bengal Railway in 1947 and arrived in Dacca to take up his duties shortly after Independence. He was one of the very few officers in East Pakistan. In June of 1948, Kalam was one of only two officers present at Eastern Bengal Railway Headquarters. Although a junior officer, Kalam was posted at the Saidpur workshop. He wrote, 'Before reaching the age of twenty-five I found myself in sole charge of two thousand five hundred men and entrusted with the manufacturing of whatever was needed not only by the Railway but also the Port, the Posts and Telegraph and several other departments, all of whom had been deprived of their supply sources from India.' Kalam also wrote about the hardship of life in the Eastern Bengal Railway, even for an officer. While on deputation with the Pakistan Army,

Kalam wrote, 'I spent ten weeks in the sweltering heat without even an electric fan in the "basha" or thatched quarters.' Kalam also wrote of a civil emergency where city authorities in Dhaka called on Pakistani railway workers for assistance. A man was stuck inside a vertical overflow pipe connected to the city's main overhead water tank. Kalam wrote, 'No one except the railways had the facilities at the time either to cut or remove the pipe.' It was a difficult operation as the pipe had to be supported and cut using a gas-cutting machine. Kalam recollected how civil authorities expected Pakistani railway workers to shoulder the burdens of the operation and how his colleagues found it perfectly natural that railway workers were being tasked with such operations that were clearly beyond their usual remit.[292]

Institutional Lifelines: India

During this difficult time, the Indian railway workers took advantage of several institutional lifelines. The most important of these helped keep their hunger at bay. They took advantage of railway canteens that served 'inexpensive and nourishing' meals at their workplaces. In the period 1947–1948, railway workers were patronizing 26 such canteens across the country. Every day, these canteens served 26,000 staff members. Some offered beverages and light snacks, while others had full meals available to patrons. Over the course of the following year, the number of such canteens doubled, and the daily footfall in terms of patrons increased to 53,000 per day. By the 1949–1950 period, some 63,000 railway workers were patronizing 69 railway canteens on a daily basis.[293] Supplementing these canteens and the grain shops mentioned earlier, Indian railway workers also survived the threat of hunger through an ever-expanding Dearness Allowance. In the period 1947–1948, most railway workers received a 17.5 per cent DA, with monthly minimums ensuring that the lowest-paid employees received an even higher

DA. Those who did not hold officer-level positions could further supplement their DAs with rations from the grain stores. The following year, the DA rates rose, especially for laborers at the lower end of pay scales. All railway workers received 17.5 per cent DAs plus Rs 5 per month. For the lowest-paid employees receiving less than Rs 40 per month and living in the most expensive parts of the country, the minimum DA stood at a substantial Rs 24.[294]

In addition to their DAs, grain stores and canteens, the Indian railway workers also greatly benefited from an expanding medical care system. This was critical in India, where the British Indian state had largely failed to develop anything like a functioning public health care system. Consequently, the railway workers came to rely on the Railway Medical Service for their health-related needs. All railway workers received health care checkups on a fairly regular basis. They also benefited from preventive and prophylactic care, which helped keep epidemics at bay, especially from railway colonies. Such services were extended to the families of railway staff. Many railway workers trained in first aid and could make use of first-aid facilities widely available across the railway system. To some extent, they also benefited from specialized research into occupational ailments and diseases caused by railway service or prevalent in areas where railway workers worked. The workers and their families also made use of maternity and pediatric services available to them. Several railway hospitals provided specialized medical services. For those in remote areas, traveling medical staff, including surgeons, provided access to healthcare.[295] During the period 1948–1949, the service expanded accessibility to all railway workers and their families on the same scale and conditions, approaching the idea of providing the highest level of care for all. Hospital services expanded with increases in the number of beds and equipment such as X-Ray machines and electro-medical apparatus. Many railway companies also set up blood transfusion services for the first time. The least-paid sections of the railway workforce also gained access to vitamins free of cost. That year onwards, many railway workers were also able to make use of free treatment at select non-railway hospitals.[296] In the period 1949–1950, the Railway Medical Department vastly expanded its malaria prevention programs, leading to a significant reduction in malarial infections.[297]

The third significant shift in the Railway Board's priorities that substantially benefited the railway workers came in the form of housing. This was of great significance because, until this time, housing privileges were restricted to better-paid and higher-ranking railway personnel only. In the period 1947–1948, the Indian Railway Board sanctioned the provision of housing for all railway workers. By the end of the period 1949–1950, almost 10,000 railway workers and their families received subsidized or even rent-free accommodation under the initiative. The houses had most benefited railway workers who held essential jobs where they could be called on to work at short notice. Having homes near their worksites substantially eased their lives. Over 7,000 of these had been built, especially on the Assam, Bengal Nagpur, Bombay, Baroda and Central India, and the Oudh and Tirhut companies. Another thousand railway workers, especially those among the least-paid workers in the system, were able to move into newly built houses.[298] Of particular significance was the relatively high quality of these houses. The lowest-grade homes, as most of these were, consisted of two 10–12 feet rooms. The houses had their own courtyards where workers could build their own gardens and came with kitchens and bathrooms. By the abysmal standards of housing in India, these were and remain model homes.[299]

Indian railway workers headed to Chittaranjan were particularly well placed to benefit from this progressive vision of railway housing. The town planners prevented segregation based on pay scales and yet enabled the lowest-paid workers to easily access the worksites, shops and other places of social activities. Their children could enroll in excellent railway schools and there were many playgrounds, cinemas and clubs. Pharmacies and a hospital ensured a high degree of medical care in a region that lacked such facilities. The eradication of malaria from the region and the gentle climate turned the city into a 'health resort' in the popular imagination.[300]

There were several institutional initiatives in the cultural realm that also benefited the Indian railway workforce. The Indianization project accelerated after Independence as the Indian Railway Board was left with little incentive to prioritize the recruitment of British personnel. This had significant consequences for cohesion in the workforce. At both the levels of the officer and skilled labor, British recruits had enjoyed higher salaries, gratuities, allowances and bonuses, all under the excuse that India was far from their native land. British officers and other personnel even enjoyed special leave privileges denied to their Indian counterparts. British railway workers lived segregated in railway colonies in better housing as compared to their Indian peers. The medical system, educational facilities extended to their children, and even social clubs were segregated on a racial basis. All such institutional practices had corroded solidarity and cohesion in the railway system. With the coming of Independence, all such discriminatory practices disappeared. Similar policies affected the Anglo-Indian population. In a reversal of the American one-drop rule, Anglo-Indians benefited from even a single European ancestor. It gave them higher salaries, better quality housing and even some access to the medical, educational and social facilities open to British railway workers.[301] Of particular significance was the decision of the Government of India to eliminate the Auxiliary Force. This was a volunteer paramilitary organization composed entirely of British and Anglo-Indian members, designed to defend the British Empire in India. British and Anglo-Indian railway personnel contributed to several railway regiments. After Independence, it was replaced by the Territorial Army open to all Indian citizens. Many railway workers volunteered to serve in the railway units prepared to assist at times of emergency. The elimination of race-based privileges and replacing them with occupational affiliations assisted in the cohesion of the railway workforce and ultimately their successful survival in this difficult period.

In addition to the removal of racial barriers, Indian railway workers were also able to survive the challenges of these years with many cultural avenues available to them through their employment. All over the railway system, railway workers enjoyed access to railway institutes. These were social spaces designed for the workforce to engage in social activities. While membership fees may have inhibited the least-privileged from entry into these institutes, the fees were quite nominal and levied in proportion to the employee's salaries. Railway workers at these clubs were able to purchase food, drinks and enjoy a variety of games and sports with their families. The larger institutes had cinema halls and spaces for theatrical productions. There were libraries, reading rooms and card tables. There was ballroom and classical dancing. Many institutes offered members facilities for boxing, tennis, field hockey, soccer, basketball, rugby, golf and cricket. The Indian Railways hockey, cricket, soccer and boxing teams were among the strongest in the country. Many railway workers went on to gain international recognition on the strengths of their skills on the hockey and cricket fields.[302] All such activities provided railway workers with opportunities to relax, forge friendships and build solidarity that helped them survive the challenges of the period.

Finally, for many railway workers, institutional support came in the form of schooling and educational opportunities for their children. While Indian Railways had provided their British employees with schooling for their children, these opportunities expanded after Independence. By the end of the period 1949–1950, the Indian Railway educational budget became quite substantial. There were 135 railway schools in operation across the Indian railway network, with the largest number on the Bengal Nagpur Line. Three schools operated in the Chittaranjan Railway Colony alone.[303] During the early years of Independence, the number of such schools expanded considerably, providing a high quality of education for many railway children. The provision of subsidies opened these schools to children of even less well-paid employees.[304]

Institutional Lifelines: Pakistan

As in India, Independence brought about a sea change in attitudes towards the Pakistani railway workforce. In contrast to the callous indifference and brutal exploitation of the Raj era managerial class, the Pakistan Railway Board, post-Independence, demonstrated a marked improvement in its commitment towards the welfare of the railway workforce. Towards this end, the institutional lifelines of the Pakistan railway system, dating to this period, became significant sources for the survival of Pakistani railway workers.

Like their counterparts in India, Pakistani railway workers benefited from canteens which provided tea on the EBR and cooked meals on the NWR. The canteens in the NWR were particularly helpful as large numbers of refugee staff came to rely on them for sustenance. At Lahore, Multan and Rawalpindi, thousands of railway workers purchased subsidized meals at Rs 2 or received food at no cost. The Pakistan Railways Report, 1947–1948, states, 'It can safely be said that these canteens went a very long way towards rehabilitating the destitute staff transferred from India in as much as thousands having little means of subsistence were saved from hardship if not starvation.'[305] The popularity of the canteens did not diminish with the Partition crisis. In fact, the following year, while the

Railway Board closed the emergency canteens, NWR railway workers were able to access the services of six new canteens. The Annual Report of the Pakistan Railway Board for the period 1948--1949 states that these new canteens 'soon became popular with the staff.'[306] The following year, NWR opened six additional canteens for its staff, bringing the total up to twenty. The canteens remained popular and highly profitable for the Railway Board. That year, the first canteens offering food opened on the EBR. In addition to the cooperative canteen operated by the staff at EBR headquarters in Chittagong, by the end of the year, all important centers had refreshment rooms and canteens for employees.[307]

At Independence, Pakistan inherited its own Railway Medical Department. Like its counterpart in India, the department provided officers and skilled workers with medical care. This was quite important in British India, where even in the 1940s medical care remained severely underdeveloped and unavailable. Things were particularly bad outside large cities, and even in those, quite limited. After Independence, the Pakistan Railway Board, like its counterpart in India, began expanding these services to a larger section of its workforce. The Railway Medical Service provided periodical medical checkups for a substantial section of the workforce to ensure performance and safety. The service also provided preventive and prophylactic care to mitigate the risks of epidemics. Emergency medical services on railway property and some research into ailments and diseases of specific concern to railway workers were also among the department's duties. For gazetted officers and subordinate staff, the medical department provided treatment facilities for families including maternity and pediatric services. Pakistani railway workers in large cities had access to railway hospitals, and traveling assistant surgeons provided care in rural areas.[308]

Like in India, these services expanded with Independence. During the period 1949–1950, the Pakistan Railways Medical

Department opened three temporary dispensaries at Jessore, Darsana and Kotchandpur in East Pakistan. The dispensaries provided drugs and care to railway workers and construction workers building the Jessore-Darsana rail link on the Eastern Bengal Railway system. In West Pakistan, the department expanded medical services through the opening of a dental clinic at the Cairns Hospital in Lahore, an in-door ward to the Karachi Hospital and a dispensary at Mari Indus.[309]

Like their counterparts in India, the Pakistani Railway Department inherited the housing initiatives begun on the eve of Independence. The plans for the housing of the entire railway workforce, including guidelines for the construction of decent housing for even the least paid railway workers, were accepted by the Pakistani Railway Division. At Independence, despite all the problems faced by the new country in general, and the Railway Division in particular, all quarters under construction prior to Independence were completed. In addition, the Railway Division constructed 800 temporary quarters for railway workers in East Pakistan during the period 1947–1948.[310] The following year, over a thousand railway workers with the EBR were able to move into homes built by the Pakistan Railway Division. That year, the division completed the construction of 1,202 residences in East Pakistan. There was no new construction in West Pakistan.[311] Three hundred railway workers employed with the NWR company were able to move into residences the following year. The Pakistan Railway Division also began a mammoth housing project for Eastern Bengal Railway staff. Budgeted at a significant Rs 4.5 million, the project made substantial progress despite acute shortages of material and skilled labor.[312]

Resource constraints limited the Pakistan Railway Division from pursuing some of the other progressive initiatives that substantially improved lives in India. However, the Pakistan Railway Division did pursue a significant DA policy that helped Pakistani Railway workers survive the difficult circumstances of these first years of Independence. In the immediate aftermath of Partition, the Pakistan Railway Department reduced the Dearness Allowance given to officers and skilled laborers, most likely as an economizing measure. For the highest-paid railway workers, the allowance became insignificant. For many railway workers making less than the highest salaries, the Dearness Allowance fell from 17.5 per cent to 10 per cent. The allowance was, however, maintained for the lowest-paid categories of railway workers.[313] The following year, the Pakistan Railway Board authorized a further 'Interim Relief' package for the lowest-earning employees of the railway system. Railway workers earning less than Rs 54 per month began receiving an additional Rs 2, and those earning between Rs 55 and Rs 175 earned an additional Rs 3 per month.[314] These allowances were to rise substantially. In 1949, the first Pakistan Pay Commission issued its recommendations, based on which the Railway Board substantially increased Dearness Allowances for all railway workers. For the lowest-paid workers, Dearness Allowances now stood at Rs 26, more than 50 per cent of gross monthly pay for many workers. For employees earning between Rs 50 and Rs 100, the allowance was set at Rs 30 per month. Class III and Class IV employees, the lowest paid workers in East Pakistan, received a further Rs 6 each month.[315] All of this made a great difference to the survival of Pakistani railway workers in this difficult moment.

The 1949 Pakistan Pay Commission recommendations constituted a significant improvement in pay scales for railway workers. The decision of the Pakistan Railway Board to follow through on the recommendations was singularly important in the context of the challenging times. To varying degrees, all Pakistani railway workers benefited from the increases in pay. Railway workers native to the regions that had become Pakistan received an option to remain on their old pay scales, but it was an option that none of them accepted. The new scales were much more reasonable.[316]

The Importance of Collective Action: Trade Unions in India

The institutional mechanisms that did so much to ensure the survival of Indian railway workers did not appear solely because of the munificence of the railway managerial class. On the contrary, the historical record makes it clear that trade unions played a very important role in their establishment. For instance, the Annual Reports of the Indian Railway Board indicates that throughout this period, the AIRF engaged in collective bargaining with the Indian Railway Board over the precise issues that were central to the survival of Indian railway workers. For instance, in the period 1947–1948, the AIRF met with the Railway Board twice. During their first meeting, held 1 July 1947, just over a month before Independence, and their second meeting, held 21 and 23 January 1948, the AIRF lobbied the Railway Board over several issues that had a direct bearing on the survival of Indian railway workers. These included the continuation and working of railway grain shops and educational assistance for children of railway employees. In addition, the AIRF pushed for the rollback of retrenchment policies and the confirmation of temporary staff who had completed one or two years of service. The AIRF discussed issues arising from Partition and urged the Railway Board to reinstate railway workers convicted of political offenses under the British Raj. The AIRF also asked for some clemency towards railway workers who had been discharged for supposedly abandoning their posts during the Calcutta air raids of the Second World War. The AIRF also asked the Board to fairly implement the recommendations of the Government of India Pay Commission and an Adjudicators Award that included necessary increments in pay for railway workers. Finally, the AIRF asked the Board to consider extending the privileges of railway workers employed with the Government of India to all other railway systems in the country, specifically the privately owned railway systems of the Princely States, and the standardization of privileges across all Government of India Railway companies.[317]

Over the course of the following year, the AIRF kept up the pressure on the Indian Railway Board. In August that year, the AIRF passed resolutions demanding increases in the Dearness Allowances offered to workers to help employees cope with the sharp rise in prices felt across the country, a fair and quick implementation of the recommendations of the Government's Pay Commission and the expansion of public administration to all privately run railroad companies in India with all attendant benefits to their workers. These demands were then reiterated in the form of further resolutions passed in a general meeting called in November the same year. The AIRF also threatened a strike in February 1949 if their demands were not taken seriously.[318]

The pressure campaign did force the Railway Board into negotiations. In January 1949, the AIRF engaged in talks with the Board on the issue of grain shops and Dearness Allowances. At issue was a debate over the need for grain shops as the Railway Board proposed replacing the sale of subsidized commodities with increases in Dearness Allowances. While there was some support for the option, many railway workers preferred the security of subsidized products from Railway grain stores to trusting the vagaries of a market highly susceptible to inflationary pressures that could render cash allowances ineffective. In addition, the Railway Board's implementation of the Government of India's Pay Commission recommendations remained a bone of contention, and the AIRF forced the Board to agree to the creation of a special committee to ensure the implementation of the recommendations in a timely manner. The talks went on until mid-February and bore some positive results, sufficient for the AIRF to call off its strike ballot initiative and prevent a nationwide strike. The AIRF, through these negotiations, remained under significant pressure from affiliated and unaffiliated regional railway unions. Many of these remained unconvinced about the talks.[319]

It was also at this crucial time that the formidable Jayprakash Narayan became President of the AIRF. Under his leadership, the AIRF's advocacy resulted in many of the institutional support systems that became significant for the survival of railway workers. In the meanwhile, the AIRF entered into additional talks with the Railway Board in November 1949 discussing new issues that emerged as the dust from the turbulence of Independence and Partition settled. The AIRF demanded fairer weightage of service when fixing the initial pay scales for employees. The AIRF also pushed for the fair implementation of the Central Pay Commission's Leave Rules recommendations. The two sides discussed the conversion of temporary posts with permanent employment to ensure greater job security for the railway labor force. The AIRF also looked to the future. The Federation began negotiations on a voluntary savings scheme for railway workers that year. Finally, the older issues of Dearness Allowance and 'Pass Rules' or codes of conduct remained on the table and under discussion.[320]

Of all the interventions made by organized labor in this period, the most significant was in the implementation of the Government of India Pay Commission recommendations. These had major implications for the well-being of railway workers. Although the Commission had published its recommendations in 1947, it was only in August 1949 that the Indian Railway Board issued orders for their implementation. Railway workers benefited enormously from these recommendations. For instance, Leave Rules were now calculated at the rate of one-tenth of the total period spent on duty in place of the older measure of one-fifteenth. The leave salary for the first 60 days of leave was also enhanced to the average rather than substantive pay of the previous 12 months. These Leave Rule privileges were also extended to temporary staff after one year's service, and to skilled workers. Temporary staff, after a year's service, also became eligible to avail the Railway's Provident Fund. All of this was managed through negotiations between the Board and the organized labor. The relationship was formalized through a Joint Advisory Committee that worked on the implementation process.[321]

Trade Unions in Pakistan

Trade Unions played an equally and perhaps more important role in Pakistan. The chaos and upheavals of Partition effectively destroyed substantial sections of the labor organization in the country. This was especially true in the railways where the AIRF, which had long represented labor interests in British India received no official recognition in the Pakistan Railway Department. However, the long experience of labor organization and solidarity had created a fertile ground for such institutions that even Partition and its attendant upheavals could not quite prevent their reappearance. The Annual Report of the Railway Division (1947-1948) indicated that many trade unions had come into operation and were advocating for labor rights in the new country.[322]

The unions were certainly operating on fertile ground. The 1946 Pay Commission recommendations accepted in India were entirely on hold in Pakistan, and there was no sign that any authority in the Pakistan Railway Division was remotely interested in their implementation there. There were other issues. The NWR company management, faced with the emerging issue of surplus staff, was becoming increasingly vocal about its plans for aggressive retrenchment as the only solution. Neither the NWR company nor the EBR company management showed any inclination in expanding housing provisions to its workforce. During the period 1947–1948, in fact, the Pakistan Railway Division ceased construction on new residential projects for their workers. Finally, the high cost of living in East Pakistan was driving the workforce there to despair.[323]

By 1948, trade unions in both wings of the country had strengthened sufficiently to organize strike ballots. On the NWR company, the North Western State Railway Trade Workers' Union felt confident enough in their organizational abilities to raise the specter of a general strike across the railway system. In East Pakistan, the Eastern Pakistan Railway Employees League had gained sufficient stature to be recognized as a union by the Railway Division authorities. The league organized their own company-wide strike ballot in the early part of the year. The Railway Division's own report indicates that these strikes were averted only after concerted action by the respective railway companies. The report stated, 'The considerable propaganda carried out by the NWR, who appointed a Public Relations Officer for the purpose, proved efficacious.' In East Pakistan, the Railway Division was also able to weaken union activity by promoting two other unions thereby dividing the workforce. The report stated, 'In consequence, the former Union lost some of its popularity and the strike threat did not materialize.'[324]

But there were strikes. During the period 1948–1949, there were at least three occasions when workers walked off their jobs on the NWR system and two occasions when workers struck the EBR company. During one NWR workers' strike, almost 10,000 workers brought the region's workshops to a grinding halt. Another strike involved 600 laborers with the carriage and wagon shops of the company who were demanding the immediate release of their union president Mirza Muhammad Ibrahim. The strikes in East Pakistan were equally impressive. On two occasions, these involved 700–800 railway workers, and during one of these, they disrupted the movement of train traffic. A bigger strike drew in some 6,000 workers demanding that grain shops continue the sale of subsidized rice to railway workers. In March 1949, the Rail Road Worker's Union, a union that had been denied official recognition, threatened to organize a strike over wages.[325]

There were incremental advances. In 1949, the Pakistan Railway Division was forced to grant 'provisional recognition' to the North Western State Railway Union, and the Annual Report of the Railway Division was cautiously optimistic as it stated, 'The Labour situation of Pakistan continued to remain fairly satisfactory.' Organized labor, however, kept up the fight through the year. The biggest issue was the withdrawal of grain store concessions. Like their counterparts in India, the Pakistan Railways authorities had struggled to fulfill their obligations towards ensuring that their workers did not go hungry. Faced with burgeoning subsidy bills, the Pakistan Railway Division decided to roll back the grain store program in favor of a cash allowance to its workforce. While many railway workers were willing to accept the cash replacement, others were concerned. Although the annual reports do not explain their concerns, it is possible that the risk of inflationary pressures might have made many Pakistani railway workers balk at the idea of a cash alternative to actual food and clothing. Indeed, this had been the case in India. However, while the AIRF in India had managed to ensure that grain shops remained an option for railway workers who could choose between a cash allowance and access to grain shops, the Pakistan Railway Division did not extend a similar choice to its workforce. Instead, the grain shops were closed in 1949. This prompted at least one significant strike at the critically important Mughalpura workshop in Lahore. The strike affected the mechanical as well as the carriage and wagon shop workers. In East Pakistan, the situation was difficult. The Railway Division's report for the year indicates that organized labor was under considerable pressure from the managerial class. Nonetheless, the report makes clear that Pakistani railway unions were fighting, and that their fight was influencing the managerial class.[326]

***

The years 1945 to 1949 constituted a final great challenge for the railway workers of India and now Pakistan. Independence created several challenges specific to the railway system. The Partition had severely disrupted the functioning of this system in India and Pakistan. In India, it ruptured the railway companies operating in Assam and Bengal, and Punjab and Jodhpur with consequences for the system as a whole. In Pakistan, the railway networks required a substantial reorientation, particularly in the East, but also to a great extent in West Pakistan. Railway workers in both countries struggled to rebuild their respective railway systems under these changed circumstances. They were crippled in these efforts by the severe problems inherited from their respective countries' imperialist legacies. Neither country had the capacity to stave off hunger, with the result that the poorest railway workers worked with hunger in their bellies. Neither country had the capacity to provide their citizens with adequate healthcare nor educate their children. Indian and Pakistani railway workers, consequently, were rebuilding their respective railway systems without access to good healthcare and without any guarantees that their children could enjoy a decent education.

And yet, in the years 1947 to 1949, railway workers in India and to some extent in Pakistan executed a remarkable turnaround for their respective railway systems. By 1949, Indian railway workers were moving far greater quantities of freight and passengers than even pre-Partition British India. Through impressive efforts, Indian railway workers were able to eliminate all transportation shortages when it came to the movement of essential commodities and industrial products. All this with a significant improvement in punctuality of services.[327] Their counterparts in Pakistan put in a similarly impressive performance when it came to passenger traffic; from 70 million passengers in the period 1947–1948 to 118 million passengers in the 1949–1950 period. However, Pakistani railway workers were transporting less freight in the 1949–1950 time span than at the time of Independence.[328] A reflection of the greater difficulties faced by that country.

The survival of this workforce had much to do with the several progressive initiatives taken by their respective Railway Boards. Many Indian and Pakistani railway workers were able to stave off hunger through a combination of grain stores, co-operatives, canteens, and DA relief. The expansion of medical care, educational facilities, and housing for railway workers, especially those who were among the least paid, also made a substantial difference to the lives of Indian and Pakistani railway workers. The results of the better-paid and better-fed workforce started to become clear in the years after Independence. By the end of the 1940s, Indian and Pakistani railway workers were transporting greater freight and passenger traffic than ever before, despite all the losses and disruption of Partition. In all of this, however, the role of organized labor was crucial. The AIRF in India and independent trade unions in Pakistan kept the pressure on their respective railway managers to provide and expand the lifelines that made the survival of the workforce possible.

FIVE

The Specter of Class Conflict

THIS BOOK IDENTIFIES some crucial and particularly difficult challenges that Indian, and after 1947, Pakistani railway workers overcame to survive the 1939–1949 decade. However, this does not mean that the Second World War, India's independence struggle, Partition, and the immediate post-colonial moment were the only challenges facing Indian and Pakistani railway workers in this period. To the contrary, the set of workers, by virtue of employment with a modern transportation system in a capitalist and imperialist economy, were subject to many other forms of class conflict that are endemic to enterprises such as the railway system. These included but were not limited to poor and unfair wage and pay scales, harsh and unsafe working conditions, imperious and unsupportive managers, and, finally, the ever-unrelenting pressure to do more for less. Railway workers and the managerial class well understood the adversarial nature of their relationship. Railway workers were aware that their employers and managers had every incentive to exploit their labor. On the other hand, the managerial class in the railway system were equally conscious that the railway workforce had every incentive to negotiate and renegotiate the work process to their own advantage. All this made class conflict inevitable.

The events discussed in the earlier chapters of this book fundamentally informed the nature of class conflict in this period but to varying degrees. While every clash between labor and management that unfolded during the Second World War was related to the war, its unfolding was often independent of this relationship. Similarly, the Independence struggle, the Partition crisis, and the difficulties of Independence informed class conflict in this period; not all struggles that unfolded directly linked with the course of these great events. This chapter, therefore, discusses the survival strategies railway workers deployed to manage class conflict that was not necessarily a direct fallout of the larger crises affecting India and its working people in this period to establish a fuller picture of survival strategies of this era.

As with the crises of the Second World War, the independence struggle, Partition, and the initial years of Independence, Indian and Pakistani railway workers deployed multiple survival strategies to manage class conflict at their worksites. The historical records make much mention of two such strategies. The first is theft. This form of resistance made much sense to laborers who did not receive a survivable income. It was a very real problem in British India, especially during the troubled years of the Second World War when terrible administrative policies led to unconscionably high price increases and made the specter of hunger all too real for hundreds of thousands of railway workers. Theft was also a problem for some better-paid railway workers who felt, for perhaps entirely understandable reasons, that they were getting paid far less than fair wages. There were many reasons for this, some intractably linked with the contradictions of an imperialist economy and others with the outcome of prevailing market conditions that created enormous opportunities for employees to even the odds in an unequal struggle with their managers and supervisors. The second strategy came in the form of ignoring or shirking rules and responsibilities. Again, there were several reasons for this. Many of the rules and regulations were impractical and contradictory. The safest and easiest path for railway workers to do their job or simply survive at their jobs was to ignore them. For others, it was another way to even the odds; a path to extract a fairer deal in a job characterized by fundamental exploitation.

But more effective forms of the strategies were, once again, collective in nature. There is one particularly striking record of workmen collectively threatening and intimidating management in order to prevent a sharp worsening of working conditions at the Kanchrapara workshop. But there are several records of strikes that rocked the functioning of the railway system with some regularity in this period. The strikes, unlike the individual survival strategies, certainly gained the attention of the managerial class. In fact, the strikes often gained national attention. They were not always successful. And sometimes they petered out or were beaten out before achieving the stated objectives.

The significance of this history lies in its power to remind us that Indian and Pakistani railway workers in this period weren't just coping with great, epoch-changing tragedies. While fighting in the struggle against fascism, Indian railway workers were also dealing with callous and exploitative management. At the same time, as they played their part in India's independence struggle, they were also engaged in struggles to establish a reasonable working environment, which included safe and fair working conditions. During the Partition crisis, as thousands of railway workers braved the dangers of the Punjab countryside, others fought to ensure that their sacrifices during the war were not rewarded with retrenchment. Finally, during the hard years in the immediate post-Independence period, railway workers, in addition to their nation-building duties, were also forced to fight to secure their survival in a world of unsympathetic managers and economic dislocation.

This history also reminds us of and reinforces the argument that railway workers used multiple survival strategies to cope with the challenges of this period. More importantly, however, this story underlines how Indian and Pakistani railway workers depended to a significant degree on their ability to organize and work collectively even during challenges thrown up by class conflicts. In all of this, the role of trade unions became particularly important. No institution could mobilize large numbers of laborers to confront and oppose recalcitrant management or even the Indian Railway Board itself quite like trade unions. The evidence is clear. While Indian and Pakistani railway workers often resorted to individual survival strategies as a daily form of resistance, these could only function as a coping mechanism. It was rarely possible to make big changes through individual initiatives. Those required collective action, and that was largely possible through the painstaking organization that was the result of years of union building. The history of class conflict in the 1939–1949 era demonstrates once again that there is no substitution for organized labor.

Everyday Initiatives

Historical records indicate that there were multiple forms of individual action ubiquitous in the railway system throughout this period—among them, theft and corruption, and the shirking or ignoring rules and responsibilities. These strategies made it to the historical records because of their capacity to damage the interests of the railway managerial class. The former directly, either through the theft of valuable material and parts or loss of revenue and trust. The latter entered the archive when the disregarding of rules and regulations disrupted the smooth functioning of the railway system. There are several sources listing instances of such forms of resistance. Records of theft made their way into police reports, and corruption found mention in the annual reports of the Indian Railway Board.

Theft

Two records from the Bombay Police demonstrate that railway workers across the ranks engaged in thievery. In July 1940, for instance, the police in western India discovered a group of railway workers involved in the theft of gold. The theft came to light when a railway gangman reported discovering a bar of silver lying on the tracks between Ankleshwar and Broach railway stations in western India. His report resulted in a search of the Delhi Express that had just passed by. The police discovered the theft of a Rs 1,000 silver bar and 3,000 gold sovereigns worth Rs 84,000. A railway gateman at Maiyagam was involved in the theft. An associate had broken open the wagon lock and hidden it in the train with the gold. He had used the silver bar to break out of the wagon when the train was passing over the Nurbudda viaduct. The gold had then been dropped off at Miyagam as prearranged and picked up by the gateman who had hidden it near his quarters.[329]

In the second instance, this time in 1947, the railway police uncovered a significant scam to illegally transport yarn from Kattigiri station to several destinations in west-central India. The stationmaster at Kudchi railway station played a key role in delivering the illegally transported yarn to clearing agents without obtaining their endorsements on railway receipts as required by regulations. All of this was in violation of the Cotton Textile Ordinance, 1946 and the Essential Supplies Ordinance, 1946. The police attached a substantial 46,266 worth of yarn during their operations.[330]

A more detailed and extensive record appears in D.V.

Reddy's memoir. The memoir carries detailed reminiscences of Reddy's most challenging early posting as Works Manager at the Kanchrapara (locomotives) workshop during the period 1948–1949. Reddy described Kanchrapara as 'one of the world's worst workshops in the matter of labor conditions,' by which he, of course, meant that the labor force was particularly successful at challenging his authority. The Kanchrapara workshop was, in the pre-Partition period, a part of the BAR company. Located some 30 miles north of Calcutta, it belonged to the small portion of this railway company that remained on the Indian side of the border as a part of the Sealdah Division. After Independence, the Indian Railway Board merged the division with the East Indian Railway company, and otherwise left the system, more or less, undisturbed. Reddy's appointment came as the board was integrating the division into the East Indian Railway company.

As Reddy made himself familiar with the workshop and its functioning, he couldn't help but notice significant theft at the erecting shed. There were two metal enclosures located on either side where the workshop staff stored spare parts. As a rule, locomotive workshops kept only sufficient spares to last a month. At Kanchrapara, however, the metal enclosures were 'filled to overflowing.' Reddy noted that many of these stores were valuable and some of it was scrap. The former had clearly been overdrawn from railway stores while the latter consisted of unwanted components. This created significant opportunities for theft. Reddy wrote, 'It was not possible to exercise any check over the stocks of new components or the disposal of unwanted components or scrap in the confusion that prevailed, giving plenty of scope for unauthorized removal of easily marketable valuable material, often openly through the main gate during lunch recess or in the evening.'[331]

A second, equally startling, discovery indicated that theft was not just a subaltern problem. The erecting shop had a cab roof repair section with an attic full of material. Reddy recalled climbing up a ladder one morning to see what was stored in that attic. 'I was shocked to find a couple of wagon loads of cut-to-size scantlings of first-class Burma teakwood,' he wrote. Reddy's shock stemmed from the high value of the product. Unable to fathom what the teakwood was doing in the attic of the cab roof repair section, Reddy approached his foreman. The foreman claimed that the teakwood scantlings had been stored for use as cab roof repairs, but this was quite impossible. Indian railway cab roofs were always repaired using cheap 'country wood,' that too, of scantlings of an entirely different size. In fact, Burma teakwood was highly unsuitable for such repairs. They were more often used in the construction of larger pieces of domestic furniture. Uncertain of what he was supposed to do, Reddy ordered the entire supply to be moved to the furniture section of the neighboring carriage and wagon workshop. It was only later that Reddy discovered the contours of what was undoubtedly a racket. Unlike the theft of scrap though, this involved officers. Reddy wrote, 'I later learnt that most workshop officers on the old Bengal and Assam Railway had their furniture worth a few thousand rupees for each made in the workshop on a sanctioned work order for which they were charged nominally.'[332]

Corruption

The strongest evidence of corruption comes from the annual reports of the Indian Railway Board. In the period 1942–1943, driven by the exigencies of war, Indian railway authorities concluded that corruption had become a problem sufficient to require the establishment of specialized police and staff. Supporting the drive were the regular court systems as well as specially created tribunals. The record from that year speaks of 'a number of convictions.'[333] The scale increased the following year. The Indian Railway Board's annual report for the 1943–1944 period states, 'In order to expedite the final disposal of cases put up for trial the Government increased the number of Special Tribunals dealing with cases of corruption on railways...' The top echelons of the railway bureaucracy understood that much of this was a function of the war, though they put it down to 'conditions [that] afford for malpractices both on the part of the public and railway servants.' There was no word on the crushing increase in workload or the skyrocketing cost of living.[334]

In the period 1944–1945, the Special Railway Staff and the Special Police Establishment worked on 113 cases. Eighty-three of these cases went to trial, either in courts or before tribunals. The courts and tribunals convicted 55 employees, a total of 142 over the past three years. The cumulative data throws some light on the railway workers with authority over the allocation of wagons, the dispatch of restricted goods and the reservation of berths, who deployed corruption as a form of resistance.[335] In the 1945–1946 period, the Special Railway Staff and the Special Police Establishment ensured the conviction of 41 employees. Many served in the Traffic and Commercial Departments of the Railway companies.[336] Railway authorities continued to escalate their campaign against corruption. In the period 1946–1947, in addition to the prosecution of 68 cases, the railway authorities instituted disciplinary action against 18 employees who had been cleared by the courts and tribunals. Three of the 18 lost their jobs. Towards the end of that year, the Railway Board issued 'a stern warning' that 'very severe action would be taken against any railway servant found guilty of having received illegal gratification or having indulged in corrupt practices.'[337]

Corruption remained a significant issue in independent India. Even amid the chaos of Partition, the Indian Railway Board continued with its anti-corruption drive. In the period 1947–1948, the Board prosecuted 38 cases leading to 28 convictions. In addition, railway authorities discharged four employees against whom investigative authorities had been unable to find sufficient evidence for a court prosecution.[338] In the 1948–1949 period, the Board prosecuted 37 cases leading to 31 convictions. In addition, railway authorities discharged three employees against whom the railway authorities had been unable to find sufficient evidence for a court prosecution.[339] Finally, in the 1949–1950 period, the Board prosecuted four cases leading to the conviction of 36 individuals. This year, the Railway Board also implemented a new method of policing based on a decentralized approach. Each railway company now had its own anti-corruption organization. These organizations worked closely with the Special Police Establishment in the investigation and prosecution of cases. The report from this year also shed some light on areas where corruption was particularly prevalent. Railway authorities highlighted limited booking facilities and complications in rules and regulations as specific problems.[340]

The Railway Board in newly created Pakistan appeared equally determined to root out corruption in their railway system. The Annual Report of Pakistan Railways for the year 1947–1948 lamented that an anti-corruption department couldn't be organized for the Eastern Bengal Railway but on the NWR, the special police were able to arrange for the conviction of seven employees and the discharge of an additional 17 during the year. The general manager of NWR issued a personal appeal asking his employees to 'desist from corrupt practices.'[341] The following year, the Pakistani railway authorities discharged 25 employees from service on charges of corruption. The authorities also arranged for the printing of 10,000 posters, which proclaimed in English and Urdu, 'Who is the State's enemy no. 1?' That year's report claimed that these posters were put up 'at stations, Parcels and Goods Offices, Workshops, etc.'[342]

These records outline the policing of theft and corruption, detailing the rigor and zeal with which railway authorities hoped to impress upon the historical archive. There is no word on the motives behind the individuals mentioned as 'prosecuted' or 'discharged' in these records. There is no discussion on what drove these individuals to make those fateful choices that came back to haunt them. India in this period was a wretchedly poor country. Did a low-paid gateman steal thinking of treatment for a dying relative in a country without a functioning public health care system? Did a clerk hand out a contract for a minor kickback hoping to pay for the education of a child, in a country with a literacy rate under 20 per cent? The records are silent on these issues. The records are also silent on the scandal of institutionalized racism in the railways. Railway companies paid high salaries to British administrators to run a system that could, and eventually did, run quite well without them. The records are also silent on the disastrous policies that prevented the indigenization of technical expertise. In the 1870s, Indian technicians had sufficient ability to manufacture sophisticated locomotives, and yet, by the early twentieth century, Indian Railways relied almost exclusively on imported rolling stock.[343] In the 1939–1949 era, catastrophic decisions like these cost Indian Railways far more than the minor incidents of corruption that the Railway Board was so keen on eradicating.

A more intimate record of corruption comes from D.V. Reddy's memoir. Once again, this illustration dates to his stint at the Kanchrapara workshop during the period 1948–1949. Upon pressing his supervisors to run a tighter ship, and in particular, ensure that scrap did not accumulate, workshop supervisors had asked Reddy for additional assistance. They asked for *khalasis* (unskilled manual laborers). Reddy, however, was suspicious. In his experience, the number of khalasis had increased across railway workshops through the war years, and there had been no reduction in these numbers in the years since. He suspected that his workshop was, if anything, already overstaffed. His own investigations into the hiring of khalasis in the form of surprise inspections revealed that many khalasis marked present were absent on the shop floor. Despite ordering his supervisors to locate these men, they could not be found. Reddy, however, had his suspicions, 'I suspected that the absent men worked as domestic servants for some of the supervisors.' When he sent a circular asking his supervisors to ensure that no leakage of khalasis occurred through surprise checks, there was much resentment. Reddy noted that after his surprise inspection and circular things got better: 'I found most shops and connected yards clean thereafter and the foremen did not press me for additional khalasis.'[344]

Disregarding Instructions/Shirking Responsibilities

There are several records of railway workers disregarding instructions and shirking responsibilities. Some of the most detailed instances of such forms of behavior can be fleshed out in the records of serious accidents. These chronicled reports were usually bureaucratic face-saving documents, rarely engaging with serious structural problems. Their authors are all too eager to blame individuals for failures and accidents rather than overall systems. Nonetheless, they often reveal practices of railway workers disregarding instructions and/or following protocols. Once again, it was not clear what the motives of the railway personnel involved were, nor whether the practices were genuine mistakes or regular practices that for a combination of factors had resulted in terrible accidents.

In May 1940, for instance, a collision at the Jekot railway station on the Bombay, Baroda, and Central Indian Railway occurred partially when the Jekot stationmaster permitted a freight train to move beyond distant signals when an 'All Clear' signal was in force for the Frontier Mail. The distant signal is the first signal an engine driver sees when approaching a signal box. In the off position, the distant signal indicates that all Stop signals ahead controlled by the box are off and that the driver may proceed. The importance of the distant signal lies in the significant distance a train must necessarily travel before it can come to a complete halt. In this instance, not having the distant signal on the on position had allowed the driver of the freight train to move into the path of the Frontier Mail leading to a fatal collision. Twenty people died, and many more were injured.[345]

A similar accident at Khodri railway station in the same year indicates that this was a common practice. At Khodri, railway investigators discovered that the 531 Down, a light freight train, had crashed after entering a catch siding, breaking through a buffer stop and plowing into an eight-foot-high pile of cinders. The catch siding refers to a special track designed to help runaway trains come to a halt. In this case, the 531 Down had, however, entered the catch siding at a much higher speed than what the siding had been designed to handle. Consequently, the train had hit the buffers at the end of the siding at high speed, breaking through them and steaming into the cinder pile. The entire engine crew consisting of a driver and two firemen died in the accident. In this case, too, the railway investigators concluded that the fault lay with the stationmaster's office. A newly appointed assistant stationmaster, under the supervision of an experienced stationmaster had permitted the 531 Down to approach without ensuring that the points of the catch siding were set and locked on the main line. The railway investigators discovered that this was standard practice and was freely admitted to by both the assistant stationmaster as well as his supervisor. When pressed, the investigators discovered that the proper observation of the regulations was impractical. The stationmaster testified, 'That if he observed it trains would be delayed, and he would be called to account.' The investigators confirmed that an older set of timetables did make it quite impossible for stationmasters to observe the rules. Disregarding them was a necessary survival strategy. This accident investigation also left behind another illustration of railway workers shirking their responsibilities. The investigators noted that guards and firemen on board trains were often unhelpful witnesses. Too often blamed for accidents, guards and firemen had learned to simply state that they were focused on their primary duties, whether it be watching out for signals or firing the engine or anything else. In this case, the guard simply stated that he had been watching the signal and proved singularly unhelpful to the investigators.[346]

Investigations into another accident revealed how a railway gateman had fled after a terrible collision between a bus and a light engine. This accident occurred on the Bengal Nagpur Railway between Benapur and Narayangarh. The light engine, on special deployment to help transport the provincial Governor's train, crashed into the bus on a level crossing. The accident occurred in heavy rain. Subsequent investigators concluded that the level crossing ought to have been closed, and therefore, the level crossing operator was entirely responsible for the accident. However, the investigations also revealed that the light engine was on special duty, and therefore not a scheduled train. Moreover, the gateman did not have shelter from the rain close to the tracks. Consequently, in a heavy downpour, with no train expected, the gateman had retreated to a shelter located at a slight distance from the tracks. The accident was, therefore, quite inadvertent. Either way, the gateman had fled, 'absconded' in the official archive. He had enough sense to understand that he was to be made a scapegoat for a railway system that clearly prioritized the comfort of provincial governors over the safety of his ordinary subjects. Survival in this case came in the form of flight.[347]

Once again, it is from the memoirs of D.V. Reddy that we get the most detailed description of such practices among railway workers. Reddy came across and wrote of numerous instances of railway workers disregarding instructions and shirking responsibility during his tenure as workshop manager at Kanchrapara. Among the first instances, Reddy came across occurred in the bureaucratic section of the workshop. Reddy was asked by clerical staff to approve a draft statement reporting that the workshop had repaired/completed maintenance on no less than a dozen locomotives. Considering that the month in question was February, with only 29 days, Reddy was suspicious. His concerns turned out to be entirely justified as he discovered that only nine locomotives had left the workshop. Of the remaining, one had failed a trial run and had been sent back for further repairs, while two others were still in the advanced stages of assembly. Reddy wrote, 'I asked the dealing clerk...the reason for including these three locomotives in the month's out-turn. He told me that it had been the practice for many years to show a 12-engine out-turn for a month, even if fewer engines had been dispatched...This clerk advised me in all sincerity to follow the established tradition and keep out of trouble.' Reddy claimed that he disregarded the clerk's honest advice and asked him to report only those locomotives that had completed repairs. This apparently caused much consternation, especially for the erecting shop foreman who 'had to put himself out a great deal more to attain the targeted out-run.'[348]

This bureaucratic instance of shirking responsibilities and disregarding rules and instructions was mirrored perhaps more egregiously on the shop floors. Reddy claimed that he noticed that supervisors did not put any pressure on their subordinates. This led to significant delays. While workmen in such a workshop were typically expected to strip a locomotive arriving for a regular overhaul in a matter of two days at Kanchrapara, the process took seven. Similarly, workmen there took a week to clean and inspect the stripped-down parts when the expected time was no more than two days. The consequences of the slow work were significant since workers could not begin indenting for components in stock or furnishing measurements for machining new components until these steps had been completed. It had repercussions on the availability of repaired or new components, leading to delays in the reassembly of the locomotives.[349]

One example of how delays in the initial stages had repercussions on the turnaround time for locomotive overhauls was the amount of time it took to repair boilers. Reddy noticed that laborers at the Kanchrapara workshop did not remove the boiler until a week or two after the arrival of a locomotive. This was considerably over the expected two days that such work typically required. Aggravating the delays was the institutional disregard for stocking norms. Reddy wrote that well-run locomotive workshops kept stocks of spare boilers for different classes of locomotives. The stocks were designed to ensure that no locomotive was kept waiting in case a boiler needed extensive repairs. Despite authorization, the managers at Kanchrapara had, however, neglected to maintain such spare stocks of boilers. Additionally, Reddy pointed out that tenders, the rear portion of a locomotive that stocked coal and water, took very long for repairs and overhauls. Aggravated and frustrated by all that he saw, Reddy wrote, 'Poor output from the workmen and indifference of the supervisors combined with the abnormally heavy repairs to the locomotive frame, cylinders, boilers and tenders piled up delays.' Reddy estimated that the turnaround time averaged around 70 working days in place of the expected 25.[350]

However, nothing caused Reddy as much outrage as his surprise inspections of the night shift. Reddy called it 'a farce.' He wrote, 'The men and supervisors worked for a couple of hours in the beginning of the shift, had their dinner which they brought with them and thereafter slept on the shop floor for the remaining six hours.' A clearly exasperated Reddy added, 'They had, over the years, established a right to two hours' work and six hours sleep and the quiet night shift was even preferred to the day shift by many.' Reddy also had much to say about housekeeping in the shops. These, according to Reddy, 'had been neglected over the years.' His descriptions were certainly quite startling: 'Scrap had accumulated in mountainous heaps,' some of which consisted of 'very heavy accumulations of non-ferrous scrap.' Reddy claimed that many hundreds of expensive heavy bronze axel boxes lay in the open yard. He pointed to a 200-strong 'Yard Gang' that was specifically meant to keep this from occurring but had 'not functioned effectively and had even forgotten what their day-to-day tasks were.' Reddy also suspected that the arrangement suited thieves. He wrote, 'The valuable scrap which had been so abandoned gave ample scope not only for pilferage but also for large-scale organized thefts.'[351]

Finally, there was the problem of overtime. Calling it a racket, Reddy provided a detailed overview of the typical workday at Kanchrapara. Men arrived at work very early, at 6.30 a.m. There were two scheduled tea breaks for them, at 8 a.m. and 2 p.m. Both breaks were scheduled for 15 minutes. A lunch break started at 10.30 a.m., but Reddy did not note how long the break was sanctioned for. He claimed that in practice, work never started at 6.30. Instead, the laborers took considerable time to collect their tools and chatted with their friends. Then, Reddy wrote, 'They had hardly started on their work when they abandoned it for tea.' This 8 a.m. tea break, like the later 2 p.m. tea break, though scheduled for 15 minutes, ended up lasting much longer. Very often, the workmen serving tea took time to bring the urns in which tea was served from the canteens. There were never enough urns nor enough men to serve the tea either. Consequently, it was often over half an hour before all the workmen had even received their due cups of tea. The men only returned to their workstations between 9 and 9.30, anywhere between an hour and an hour and a half. Reddy indicated that supervisors occasionally tried to hurry the men back to their stations, but they were ignored.[352]

Reddy called the tea recess 'a scandal.' But the lunch hour did not proceed much better. The workshop closed at 10.30 a.m. for lunch, but the workmen typically downed their tools and began cleaning up by 10 a.m. Lunch was, moreover, taken at home, extending the break until the workmen returned. In Reddy's assessment, the total work time during the morning stood at one hour only, and the afternoon was similarly spent, with just one hour's work. Reddy claimed that he put in considerable effort into coaxing his workers to increase their efforts. To this extent, he urged sections of the workforce to increase their pace to try and earn bonuses. To this the railway workers responded with a 'You keep your bonus. We will keep our health.'[353]

Reddy's memoir listed several possible explanations for such behavior other than a culture of shirking responsibility. For instance, he indicated that the war had certainly affected the ability of supervisors and their officers to prioritize the maintenance of a clean workshop. Elsewhere, Reddy noted that the workshop lacked the machinery necessary to process some of the scrap and its accumulation therefore became a problem without simple solutions. There may have been other factors. Partition had certainly created new strains on the Kanchrapara workshop as the Eastern Bengal Railway system lost workshops to East Pakistan. But Reddy's own assessment was that this was largely a case of workmen and supervisors shirking responsibility. And Reddy may have been correct.

Violence and Intimidation

Once again, it is from D.V. Reddy's memoirs that we get the clearest illustrations of railway workers resorting to violence and intimidation. And, once again, the best evidence comes from the Kanchrapara workshop where Reddy served as works manager. Early in his stay, Reddy discovered that pilferage at the workshop was sustained through violence and intimidation. Referring to the theft of spare parts and scrap, he claimed that railway workers stole with relative impunity, marching out with their goods through the workshop's main gates. The gates were manned by security personnel; however, he wrote, 'checks by them were not only resented but resisted by the men.' This resistance came in the form of organized violence. Reddy wrote, 'When the security staff were unwise enough to impose a check on the men going through the gate and apprehend a worker or two carrying on his person stolen railway material, the men surrounded the staff, beat them up and released the miscreants.' Clearly there had been several instances of this kind of confrontation, working out in favor of the railway workers. Reddy wrote, 'The security staff gave up searching men going out of the gate, having by then imbibed the wisdom in the saying 'Discretion is the better part of valor.'[354]

But it was developments later in his stay that make for more compelling drama. Reddy's trouble began when one of his foremen at the General Iron Foundry wrote him a letter complaining about a subordinate. This subordinate, a trade union representative, apparently did not work at all and spent much of his time inciting workers on the shop floor. The foreman wrote that this man was making his work quite impossible. Reddy did not want a confrontation with organized trade unions but felt that he could not ignore the letter either. Consequently, he invited the union representative for a meeting. The meeting went badly. The conversation quickly degenerated into an open argument. The next day, Reddy met with union representatives for a scheduled bi-monthly meeting. This meeting turned into an even bigger fiasco. Both sides began shouting at each other, and the union representatives forced the meeting to a halt.[355]

The situation escalated sharply. The next morning, as Reddy ate lunch at his residence, he was rudely interrupted by a phone call informing him that the entire workforce of the locomotive workshop was refusing to return to their stations at the end of this lunch break. On the contrary, they had gathered outside Reddy's office insisting that he come out and meet them. Reddy was having lunch with a colleague. Both hurriedly drove towards the workshop, a little over a mile from Reddy's residence. Reddy later discovered that union organizers had been busy that morning organizing the workers to ensure that they acted collectively. The foreman, either out of sympathy for the workers or for other reasons, did not warn management. In many ways, this prevented a serious escalation. Reddy was quite clear in his memoir. Had he been forewarned, he would have informed the police 'and reinforced security arrangements.' As he drove through the gates of the workshop, Reddy saw the crowds gathered close to his office. They greeted him with threats. Reddy wrote, 'I had a premonition of impending disaster. I said my prayers as I continued to drive towards my office.' The attack began as soon as the car came to a halt. Reddy had driven up to his garage and brought the car to a halt when the angry workers let loose a shower of 'brickbats' into the convertible. Reddy was hit by several of these even before he had set foot out of the car. When he did manage to get out of the car, Reddy found himself assaulted by several workmen. He wrote, 'I was manhandled and beaten with fists and umbrellas.' Surrounded and hemmed in by the crowd, Reddy couldn't even run.[356]

There had been several developments during the previous day that Reddy had been unaware of. Many railway workers had heard that Reddy had ordered the suspension of payments of all arrears to the workmen. These were arrears that had resulted from the flawed implementation of the Pay Commission recommendations, which the Railway Board, under pressure from the AIRF, had acknowledged and was attempting to make good. The idea that Reddy, out of sheer spite, had blocked these payments had certainly contributed to the general anger of the workforce. Indeed, Reddy recalls hearing cries of '*Sala ko maro; hamara paisa rokta hai.*' (Beat the bastard up. He stopped our money from coming in.). Later Reddy heard a further rumor that some officers had been involved in the incident as well. There had been some resentment among the older BAR officers of Reddy's brash new style. This may have extended to some anger and resentment over Reddy's putting a stop to their theft of Burmese teak for personal use. Though Reddy never found any evidence to support this idea.[357]

Reddy's colleague who had been unlucky enough to have accompanied him that morning had enough sense to scream 'I am new. I have been at Kanchrapara for only two days only. [*sic*]' The workers left him alone. Reddy himself escaped serious injury thanks to the intervention of some kindhearted workers who pulled him away from the mob. Reddy wrote, 'I thought they were dragging me to some place to finish me off.' But instead, he found himself pushed into an old Works Manager's office, some 50 feet away. The men then stood at the entrance protecting their boss from their own angry colleagues. In the meantime, other senior officers had been alerted to the violence, as had the police. Both arrived on the scene and were able to disperse the crowds. Reddy escaped with light injuries. His doctor told him that he was severely bruised, but nothing more. Reddy also chose not to escalate the situation further by pressing charges against the union leaders who he suspected of organizing the whole affair. Instead, he took off on a fortnight's holiday.[358]

Reddy was fortunate and he knew it. He somberly recalled in his memoir how in less than a month after his own experience, angry workers had burnt six white officers of Jessop and company in their factory's blast furnace at Dum Dum, barely a few miles from Kanchrapara. Franz Fanon argues that the violence of the oppressed is forced upon them by the oppressor. Reddy sensed this to be true and feared for the consequences in a free India.[359] After a century of imperialist capitalism,

Indian laborers, who had been at the receiving end of great violence, sensed possibilities of a world where they could fight back. A new country had emerged that was filled with the promise of fairness. Many workers chose. Therefore, to fight back using the same tools that had driven their exploitation and persecution for as long as they could remember. The lure of threats and intimidation and individual and collective violence became strong under these circumstances.

Moreover, the effectiveness of such actions seemed in little doubt. Certainly, it seemed to have worked with D.V. Reddy. The violence forced Reddy to temporarily retreat. In fact, his memoir indicates that he left town for a fortnight's holiday to recuperate from the shock. He also lobbied his seniors extensively, seeking a transfer elsewhere. He was able to return to his duties 'feeling much better.' A few weeks later, during Independence Day celebrations, Reddy addressed the staff appealing to them 'to forget the past, to look ahead and by special effort to improve the out-turn of Kanchrapara shop.' And indeed, over the following months, Reddy was able to significantly improve the out-turn of locomotives at the workshop. Nevertheless, by December, Reddy could sense 'antagonism building up again... The men seemed to have reached the limit of their stamina for sustained work. They could only be driven so far and no farther.' Reddy requested the chief mechanical engineer leave for four month, which was sanctioned. He wrote, 'I packed up my furniture, locked it up in one room of the bungalow, with my successor's permission and left Kanchrapara with my wife and baby daughter.'[360]

Collective Action: Going on Strike

Indian and after 1947 Pakistani railway workers deployed collective action to go on strike on multiple occasions through the 1939–1949 period. Some of these have already been discussed in earlier chapters. The scale and ambition of these strikes varied. Some were relatively localized and fought for limited gains, while others were regional and fought over issues that affected a large number of laborers. Strikes were significant and therefore gained considerable attention. Even some regional strikes found a notice in newspapers, and the South Indian Railway strike of 1948 made it to the official archive through an extensive discussion in the Annual Report of the Indian Railway Board. While the effectiveness of strikes is difficult to gauge, since the historical records rarely provide insight into the precise relationship between strike action and management-level responses, there is little doubt that it was an exceptionally successful method of gaining attention. It is to demonstrate this point; that strikes were exceptional examples of collective action in the contours of class struggle as it unfolded in this era.

The 1941 Great Indian Peninsula Railway Strike

In 1941, as noted in the first chapter, Indian railway workers faced the twin challenges of rising inflation and sharply increasing workloads. They were also challenged by the loss of equipment and skilled labor lost either overseas or to the military departments of government. Through this period, Indian railway workers were represented by the AIRF in their negotiations with the Indian Railway Board. In 1941, the central issue of discussion was concerning mechanisms with which laborers could cope with the rising cost of living. This was an issue that cut across all categories of labor both within and outside the Indian railway system. In fact, over the course of the year, government employees in several departments of the Central as well as provincial administrations were able to negotiate wage increases or adjustments to keep up with galloping inflation. As noted in an earlier chapter, the AIRF negotiated with the Indian Railway Board during meetings held in January and March 1941 on the issue of rising prices and measures that the Railway Board had to take to mitigate the effects of those rising prices.[361]

Although the Federation was successful in negotiating some concessions from the Board, many of the railway workers' unions affiliated with AIRF were disappointed. Railway workers affiliated with the GIPR company union were frustrated by the limited nature of the gains that AIRF had managed to negotiate. One section of this workforce escalated this confrontation through a strike action. The strike was planned and put into place at the Parel workshop of the GIPR company located in the northern section of Bombay. The strike began on 6 November. Seven thousand workers of the Parel workshop went on strike. *The Bombay Chronicle* reported on the commencement of the strike in considerable detail. The strike began at eightin the morning. Workers streamed into the workshop just as the 'whistle was blown.' The 7,000 workers, 'quietly walked into the workshop in a queue but immediately went on a stay in strike' and 'peacefully squatted on the floor.' Their numbers were reinforced 'by a complement of 1000 workers brought in from Dohad Workshop [about 350 miles north of Bombay].' The workers continued their strike through the day. The *Chronicle* stated, 'After an hour's lunch interval the workers were again allowed into the workshop at 1 p.m.' The *Chronicle* claimed that the strike caught the workshop managers quite by surprise. Itstated, 'The only intimation of it to Mr. Lamb, the Manager, was when the workers started shouting and refused to do the work in the morning.' The workers resisted all efforts at intimidation. The *Chronicle* reported, 'At first the notice asked the workers to immediately take up work with a warning that disciplinary action would be taken if they did not comply with the notice by 11:45 a.m. The workers remained adamant. A second notice was put up subsequently and it appears that they were told that the day's wages would be deducted. But the workers were still unmoved.'[362]

Records of this particular strike clearly demonstrate tensions between the conservative AIRF and its more aggressive regional counterparts, in this case, the GIP Railwaymen's Union. The Parel strike had been organized by the union. The workers had demanded an increase in their Dearness Allowance as well as a raise in their general wages. Their negotiations with the Chief Mechanical Engineer had, however, stalled as the workers had only been offered special grain shops, which the laborers rejected. The *Chronicle* quoted the GIP Railwaymen's Union secretary as stating, 'The workers demanded…Rs. 7-8-0 [seven rupees eight annas] up to Rs. 200…The CME [Chief Mechanical Engineer] insisted upon opening grain shops. The workers refused the idea and called on strike.'[363] On 11 November 1941, an additional 4000 laborers from the GIPR workshop at the nearby Matunga neighborhood joined the strike, increasing the number of workers on strike to 11,000. The Matunga workshop workers demanded similar increases in their Dearness Allowance and a general increase in their wages. The *Chronicle* also indicated that the state had become involved, attempting to intimidate the workforce. It reported, 'The police are keeping a strong 'bandobust' near both the workshops.'[364]

The *Chronicle*, on 16 November, carried details of high-level negotiations that indicated differences between the aggression of the AIRF and the GIP Railwaymen's Union. While the AIRF negotiators had been satisfied with a DA of four rupees eight annas per month for all employees drawing less than Rs 70 per month, the Matunga and Parel Workshop laborers demanded a DA of Rs 7 per month for all employees drawing less than Rs 200 per month. The *Chronicle* also reported that the workshop managers had declared a lockout, forcing the laborers off the premises. The railway managers sought to increase pressure on the workers with plans to put up notices with promises to waive all penalties if the laborers returned to work immediately. On the other hand, laborers who refused risked forfeiting wages for days lost and re-engagement on new and lower-wage scales. The *Chronicle* reported that 'This has created a serious problem to the strikers as well as the GIP Railwaymen's Union. Informal consultations are in progress.'[365]

On 18 November, the *Chronicle* reported: 'At a meeting of the strikers of the GIP Railway workshops at Parel and Matunga, held at Kamgar Maidan, Parel, this evening, a resolution approving the recommendations of the Conciliation Committee and urging the strikers to resource their work from Tuesday was passed.'[366] The strike had been reasonably successful. The expansion of the strike to the Matunga workshop had forced the Railway Board to offer the workers an enhanced War Allowance, though one still lower than what the government had offered staff in other sectors.[367] However, the role of the AIRF in restraining the GIPR union workers was once again, striking. In an official statement, S. Guruswamy, General Secretary of the AIRF, urged the GIP Railway union to 'persuade the railway authorities and the men concerned to terminate without prejudice the present deadlock.' He further stated, 'Any independent, hasty or drastic action on the part of any section of labor in the present situation can only result in discrediting the method of reaching agreements through trade unions and dividing the rank and file of railway workers in various parts of the country.'[368] The appeal did not go unheeded. There are no further newspaper reports of strikes at the workshops that year.

The South Indian Railway Strike of 1948

The second strike discussed in this chapter affected the South Indian Railway company during the high summer of 1948. The strike was significant enough to enter into the records of the official archives, including, for the first time, a substantial discussion in the Indian Railway Board's Annual Report. The report makes clear that Independence had not translated into a resolution of class conflict in the Indian railway system. To the contrary, Indian railway workers continued to deal with substantial hardship. More importantly, they were willing to fight to seek redress for their grievances.[369]

In late August 1948, the AIRF held its annual convocation in the railway town of Liluah, located on the outskirts of Calcutta. During their convocation, the AIRF passed three resolutions, which shed light on the main grievances of the Indian railway workers at this moment. The first resolution addressed the very real issue of hunger. The government's deregulation of agricultural commodities, discussed in the previous chapter, had led to sharp price increases of many necessities. The effects of this escalation in the cost of living had been exacerbated by the Indian Railway Board's curtailment of Railway grain store concessions. Indeed, the total number of grain stores showed an absolute decline in the years after Independence. The AIRF protested this curtailment and also demanded an increase in cash dearness allowances corresponding with the increase in the cost-of-living index. The second resolution raised the issue of implementing the recommendations of India's first Central Pay Commission. The resolution clearly indicated that Indian railway workers were frustrated at the manner in which the Indian Railway Board was implementing the Pay Commission resolutions. The AIRF, through this resolution, tried to make clear just how important this issue was. The AIRF threatened to take out a strike ballot if the Board failed to act. The third and final resolution demonstrated a considerable degree of broadmindedness among the organized railway workers of India. For it dealt with the plight of railway workers employed by the various independent railway companies then still functional across the country. These were largely the railway companies operated by the Princely States of India, then in the process of merging with Independent India. The railway workers employed in these companies did not have the same service conditions and pay scales as their counterparts employed by the Indian Railway Board. Indeed, considering the regressive nature of the Princely States, railway workers in these companies were likely much worse off than their counterparts in Government of the India Railways. The third resolution, therefore, called on the Government of India to take over the administration of these independent railway companies and implement conditions of service and scales of pay that matched those in place for railway workers employed by the Indian Railway Board.[370]

This convocation was followed by a meeting of the AIRF's general council. At this meeting, the council passed several resolutions, two of which further highlighted the pressing issues raised in the first two resolutions passed in the AIRF's convocation. These reiterated the anger felt by many railway workers about the cash DAs offered by the Indian Railway Board as well as by its policy of curtailing in-kind relief provided by railway grain shops. The Council also reiterated its frustration with the Board's implementation of the Central Pay Commission's recommendations. The anger and disappointment was palpable. The AIRF, while not closing the door on the possibility of resolution, proceeded to act on its earlier threat of issuing a strike ballot. It called on all affiliated unions to issue strike ballots. If these were favorable, the AIRF proposed notifying the Board of a general strike the following February.[371]

The threats showed some results. In January 1949, N. Gopalaswami Ayyangar, then minister of transport and railways, met with the AIRF to hammer out a compromise and prevent the general strike. At their meeting in Bombay, the two sides discussed the issue of grain shop facilities and cash dearness allowances. The disagreements over the implementation of the first Central Pay Commission recommendations were also on the table. The two sides agreed to establish a joint machinery to resolve disputes between labor and management. The two sides also agreed to establish a committee to resolve the disagreements over the implementation of the Central Pay Commission recommendations. They even decided to continue their negotiations. These resumed in Delhi and continued through early February. The talks showed some promise. The Federation chose not to act on the strike ballots that had been issued by trade unions on the East Indian, Oudh and Tirhut, Eastern Punjab, Bombay, Baroda and Central India, and South Indian Railways. These had been favorable. Many affiliated trade unions remained skeptical. Indeed, some trade unions ignored the AIRF's stay order and gave notices for a general strike on 9 March 1949. On that day, railway authorities noted multiple attempts at sabotage, though the general strike was averted.[372]

It was in this context that the South Indian Railway Labor Union struck work in April 1948. During the last week of that month, exhausted engine crews at multiple locations refused to continue operating trains after completing eight hours of continuous service. Their action spread across the railway system culminating in an official call to strike by the South Indian Railway Labor Union on the night of 9–10 May 1948. It was a token 24-hour strike meant to warn the company management of the widespread anger of the railway workforce. According to the Railway Board's own records, 3,000 loco shed and running staff joined the strike. They represented over a third of the total workforce. Some 700 workmen employed in the Golden Rock Railway workshop also walked off their jobs. The strike affected other departments of the railway system where Class IV staff, the most underprivileged and least-paid workers, joined in the struggle. The South Indian Railway Board were forced to restrict services in affected sections, though they were able to maintain normal services elsewhere. Railway workers also resorted to sabotage. Specifically, removing fishplates and tampering with tracks. The South Indian Railway Board was able to restore much of the system's services only on 13 May, though even then localized strikes disrupted services at multiple stations. The strike, in fact, continued into early June. Groups of workers took localized action disrupting services in their locality over limited periods of time. Railway workers kept their managers guessing by going on strike and then rejoining service in brief intervals. It was only on 6 June that most workers reported for duty and the South Indian Railway Board could declare a return to normal services.[373]

The strike made national headlines. On 10 May 1948, *The Bombay Chronicle* carried a front-page report under the headline, '24-Hour General Strike on S. I. Railway,' noting the start of the strike. In contrast to the tame, bureaucratic language of the official archive, the *Chronicle* reported on the harsh repression unleashed by the railway and state authorities. In the hours leading up to the strike, the police arrested several railway workers. The *Chronicle* stated, 'Mr. Sivanadhaya, railway guard and another railway employee, both of whom are alleged to be active workers of the Communist-controlled South Indian Railway Labor Union were arrested last evening under the Public Safety Act on a warrant issued by the Madura District Magistrate.' The *Chronicle* also reported additional arrests during the hours leading up to the strike.[374]

The 11 May 1948 issue of the *Chronicle* carried further news of the strike. In addition to details of service disruptions, the report demonstrated that in places the strike had brought services to a complete halt: 'Trichy Junction which is the nerve center of the SIRly [*sic*] system and which is very busy everyday, today presented a somewhat deserted appearance.' The report carried further evidence of police suppression. The police arrested over forty railway workers that day, and in places, public authorities had placed prohibitory orders preventing public protests. The *Chronicle* stated, 'About 30 people were arrested by the police for attempting to take out processions in defiance of the ban. Eleven people were also reported to have been arrested for trespassing near the Railway Locoshed.' There were additional details on sabotage. Railway workers had placed boulders on tracks near the Virudhunagar station, some 30 miles south of Madurai; and at two places near Tenkasi and Palni, Southwest of Madurai, railway workers removed fishplates from the track. Most striking however, were reports of solidarity strikes. The *Chronicle* reported, 'The Municipal Conservancy Staff, Tannery Workers at Sempattu, Handloom weavers and cigar workers in Woraiur have also struck work in sympathy with the strikers in the railways.' In addition, a number of cleaners at the Indian Refreshment Room in Trichy went on strike in solidarity with the railway workers.[375] The *Chronicle* also reported on a strike carried out by railway workers in Calicut. Located in the southwestern corner of the subcontinent, the city was located over 400 miles west of Madras, the epicenter of the south Indian railway strike. The 24-hour 'sympathy strike' in Calicut was carried out by determined locomotive drivers and firemen. They were supported by many coolies there.[376]

In fact, it is also worth noting that this was hardly the only strike unfolding on the Indian Railway system in 1948. During the very same week, a large group of railway workers in western India went on strike demanding increased rates of pay. The railway workers, employed with the GIPR company went on strike on 2 May 1948. Initially numbering 3,000, the striking workers doubled in strength, and the strike went into its second week. The railway workers had been designated as temporary staff by the GIPR company and were paid significantly lower wages than permanent staff. This practice, while accepted earlier, was no longer an official policy. Indeed, the Central Government Pay Commission had recommended that temporary workers receive the same pay rates and grain shop concessions as their permanent counterparts. Ram Joshi, the convener of the strike committee, pointed out that the GIPR was entirely in contravention of these recommendations. Their strike brought both critical Ghat sections just outside Bombay to a halt. It took the interventions at the national level to bring the strike to a halt. Negotiations between Jayprakash Narayan, then president of the AIRF, and S.S. Vasist, general manager of the Indian Railways, resulted in a breakthrough, which included assurances 'that there would be no victimization of the strikers on their resuming work.'[377]

On the other end of the country, on 18 May, many railway workers on the BAR company struck work. This strike was driven by increasing threats to the safety of the workforce. Parochialist politicians in Assam were urging mobs to attack ethnic Bengali employees of the BAR company. The laborers struck work and demanded better security measures. On 25 May, *The Bombay Chronicle* reported, 'The strike follows, according to the Gauhati correspondent of the "Amrita Bazaar Patrika" from the detention of an Assamese ticketless traveler on May 7 by a Bengali railway worker.'

***

This chapter seeks to highlight the survival strategies that Indian and, after 1947, Pakistani railway workers deployed during the 1939–1949 period to survive class conflict at their worksites. As stated earlier, this is not to suggest that there was no element of class conflict in the great moments of crisis in this decade. To the contrary, the research presented in earlier chapters on the Second World War, the culmination of India's freedom struggle, the Partition, as well as the first years of Independence were all moments of crisis characterized by multiple dimensions of class conflict. Instead, this chapter has sought to shed light on the class conflict that characterized life and work on Indian Railways that was not necessarily directly linked with the great crises of this decade. Rather, this chapter examines class conflict as a product of labor in a modern, mid-twentieth-century transportation service. This is not to suggest that the class conflict examined here had nothing to do with the great crises of this decade; the chapter does not highlight those linkages. The advantage of such an approach lies in the uncovering of the several survival strategies that persisted through the decade, with railway workers deploying them through the vast changes that swept through the Indian subcontinent in general and the region's railway systems. Hence this chapter seeks to uncover the survival strategies that helped Indian and, after 1947, Pakistani railway workers survive the specters of class conflict in this era.

The data indicates that Indian and Pakistani railway workers used several different strategies to survive the specters of class conflict in this era. Many of these strategies can be characterized as instances of everyday resistance. These include criminal activities, namely theft and corruption. The chapter recounts several instances of both. The historical evidence is replete with examples of petty thievery and more serious organized criminal activity. The Railway Boards from India and later Pakistan outline the persistence of corruption and the railway managerial class's long and seemingly Sisyphean struggle to eradicate it. They also included the shirking of responsibilities and the disregarding of instructions. The former includes instances of individual railway workers seeking to protect their interests by simply walking away from their responsibilities, as well as individual railway workers disregarding nonsensical or contradictory instructions in order to keep the railway system functional. The data, however, indicates that railway workers relied on collective action as a survival strategy. A rare record from the memoir of D.V. Reddy provides us with a frightening glimpse of violence when a group of workers attacked Reddy, as well as compassion when a group of workers saved his life. More often, however, the historical evidence provides us with rich histories of organized strikes. These occurred throughout the decade 1939–1949 and across the Indian subcontinent. Evidences presented in earlier chapters also indicate organized strikes breaking out in Pakistan after 1947.

The significance of the data from this chapter lies in the demonstrable pattern indicating that acts of collective action, especially strikes, remained much more significant as a survival strategy than acts characterized as everyday resistance, especially when carried out in an individual capacity. Acts of everyday resistance, when carried out in an individual capacity or even as a small group, never actually changed the circumstances of the workplace. Acts of theft or corruption could help a single railway worker or even a small group of railway workers make some ill-gotten wealth. The shirking of responsibility or the disregarding of instructions could, similarly, help an individual railwayman or even a small group of railway workers protect their interests on a day-to-day basis. But, neither set of actions could bring about change to the railway system itself. That required something more—collective action, possible only through trade union organization.

Conclusion

THE DECADE 1939–1949 remains the most turbulent in modern Indian history. During the first half of this decade, India's British masters dragged the country into a war with Germany and Italy. Later, into a war with Japan. It was and remains India's bloodiest war of the twentieth century. Among the many cruel ironies of the war was the way it went on to be remembered as a war fought by the forces of Liberalism (in alliance with the Soviet Union) against the forces of fascism. And yet, India's British masters ran a despotic and authoritarian Empire in India, characterized by great cruelty, ruthless exploitation and a callous disregard for human life and the dignity of their Indian subjects. These years were also marked by the culmination of India's long struggle for freedom from British rule. There were two major nationwide confrontations. The first was in 1942, commencing with Gandhi's call for a final 'Do or Die' struggle to end British rule in India. Remembered as the Quit India movement, it became the largest and most violent uprising against British rule in India in almost a century. It was crushed by a brutal and ruthless application of raw military power. The second in 1946, though less intense, ended up playing a more decisive and successful role in bringing about the end of British rule. Waged by civilians and, importantly, sections of the British Indian armed forces, this struggle erupted in solidarity with rebel soldiers of the Azad Hind Fauj. These men had joined the army of a rebel provisional government of free India, allied with Japan and diplomatically recognized by several Axis powers, crucially, the Taoiseach of Ireland. The British Indian government sought to try the soldiers of this rebel army, especially its officers, for treason. The people of India, however, overwhelmingly recognized these soldiers as patriots. Within months of this uprising, the British government announced its intention to grant India its independence. In August 1947, British rule over the Indian subcontinent came to an end. It was also, however, over the course of these very months that the region suffered its worst humanitarian catastrophe—the partition of India into two countries, India and Pakistan.

The result of complicated and exhaustively studied political negotiations between the leaders of the Indian National Congress and Muslim League and the departing British administration, Partition sought to divide the country along religious lines. Pakistan was meant to be a homeland for India's Muslims and covered those regions identified by census takers as Muslim-majority regions. Partition, however, led to ethnic cleansing on a scale never seen before or since. Hundreds of thousands of Hindus, Muslims and Sikhs perished in the bloodletting that preceded and followed Partition. It also created the largest refugee crisis ever seen in history, rivaling in scale the refugee crises precipitated by the Second World War. The scale and horror of these three great crises—the Second World War, the culmination of India's struggle for independence, and the partition—overshadow the great difficulties and uncertainties of the last years of this difficult decade. Two new countries emerged on the world stage, precarious in their status as post-colonial, independent countries and wretchedly poor, underdeveloped and staggeringly diverse in a world that still firmly believed in the necessity of shared cultures for successful nationhood. Both India and Pakistan faced much hardship during their first years of Independence.

A million men, women and children worked for the Indian railway system in this period. Their numbers rose through the decade, accelerating through the second half of the Second World War in response to the rising demand for rail services. This book has sought to understand how this massive workforce survived the challenges of the decade. It is an investigation into the survival strategies that this very large workforce deployed over the course of this turbulent decade. There are several features of the workforce that make such an investigation difficult and complicated. First and foremost is the sheer diversity of this million-strong workforce. In addition to the variation in gender and age, the workforce was also divided by their vocation. The operation of a railway system, in particular a railway system of the staggering scale of India's railways, was and remains a highly complex affair. It involves crew that operate trains, a highly skilled and physically challenging vocation. The trains varied in size and travelled varied distances. Some were local, commuter passenger trains, others covered vast distances. Some travelled over flat, unchanging terrain, while others crossed mountains, forests and even deserts. It also involved labor that man railway stations. These could range from small stations in tiny hamlets to those located in major metropolitan centers such as Bombay and Calcutta, which were among the largest in the world. The railway workers in such stations could expect to man counters and refreshment stalls, work as police officers or as laborers loading and unloading cargoes. Or, they could work in more operational management roles, which ranged from managing personnel to managing the running of trains. Indian Railways extended even beyond trains and their stations. The system included multiple workshops maintaining and overhauling locomotives and their carriages. The skills required for such work were quite substantial, and a large number of railway workers were engaged in these sophisticated jobs. Others maintained railway tracks or were involved in construction projects. During the Second World War, many of these tasks expanded as the railway system shifted to a role supporting the war effort.

In addition to this vast diversity of professional roles, the railway workforce was also divided on the basis of identity. Through much of this decade, racial identities were important markers of difference. In particular, the workforce was divided between laborers of Indian and European descent. The railway workforce, thanks to imperialist recruitment policies, consisted of a very large number of British officers. There was also a substantial contingent of mixed-race Anglo-Indians who held important positions throughout the railway system. The Indian component of the workforce was also quite diverse. In addition to differences in religion and linguistic identities, the workforce was also divided by caste. All these diversities led to substantial variation in survival strategies, even when facing similar or the same challenge. The survival strategies also changed over time as and when the railway workers discovered newer or better options to overcome the challenges they faced.

Indian and, after 1947, Pakistani railway workers deployed multiple survival strategies to overcome the challenges of the 1939–1949 decade. To meet the challenges of the Second World War, for instance, Indian railway workers became highly effective at developing and deploying innovative solutions to complex problems. The historical data presented in the first chapter outlines many instances of railway workers deploying such a strategy. One particularly striking instance was the multiple strategies railway engineers came up with to deal with the severe shortages of coal during the war. Most railway locomotives ran on coal, but in response to the shortages, railway engineers converted several of these from coal to oil-burning engines. In others, engineers rigged their locomotives to run on cinder. Finally, railway workers learnt to be more efficient and careful with their stocks and learnt to run their trains with lower stocks of coal than ever before. Similarly, in order to meet the challenge of India's final struggles with the British Empire, the railway workers deployed multiple strategies. Some chose loyalty, particularly British railway workers who supported the Empire openly and determinedly. Others opted to support the freedom struggle surreptitiously during the Quit India movement. During the most pressing challenge of the decade, the partition of India, Indian and Pakistani railway workers pursued multiple strategies to survive the challenges thrown up during the crisis. Some railway workers made the worst possible decision to join looters and murderers. Others made brave choices and chose humanity. Often at risk to their own safety, many chose to protect their comrades and passengers from attack. Some chose prudence and tried to emigrate to Pakistan or India, depending on their religious affiliations and career prospects. Others avoided service or passage through dangerous areas. Many took reasonable practical decisions to ensure the safety of their services, crew and passengers. The narratives mentioned in the introduction are both instances of individual railway workers demonstrating bravery and choosing humanity on an individual level to protect their comrades from the barbarism to which their countrymen were descending.

Finally, as discussed in the fifth chapter, railway workers deployed a variety of survival strategies to overcome the challenges of general class conflict through this period. Several may be characterized as individual instances of everyday resistance, be it theft and corruption or shirking responsibilities. Of the former, police and Railway Board records provide rich details. Theft and corruption were deployed as survival strategies by individuals as well as small groups working together. The culprits ranged from the least-paid workers who stole small amounts, possibly to supplement meagre wages in difficult economic circumstances, to more powerful and better-paid officers who engaged in theft and corrupt practices because they felt powerful and entitled enough to get away with this kind of behavior. Shirking of responsibilities on the other hand was often an eminently practical decision. The railway system was complex and had codes and operational systems that were sometimes contradictory, requiring railway workers to make practical decisions to keep the system functional. In other cases, however, this was also a form of reducing the burden of work. Sometimes done individually, other times, in small groups.

The most effective survival strategies, however, came in the form of collective action, and more specifically through trade union organization. During the Second World War, for instance, the historical record is unambiguous. Indian railway workers were able to move substantially greater numbers of passengers and much increased quantities of freight even though their resources were much reduced. Additionally, railway workers were able to even expand the railway network and upgrade its technologies and capabilities and make meaningful and important contributions to India's war efforts. All this, the records make clear, was possible through collective action, though the bureaucratic record referred to it as 'teamwork.' The records, however, did give due credit to trade unions for clearly stating their commitment to the war effort. Similarly, during the struggle for India's independence, the Indian railway unions stated their moral support for Congress leaders imprisoned by the British Indian state in 1942, and in 1946 the railway workers supported the Royal Indian Navy mutineers through multiple strikes in solidarity.

Collective action and trade union organization also played a crucial role in railway workers surviving Partition, the most difficult crisis of the era. Trade unions made quite clear that in this moment of crisis, while India's British masters were abandoning the country in a hurry, railway unions were calling on all railway workers to serve the country and help overcome the crisis. The role of unions, however, was not just in encouraging railway workers to man their posts. Rather, there is a case to be made that solidarity built up over the course of years and decades played a crucial role in ensuring that railway workers did not turn on each other during the crisis. Decades of class-based solidarity fostered by trade union organizations played its part in the pattern of railway workers choosing humanity over barbarism. Collective action and trade union organization also ensured the survival of railway workers in post-colonial India and Pakistan. The constant pressure of trade unions led to the post-colonial Railway Boards in India and Pakistan working towards ensuring the railway workers in their countries received decent wages, were able to keep hunger at bay and were able to gain access to health care and education for themselves and their families. This, in turn, played an important part in guaranteeing that both railway systems survived and, especially in the case of India, substantially improved in performance. In fact, as the data indicates, railway workers in both India and Pakistan were important in ensuring the survival of their countries in this vulnerable period. Finally, the evidence also indicates that collective action and trade union organization were exceptionally effective in protecting the interests of railway workers when it came to general class conflict as endemic in a modern enterprise. Whether in the form of negotiations or through outright, organized strikes, railway workers were more likely to protect their interests and change their workplaces for the better when working together through their trade union organizations.

While the events discussed in this book are located in a specific time and place (India, 1939–1949), the relevance of the railway workers and their survival strategies matter beyond this frame. As recently as September 2022, the railway workers were in the news. Not in India, where they, as noted in the introduction, still often are, but in the United States. Although passenger travel in the US has for long come to be imagined with air and automobiles, American railroads still carry substantial numbers of passengers. Between June 2020 and June 2021, American railway workers transported some 4.4 billion passenger miles, not too far behind the 6.3 billion passenger miles transported by Indian railway workers in the period 1944–1945. The figures for freight traffic are even more striking. In 2020, American railway workers transported a staggering 1.5 trillion ton-miles, far dwarfing even the busiest years from India in the period examined in the book.[378] The American railway workforce too, is substantial in number. One lakh and fifty thousand railway workers are employed across multiple railway companies. While this number is small compared to the million-strong workforce in 1940s India, or for that matter the million-strong workforce in the 1950s United States, 1,50,000 is still a significant number.[379]

This workforce, in the autumn of 2022, flexed its organized labor muscles and threatened to bring the American rail system to its knees by a strike. The railway workers had good reasons too. The American railway system had over time come to be acquired by financial institutions with an insatiable appetite for profits. This had prompted the managerial class to sharply reduce the railway workforce by 40,000 laborers between 2018 and 2020. This sharp fall in the workforce coincided with the introduction of a new Precision Scheduling Railroading (PSR) System for the freight divisions of the railway system. In effect, the new system replaced industry standard fixed schedules in favor of a 'Just in time' model of transportation. A PSR system relies on data on demand to schedule the movement of trains introducing a very high level of flexibility.[380] Theoretically, it supposedly allows railway companies to improve profits by cutting down inefficiencies in operations. In practice, however, the profitability comes from a much more exploitative model of labor management. In the United States, this came down to the creation of a labor force that had to be, for all practical purposes, on call 24/7. The railway unions threatened to strike demanding that the railway companies institute at the very least an exception for medical purposes. The railway companies, on the other hand, argued that they had instituted a points system. Each worker lost points if they were unable to make it to their stations on time, but since each worker had several points to begin with, a loss of a few through medical emergencies mattered little. Railway unions, however, pointed to the very reality of railway workers facing disciplinary action for being unable to make it to their posts because of a doctor's appointment or even surgery. The inhumanity of making such demands through the COVID-19 pandemic became a core part of their motivation to demand change.[381]

The strike threatened to cripple not just the rail industry but also the entire American economy. Reeling under supply chain issues, the American ruling class intervened in response to the strike threat. A high-level intervention from the US government played a key role in negotiating a medical exception to the points system, thereby handing American railway workers an important victory.[382] In many ways, the incident demonstrated the power of collective action.

The United States was far from being the only country facing labor unrest in the railroad transportation sector as this book was being written. Earlier, in the summer of 2022, rail workers in Britain, the land of India's former colonial masters, struck work, bringing services on British Railroads to a halt. British railway workers, organized under the leadership of The National Union of Rail, Maritime and Transport Workers (RMT), demanded cost-of-living adjustments to their wages. The demand came in response to soaring inflation, estimated at over 10 per cent that summer. The British government's stated plans of harsh austerity measures to tackle the crisis included cuts of almost $5 billion from rail transportation alone. The British railway workers rightly feared that this would translate into job losses.[383] While the strike itself was successful in temporarily bringing rail transportation across Britain to a halt, the railway workers were unable to entirely tame the British government's single-minded focus on sweeping austerity measures as a solution to the problems of its capitalist economic structures. There were, however, two particularly striking features of the movement relevant to the subjects covered in the book. On 23 June, a clearly anti-railway worker audience member on the British Broadcasting Service television program, Question Time, aggressively suggested that British railway unions were acting like 'dinosaurs,' and were surely headed for extinction. Mick Lynch, general secretary of the RMT, however, was ready. He responded with a plucky 'Well, they were around for a very long time.'[384] The relevance of the exchange lies in Lynch's point that the relevance of trade unions and collective action should not be underestimated. There is certainly much to be said for this. Seventy years after the events discussed in the book, railway workers, this time in advanced capitalist countries, are still capable of bringing entire transportation systems to a grinding halt.

There is at least one more point of convergence between events in Britain in the summer of 2022 and the events covered in this book. During the Second World War, Indian Railway Unions demonstrated a striking commitment to anti-fascism, prioritizing the war against fascist powers and calling on railway workers to support the war effort. This was even though the British government in India barely qualified as a Liberal government of any form. To the contrary, the brutality of its response to Gandhi's Quit India movement, including the use of air power on unarmed railway workers doing their jobs, was certainly comparable to the worst forms of imperialism anywhere. This kind of political maturity was echoed in the internationalism demonstrated by British railway workers a few months after their strike. When American railway workers accelerated their own campaign against railroad companies, the British railway workers expressed their support.[385]

The significance of such internationalism and class-based solidarity lies in their possibilities towards the rescue of collective life. As pointed out in the Tricontinental Institute of Social Research dossier 'Ten Thesis on Marxism and Decolonization,' the twinned forces of Neoliberalism and Globalization have effectively eroded collective life and accelerated the atomization of society.[386] Trade Unions, through the possibilities of collective action, have historically been and remain powerful tools to reverse this kind of atomization and revive collective life. While this is certainly true today, as evidence of the internationalist solidarity demonstrated by the British Railway workers towards their American counterparts, it was also true in the last days of British India. While the eviscerating forces of imperialism twinned with religious sectarianism schemed to tear Indian society apart in a frenzy of communal violence, Indian railway workers, with their long histories of trade union-led collective action, were able to maintain ties of solidarity that overcame the toxic factionalism that religious extremism had brought to their communities. The evidence is overwhelming. There is no substitute for collective action. Trade union organization has in the past and continue to hold out humanity's best possibilities for a better future.

Acknowledgements

This book was made possible through the support of many. First, I benefited from the constant support and good wishes of my colleagues at Saint Francis University, Loretto, Pennsylvania. My historian colleagues Denise Damico and Lori Woods as well as the political scientists Mark Gentry and Joe Melusky. Your support led me on. Faculty affiliated with the Julin Grant Writing Circle read and gave feedback on early drafts from the book; I thank Art Remillard, Kirk Weixel and Tim Bintrim. I also thank Sarah Myers, now at Messiah College, but through much of the early writing process my colleague at Saint Francis University. I thank my Dean, Pete Skoner, for urging me on past the finish line. Finally, I thank our university President, Fr. Malachi Van Tassel. His early support for the book stayed with me over the four years that it took for me to finish. Many other well-wishers supported me through this process; Briana Keith, Jessica Cammarata, Marcia Kokus, Renee Hoffman and Shlomit Flascher Grinburg in particular. The book was much strengthened through the support of student researchers, funded by the Office of Student Research. I thank Balazs Harrgitai for this support. Four students provided valuable research assistance in the making of this project. I thank Andrew Burman, Cory Kumph, Kyra Udzelia and Sarah Zakrzswisky. I also thank the

University for allowing me to go on sabbatical and finish the book.

Friends and mentors at other institutions also supported this work through feedback and generous encouragement. I thank Prasannan Parthasarathi, Kevin Kenny, Sugata Bose, Navyug Gill, Sarvani Gooptu and Aryendra Chakravarty in particular. Also, Sunil Kumar, editor at the *Indian Economic and Social History Review,* for his thoughtful feedback and support for the article that came out in that journal. I thank the staff at the British Library for their invaluable assistance in locating the many primary source material that went into the writing of this book. Finally, I thank Ravi Singh at Speaking Tiger Books for recognizing the exciting possibilities offered by the book.

This book was completed under adverse medical conditions. I thank my wife Frances for her love and care through those difficult days. This book is dedicated to her. I also thank my son Neel and daughter Tara. They were my inspiration through the making of this book. I also thank my parents, Indra and Indrani Bose. Their love and support helped make this book possible. I also thank my in-laws, James and Patricia Nebus, for their affection and support. My extended American family, Brian and Sakti Kunz, Suvendra Nath Dutta and Rajakumari Daggumalli, Arunendro and Rajendro, Lakshmimoni, Reshmi, Ani and Ro, Gora Mama and Rakhi Mami, Rohan, Shagarika Ghosh, Juni Didi and Juan Carlos. The Everharts, Henzes, Looneys, Nebus and Shiftouri, Owens, and Walshes. It was good to have you all in my corner. The same goes for my extended family in India. The Bose, Baidya, Dutta, Gooptu and Hui families have provided me with a sense of support that can never be adequately expressed. I also thank Gayatree Chatterjee and Alakanada Dutt. One family member who inspired this book is my grandfather Nirendra Nath Dutta. He served the Indian Railways and was the first to pique my interest in railway history. I wish he had lived to see this book.

Finally, I'd like to thank the many friends who shared in the journey. Rajarshi Mitra, Devatanu Banerjee, Anirudh Dutt, Pranav Chandrashekhar, Mayank Jain, and Suhaan Mehta. Your support meant a lot. Our wonderful neighbors, the Cannons, Baileys, Feschemeyers, Keens, Aragon-Ramirezs, Randolphs, Shreckengrasts and the Werles, thank you for all the support and encouragement. Our friends, Mark and Maureen, Mark and Samira, thank you too. My wonderful doctors, Jan Drappatz, Brian McCleary and Brad Zacharia, and nurse Lauren Theis, your care made this book possible.

Notes

Introduction

1. D.V. Reddy, *Inside Story of the Indian Railways: Startling Revelations of a Retired Executive* (Madras: M. Seshachalam & Co., 1975), 140–142
2. Ibid.
3. Ibid.
4. Kabir Taneja, 'A Train to Partition: My Grandfather's Narrow Escape from Death Was a Small Triumph for Humanity,' *Huffpost*, 15 August 2017, accessed 17 May 2023, https://www.huffpost.com/archive/in/entry/a-train-to-partition-my-grandfather-s-narrow-escape-from-death_in_5c10f2d0e4b085260ba754fc
5. Ibid.
6. Ibid.
7. Ibid.
8. For an overview of this literature, see John Hurd and Ian Kerr, *India's Railway History: A Research Handbook* Handbook of Oriental Studies, Section 2, South Asia Series. (Lieden, NL: Brill, 2012), 32–35.
9. Ian Kerr, 'Chugging into Unfamiliar Stations: A New History of India's Railways,' *Economic and Political Weekly*, 7 May 2016.
10. Bibek Debroy, Sanjay Chadha, and Vidya Krishnamurthi, *Indian Railways: Weaving of a National Tapestry* (New Delhi: Penguin Random House, 2017).
11. Arup Chatterjee, *Purveyors of Destiny: A Cultural Biography of the Indian Railways* (New Delhi: Bloomsbury, 2017).
12. Kerr's *India's Railway History* has an excellent overview of this literature. See John Hurd and Ian J. Kerr, *India's Railway History*, (Leiden, NL: Brill, 2012), 47–48.
13. Ian Kerr, *Building the Railways of the Raj: 1850–1900* (New Delhi: Oxford University Press, 1997)
14. Laura Bear, *Lines of the Nation: Indian Railway Workers, Bureaucracy, and the Intimate Historical Self* (New York: Columbia University Press, 2007); Nitin Sinha, 'The World of Workers' Politics: Some Issues of Railway

Workers in Colonial India 1918–1922,' *Modern Asian Studies*, 42, 5, (Sept. 2008): 999-1033.

15. For additional details on this heroic achievement, see Priya Aggarwal, 'The Role of Indian Railways in COVID-19 Crisis Management,' Global Railway Review, accessed 8 December 2021, https://www.globalrailwayreview.com/article/123127/indian-railways-covid19-crisis-management/
16. Vidu Badigannavar, John Kelly, and Manik Kumar, 'Turning the Tide? Economic Reforms and Union Revival in India,' *Industrial Relations Journal*, vol 52, no. 4 (2021): 364–85, accessed 17 May 2023, https://doi.org/10.1111/irj.12340.
17. Mansoor Raza | Hasan Mansoor, 'On Death's Door: Trade Unions in Pakistan,' *Dawn.com*, 1 May 2016, accessed 17 May 2023, https://www.dawn.com/news/1255333
18. See Ministry of Labour, Government of India, *Annual Report on the Working of the Payment of Wages Act, (IV) of 1936 on Railways including a Note on the Employment of Children Act, 1938, 1946–1947*, Manager of Publications, Government of India Press, New Delhi, 1949) India Office Records and Private Paper, British Library, London.
19. R.A. Gopalaswami, 'Table B-III: Employers, Employees, Independent Workers in Industries and Services by Divisions and Sub-Divisions,' *Census of India, 1951. v. 1, India, Pt. II-B, Economic Tables (General Population)*, 1954.

1. Defeating 'Fascist Hordes'

20. Morris David Morris and Clyde B. Dudley. 'Selected Railway Statistics for the Indian Subcontinent (India, Pakistan and Bangladesh), 1853–1946-47,' *Artha Vijnana: Journal of the Gokhale Institute of Politics and Economics*, vol 17, no 3 (September 1975), qtd. in Ian Kerr, ed., *27 Down: New Departures in Indian Railway Studies* (New Delhi: Orient Longman, 2005), accompanying CD-ROM.
21. Srinath Raghavan, *India's War: World War II and the Making of Modern South Asia* (New York: *Basic Books*, 2016), 332–333.
22. Railway Board of India, *Full Steam Ahead: The Indian Railways–Their Problems and their Work, and their Future Plans* (New Delhi: Press Information Bureau, Government of India, for the Railway Board, 1945), 36–37.
23. Op cit, *Full Steam Ahead*, 31, 34.
24. Government of India, Railway Department, Railway Board, *Report by the Railway Board on Indian Railways for 1939–1940*, vol. 1 (Delhi, 1941), 109. India Office Records and Private Papers, British Library, London
25. *Report by the Railway Board on Indian Railways for 1940–1941*
26. Ibid, 34–35.
27. *Report by the Railway Board on Indian Railways for 1942–1943*
28. Op cit, *Full Steam Ahead*, 7, 13, 37.
29. Ibid.
30. Ibid, 37.

31. Ibid, 37–38.
32. Ibid, 7, 14.
33. Janam Mukherjee, 'Japan Attacks', *Calcutta: The Stormy Decades,* Tanika Sarkar and Sekhar Bandyopadhyay (eds.) (London and New York: Routledge, 2018) 101–102, 116.
34. 'Calcutta Bombed Again: 25 Killed in Three Enemy Raids', *The Times of India*, 24 December 1942
35. A. Kalam, *Recollections of a Railwayman* (Karachi: Royal Book company, 1995) 25.
36. Yasmin Khan, *The Raj at War: A People's History of India's Second World War* (London: Penguin Random House, 2015), 115, 110; Government of India, *Full Steam Ahead*, 39.
37. Judith Brown, 'India,' *The Oxford Companion to World War II*: eds. I.C.B. Dear and M.R.D. Foot (New York: Oxford University Press, 2003).
38. Railway Board, *Report by the Railway Board on Indian Railways for 1939–1940*
39. Yasmin Khan, *India at War: The Subcontinent and the Second World War* (New York: Oxford University Press, 2015), 174.
40. Op cit, 'India.'
41. Op cit, *Full Steam Ahead*, 15–16.
42. For instance, see Dinesh Kumar Mishra, 'The Bihar Flood Story,' *Economic and Political Weekly*, vol 32, no. 35 (5 September 1997): 2206–17
43. Amartya Sen, 'The Great Bengal Famine,' *Poverty and Famines* (Oxford: Oxford University Press, 1983).
44. See Urvi Khaitan, 'Women beneath the Surface: Coal and the Colonial State in India during the Second World War,' *War & Society*, vol 39, no. 3 (2 July 2020): 174, https://doi.org/10.1080/07292473.2020.1790473.
45. Ibid, 174.
46. Op cit, *Full Steam Ahead*, 13.
47. Shashi Tharoor, 'But What about the Railways...? "The Myth of Britain's Gifts to India",' *The Guardian*, 8 March 2017, accessed 19 May 2023, https://www.theguardian.com/world/2017/mar/08/india-britain-empire-railways-myths-gifts.
48. Op cit, *Full Steam Ahead*, 7
49. *Report by the Railway Board on Indian Railways for 1938–1939*
50. Op cit, 'Selected Railway Statistics for the Indian Subcontinent (India, Pakistan and Bangladesh), 1853–1946-47', qtd. in Kerr, *27 Down.*
51. Ibid, 102–131.
52. Op cit, *Full Steam Ahead*, 20, 22.
53. Ibid, 22–23.
54. Ibid, 22–23.
55. Ibid, 23–25.
56. Ibid, 26.
57. Ibid, 26.
58. Ibid, 31, 34, 39.
59. Ibid, 35.
60. Ibid, 39.

61. Op cit, *Report by the Railway Board on Indian Railways for 1939–1940*, 107–108
62. Op cit, *Report by the Railway Board on Indian Railways for 1940–1941*, 74.
63. Op cit, *Report by the Railway Board on Indian Railways for 1942–1943*, 32.
64. Op cit, *Report by the Railway Board on Indian Railways for 1943–1944*, 34.
65. Op cit, *Report by the Railway Board on Indian Railways for 1940–1941*, 74.
66. Op cit, *Report by the Railway Board on Indian Railways for 1941–1942*, 34.
67. Op cit, *Report by the Railway Board on Indian Railways for 1939–1940*, 108.
68. Op cit, *Report by the Railway Board on Indian Railways for 1940–1941*, 74.
69. Op cit, *Report by the Railway Board on Indian Railways for 1944–1945*, 55.
70. Op cit, *Report by the Railway Board on Indian Railways for 1943–1944*, 34; Op cit, *Report by the Railway Board on Indian Railways for 1944–1945*, 56.
71. Op cit, *Report by the Railway Board on Indian Railways for 1941–1942*, 34; Op cit, *Report by the Railway Board on Indian Railways for 1942–1943*, 32.
72. Op cit, *Report by the Railway Board on Indian Railways for 1943–1944*, 34-35.
73. Op cit, *Report by the Railway Board on Indian Railways for 1944–1945*, 34.
74. Op cit, *Report by the Railway Board on Indian Railways for 1943–1944*, 34; Op cit, *Report by the Railway Board on Indian Railways for 1944–1945*, 34.
75. Op cit, *Report by the Railway Board on Indian Railways for 1940–1941*, 74.
76. Op cit, *Report by the Railway Board on Indian Railways for 1941–1942*, 34.
77. Op cit, *Report by the Railway Board on Indian Railways for 1942–1943*, 32.
78. Ibid.
79. Op cit, *Report by the Railway Board on Indian Railways for 1943–1944*, 34.
80. Op cit, *Report by the Railway Board on Indian Railways for 1940–1941*, 74.
81. Op cit, *Report by the Railway Board on Indian Railways for 1943–1944*, 34.
82. Op cit, *Report by the Railway Board on Indian Railways for 1944–1945*, 34.
83. Op cit, *Report by the Railway Board on Indian Railways for 1945–1946*, 56.
84. Op cit, *Report by the Railway Board on Indian Railways for 1942–1943*, 32.
85. 'GIP Workers Demand Increased Dearness Allowance', *The Bombay Chronicle*, 11 January 1943.
86. 'Bombay Railway Workers Rally', *The Bombay Chronicle*, 20 January 1943.
87. 'Railwaymen's Demands', *The Times of India*, 28 January 1943.
88. 'Railway Workshop Workers Demands Accepted', *The Bombay Chronicle*, 28 January 1943.
89. 'Bombay Railway Workers Rally at Kamgar Maidan', *The Bombay Chronicle*, 17 February 1943; 'Railwaymen's Demand for Dearness Allowance', *The Bombay Chronicle*, 18 February 1943.
90. 'Move for General Strike on Railways', *The Bombay Chronicle*, 8 March 1943.
91. Op cit, *Report by the Railway Board on Indian Railways for 1942–1943*, 32.
92. 'GIP Workers and Strike Issue', *The Bombay Chronicle*, 17 March 1943.
93. 'BBCI Railway Workers Grievances', *The Bombay Chronicle*, 22 March 1943.

94. 'Railway Workers Demand More Adequate Allowance', *The Bombay Chronicle*, 21 April 1943.
95. 'Railway Federation's Demand', *The Bombay Chronicle*, 12 May 1943.
96. Op cit, *Report by the Railway Board on Indian Railways for 1942–1943*, 32; Op cit, *Report by the Railway Board on Indian Railways for 1943–1944*, 34.
97. 'Railway Workshop Workers Demands Accepted', *The Bombay Chronicle*, 28 January 1943.
98. For instance, see Nrisingha Chakrabarty, *History of Railway Trade Union Movement: A Study* (New Delhi: Center of Indian Trade Unions, 1985).
99. Op cit, *Report by the Railway Board on Indian Railways for 1942–1943*, 32.
100. Statement of V.R. Kalappa, quoted in 'Hindustan Army Activities', *The Times of India*, 22 August 1942
101. 'G.I.P. Workers Manifesto', *The Bombay Chronicle*, 19 October 1942.

2. The Freedom Struggle

102. *Report by the Railway Board on Indian Railways for 1942–1943*, 33
103. 'Firing', *The Bombay Chronicle*, 24 August 1942.
104. 'Mobs Fired on From Patrol Train', *The Bombay Chronicle*, 21 August 1942.
105. 'Bomb Found in Sind Express', *The Bombay Chronicle*, 28 October 1942.
106. 'Suspicious Looking Man Arrested', *The Bombay Chronicle*, 6 December 1942.
107. *The Bombay Chronicle*, 17 December 1942.
108. 'Miraculously Saved', *The Bombay Chronicle*, 5 October 1942.
109. Op cit, 'Selected Railway Statistics for the Indian Subcontinent (India, Pakistan and Bangladesh), 1853–1946-47', qtd. in Kerr, *27 Down*, 25, 28, 34, 37, 100.
110. William Richardson, 'The Mutiny of the Royal Indian Navy at Bombay in February 1946,' *The Mariner's Mirror*, vol 79, no. 2 (May 1, 1993): 192, accessed 18 May 2023, https://doi.org/10.1080/00253359.1993.10656 448
111. 'Statistics Connected with the Congress Disturbances for the Period Ending 31 December 1943, by provinces and Central Departments,' National Archives of India, qtd. in Francis G. Hutchins, *India's Revolution: Gandhi and the Quit India Movement* (Cambridge, MA: Harvard University Press, 1973), 232
112. Bibek Debroy, Sanjay Chadha, and Vidya Krishnamurthi, *Indian Railways: Weaving of a National Tapestry* (New Delhi: Penguin Random House, 2017), 216.
113. K.G. Mashruwala, *Harijan*, 23 August 1942, qtd. in Hutchins, *India's Revolution*, 222.
114. 'Vandemataram, Circular No. 8, Bihar', 'All India Congress Committee, Instruction No. 12, To the Peasants of India', Home File No. 3/19/43, National Archives of India, qtd. in Hutchins, *India's Revolution*, 224.
115. Op cit, 'Statistics Connected with the Congress Disturbances for the Period Ending 31 December 1943, Central Departments'

116. Op cit, 'Vandemataram, Circular No. 8, Bihar,' 'All India Congress Committee, Instruction No. 12, To the Peasants of India'
117. 'Improvement in Bombay Riot Situation', *The Times of India*, 13 August 1942.
118. 'Mob invades Railway Booking Office', *The Bombay Chronicle*, 13 August 1942.
119. 'Forty Yards of P.W. Removed on M.S.M. Ry', *The Bombay Chronicle*, 17 August 1942.
120. 'Incidents of EIRY', *The Bombay Chronicle*, 22 August, 1942.
121. 'Arms and Explosives Discovered', *The Bombay Chronicle*, 1 November 1942.
122. 'Attack on Bolepur Station', *The Bombay Chronicle*, 11 September 1942.
123. 'Boy Killed in Bomb Explosion', *The Bombay Chronicle*, 1 December 1942.
124. 'It was Due to Sabotage', *The Bombay Chronicle*, 6 October 1942.
125. 'Fish Plates Removed: Telegraph Wires Cut', *The Times of India*, 13 November 1945.
126. 'Troops Man Positions in Calcutta', *The Times of India*, 24 November 1945.
127. 'Demonstration on Railway Platform', *The Times of India*, 15 December 1945.
128. 'Mobs run Amok in Bombay', *The Times of India*, 25 January 1946.
129. '36 Dead, 300 Hurt in Calcutta Riot', *The Times of India,* 14 February 1946.
130. Op cit, *India's Revolution*, 228, 251–252.
131. 'Station Master Arrested', *The Bombay Chronicle*, 29 August 1942.
132. 'Order not to be Renewed: Arrests and Raid in City', *The Bombay Chronicle*, 1 September 1942.
133. 'Train Derailment Judgment', *The Bombay Chronicle*, 5 October 1942.
134. 'Railway Chowkidar Among Others Arrested,', *The Bombay Chronicle*, 13 October 1942.
135. Inder Malhota, interviewed by Gillian Wright, *India Office Library and Record Interview*, 25 November 1987, MSS EUR R193/11 British Library, London.
136. Op cit, *Report by the Railway Board on Indian Railways for 1942-1943*, 33.
137. Op cit, *Report by the Railway Board on Indian Railways for 1939–1940*, 100–101.
138. Op cit, *Report by the Railway Board on Indian Railways for 1946–1947*, 52–53.
139. David Gilmour's *The British in India: A Social History of the Raj* (New York: Farrar, Straus and Giroux, 2018) has a short discussion on such mavericks, 414–421.
140. 'National Archive of India, Home File No. 3/21/42 Poll. (I)', qtd. in Hutchins, *India's Revolution*, 217–218
141. Roy Edward King Nissen, interviewed by David M. Blake, *India Office Library and Record Interview*, 17 July 1989, MSS EUR R189/1-4, British Library, London, Part 8, Side B.
142. Sujata Gidla, *Ants Among Elephants: An Untouchable Family and the Making of Modern India* (New York: Farrar, Straus & Giroux, 2017).

143. Op cit, Kalam, *Recollections of a Railwayman*, 21, 23, 35.
144. Op cit, *Report by the Railway Board on Indian Railways for 1942–1943*, 32.
145. Statement of V.R. Kalappa, qtd. in 'Hindustan Army Activities,' *The Times of India*, 22 August 1942.
146. 'G.I.P. Workers Manifesto', *The Bombay Chronicle*, 19 October 1942.
147. Keka Bose, 'The Role of the Working Class in the Political Upsurges in Undivided India (1945-46),' *Proceedings of the Indian History Congress*, vol 51 (1990): 619–24
148. Ibid, 621.
149. Op cit, 'The Role of the Working Class in the Political Upsurges in Undivided India (1945-46),' 621; 'Looting and Incendiarism in Bombay', 'Mobs Run Amok in Bombay', *The Bombay Chronicle*, 23 February 1946; 'Looting and Arson in Bombay North', 'Difficulties of Ambulance Men', *The Bombay Chronicle*, 24 February 1946.
150. 'Jawahar Rushes Post-Haste to Bombay', *The Bombay Chronicle*, 25 February 1946.
151. 'Calcutta Ratings on Strike', *The Bombay Chronicle*, 21 February 1946.
152. 'In Calcutta', *The Bombay Chronicle*, 22 February 1946.
153. 'Raising of Naval Ratings Wages Impossible', *The Bombay Chronicle*, 23 February 1946.
154. 'Calcutta Back to Normal', *The Bombay Chronicle*, 26 February 1946.
155. 'Calcutta Still Uneasy', *The Bombay Chronicle*, 24 February 1946.
156. 'Sealdah Station Strike Ends', *The Bombay Chronicle*, 25 February 1946.
157. 'General Strike of Workers and Students', *The Bombay Chronicle*, 26 February 1946.
158. 'Hartal in Madura', *The Bombay Chronicle*, 28 February 1946.
159. Keka Bose, 'Post-War Labour Unrest: A Case Study of the South Indian Railway Strike (1946),' *Proceedings of the Indian History Congress*, vol 49 (1988):505; 'Notices of Strike Served on 8 Major Railways,' *The Bombay Chronicle*, 2 June 1946; 'Decision on Railway Strike Today,' *The Bombay Chronicle*, 5 May 1946; Asaf Ali, 'Speech of the Transport Member Introducing the Railway Budget for 1947–48 on 27th February 1947' (Indian Railway Board, February 27, 1947), https://indianrailways.gov.in/railwayboard/uploads/directorate/finance_budget/Previous%20Budget%20Speeches/19 47-48.pdf.
160. Op cit, 'Post-War Labour Unrest', 505–506.
161. Asaf Ali, 'Speech of the Transport Member Introducing the Railway Budget for 1947--48 on 27th February 1947.'
162. Op cit, 'Post-War Labour Unrest', 506.
163. Op cit, 'Post-War Labour Unrest', 506; 'All South Bound Trains from Madras Canceled', *The Bombay Chronicle*, 25 August 1946; 'SIR Strike', *The Bombay Chronicle*, 26 August 1946.
164. 'Increases for Loyalists', *The Bombay Chronicle*, 25 August 1946.
165. Op cit, 'Post-War Labour Unrest', 507.
166. '30 PC of Employees on Strike on SI Railway', *The Bombay Chronicle*, 27 August 1946.
167. 'Two Communists Arrested', *The Bombay Chronicle*, 29 August 1946;

'20,600 out of 48,500 Involved in SIR strike', *The Bombay Chronicle*, 30 August 1946.

168. 'New Turn in South Indian Railway Strike', *The Bombay Chronicle*, 28 August 1946.
169. Op cit, 'Post-War Labour Unrest', 507–508.
170. 'Three Killed in Firing on Riotous Mob in Trichy', *The Bombay Chronicle*, 6 September 1946.
171. Op cit, 'Post-War Labour Unrest,' 508
172. 'SIR Strike Called Off', *The Bombay Chronicle*, 23 September 1946.
173. *The Bombay Chronicle's* coverage of the strike is particularly illustrative.
174. Op cit, 'Post-War Labour Unrest', 509.
175. Asok Mitra, 'The Great Calcutta Killings of 1946: What Went Before and After,' *Economic and Political Weekly*, vol. 25, no. 5, (3 February 1990): 273-285.
176. U. Bhaskar Rao, *The Story of Rehabilitation* (Ministry of Relief and Rehabilitation, Government of India, 1967), qtd. in Ravinder Kaur, 'The Last Journey: Exploring Social Class in the 1947 Partition Migration,' *Economic and Political Weekly*, vol 41, no 22 (2006): 2222.

3. 'West Bound Refugee Train Passes Amritsar Safely'

177. 'Francis Mudis to Jinnah; 5 September 1947', Kirpal Singh, *Select Documents on the Partition of Punjab 1947: Punjab. Haryana and Himachal, and India and Pakistan*, (Delhi: National Books, 1991) qtd.in Kaur, 'The Last Journey,' 2223
178. Kirpal Singh, *Select Documents on the Partition of Punjab 1947: Punjab. Haryana and Himachal, and India and Pakistan*, (Delhi: National Books, 1991) qtd.in Kaur, 'The Last Journey,' 2223
179. Op cit, 'The Last Journey,' 2221-2228.
180. Navdip Kaur, 'Violence and Migration: A Study of Killing in the Trains During the Partition of Punjab in 1947,' *Proceedings of the Indian History Congress*, vol 72, part 1 (2011): 948.
181. John Mathai, 'Speech of Dr. John Mathai Introducing the Railway Budget for 1948-49, on 24th February 1948' (Government of India, Ministry of Railways (Railway Board), February 24, 1948), https://indianrailways.gov.in/railwayboard/uploads/directorate/finance_budget/Previous%20Budget%20Speeches/19 48-49.pdf.
182. 'Trouble in Amritsar', *The Times of India*, 5 August 1947.
183. 'More Rioting Incidents in Calcutta', *The Bombay Chronicle*, 9 August 1947.
184. '11 Hacked to Death', *The Times of India*, 9 August 1947.
185. 'Mr. Gandhi Tours Riot Hit Areas,' *The Times of India*, 12 August 1947.
186. 'Congress Hindu Sabha Clash,' *The Bombay Chronicle*, 11 August 1947.
187. 'Plans to Send More Troops to Punjab,' *The Times of India*, 17 August 1947.
188. 'Amritsar and Lahore Quiet,' *The Bombay Chronicle*, 20 August 1947.
189. 'Lahore and Amritsar Situation Improves,' *The Bombay Chronicle*, 24 August 1947.
190. 'Three Killed in Train Holdup,' *The Bombay Chronicle*, 25 August 1947.

191. 'Railway Goods Wagons Held Up,' *The Bombay Chronicle*, 28 August 1947.
192. 'Goods Train Burnt Near Delhi,' *The Bombay Chronicle*, 1 September 1947.
193. 'Seven Killed in Attack on Train Near Delhi,' *The Bombay Chronicle*, 29 August 1947.
194. 'Goods Train Burnt Near Delhi,' *The Bombay Chronicle*, 1 September 194.
195. *The Bombay Chronicle* states 'Patll' station, a misprint. 'Attack on Trains: Some Feared Killed,' *The Bombay Chronicle*, 2 September 1947.
196. 'Saboteurs Derail Train Near Shafiabad,' *The Bombay Chronicle*, 4 September 1947.
197. 'Thirty Killed in Train Attack', '200 Killed When Troop Train Crosses Refugee Train,' *The Bombay Chronicle*, 6 September 1947,
198. 'Attack on Passengers at Station,' *The Bombay Chronicle*, 9 September 1947, 5.
199. 'Bombs Found in Calcutta Mail,' *The Bombay Chronicle*, 10 September 1947, 3.
200. 'Attack on Refugee Train', 'Three Shot Dead by Guard of Goods Train,' *The Bombay Chronicle*, 12 September 1947,
201. 'More News from Pakistan,' *The Bombay Chronicle*, 17 September 1947.
202. 'Dehra Ismail Khan Disturbed', 'Bhatinda Incident,' *The Bombay Chronicle*, 17 September 1947.
203. 'Ordinance for Public Safety in Sindh,' *The Bombay Chronicle*, 22 September 1947
204. 'Disturbances in Dehra Dun,' 'Thrown out of Train,' *The Bombay Chronicle*, 25 September 1947.
205. 'Attack on Refugee Train,' *The Bombay Chronicle*, 22 September 1947.
206. 'Wounded Refugees Taken to Hospital,' *The Bombay Chronicle*, 25 September 1947.
207. 'Auchinlek Meets Jinnah,' *The Bombay Chronicle*, 26 September 1947.
208. 'Refugees Raid East Punjab Villages,' *The Bombay Chronicle*, 26 September 1947
209. 'Casualties in Attacks on Refugee Trains,' *The Bombay Chronicle*, 25 September 1947
210. 'West Bound Refugee Train Passes Amritsar Safely,' 'Refugee Train Attacked in East Punjab,' *The Bombay Chronicle*, 26 September 1947.
211. 'Two Hurt in Explosions,' *The Bombay Chronicle*, 29 September 1947.
212. 'Dosabhai Framji Karaka | Making Britain,' *The Open* University, accessed April 4, 2022, https://www.open.ac.uk/researchprojects/makingbritain/content/dosabhai-framji-karaka.
213. D.F. Karaka, 'From One Living Hell to Another,' *The Bombay Chronicle*, 29 September 1947.
214. 'Passengers Attacked in Running Train,' *The Bombay Chronicle*, 15 October 1947.
215. 'Mob Attack Railway Passengers,' *The Bombay Chronicle*, 29 October 1947.
216. 'Arms and Government Property Seized,' *The Bombay Chronicle*, 5 November 1947.
217. 'Refugees Attempt to Derail Train,' *The Bombay Chronicle*, 6 November 1947.

218. 'Bomb Explosion,' *The Bombay Chronicle*, 10 November 1947.
219. See Navdip Kaur, 'Violence and Migration,' and Ravinder Kaur, 'The Last Journey.'
220. Urvashi Butalia, *The Other Side of Silence: Voices from the Partition of India*. Durham, NC: Duke University Press, 2000
221. 'Non-Muslim Staff of N.W. Railway,' *The Times of India*, 3 August 1947.
222. 'Surplus Railwaymen Issue Presents Grave Problem,' *The Times of India*, 5 August 1947.
223. 'Effect of Partition,' *Report by the Railway Board on Indian Railways for1947–1948*, 8.
224. *Report on the Railway Division on Pakistan Railways*, 1947–1948, 4, India Office Records and Private Papers. British Library, London.
225. John Mathai, 'Speech of Dr. John Matthai introducing the Railway Budget for 1948–49, on 24th February 1948,' Budget Speech 1948–49, Indian Railways, 21–22, accessed 20 June 2018, http://www.indianrailways.gov.in/railwayboard/uploads/directorate/finance_budget/Previous%20Budget%20Speech es/1948-49.pdf
226. *Report on the Railway Division on Pakistan Railways*, 1947–1948, 4.
227. 'Non-Muslim Staff of N.W. Railway,' *The Times of India*, 3 August 1947.
228. 'Effect of Partition,' *Report by the Railway Board on Indian Railways for 1947–1948*, 8.
229. *Report on the Railway Division on Pakistan Railways*, 1947–1948, 7.
230. 'Effect of Partition,' *Report by the Railway Board on Indian Railways for 1947–1948*, 13–14.
231. *Report by the Railway Board on Indian Railways for 1948–1949*, 5.
232. 'Effect of Partition,' *Report by the Railway Board on Indian Railways for 1947–1948*, 13–14.
233. 'Customs Examination on Borders with Pakistan,' *Report by the Railway Board on Indian Railways for 1947– 1948*, 14–15.
234. 'Customs Examinations at Borders with India,' *Report on the Railway Division on Pakistan Railways*, 1947– 1948 (Moghulpura (Lahore) and Karachi, Manager of Publications, North-Western Railway Press, 1948, 7.
235. 'Effect of Partition: on Power Position, Rolling Stock, and Workshop Capacity,' *Report by the Railway Board on Indian Railways for 1947–1948*, 12–13; 'Effect of Partition on Power Position, Rolling Stock and Workshop Capacity,' *Report on the Railway Division on Pakistan Railways*, 1947–1948 (Moghulpura [Lahore] and Karachi, Manager of Publications, North-Western Railway Press, 1948), 6.
236. Ibid.
237. 'Effect of Partition: on Power Position, Rolling Stock, and Workshop Capacity,' *Report by the Railway Board on Indian Railways*, 1948–1949, 11.
238. Op cit, 'Non-Muslim Staff of N.W. Railway'
239. 'Effect of Partition on Traffic Arrangements, Routing and Trend of Traffic,' *Report on the Railway Division on Pakistan Railways*, 1948–1949 (Moghulpura (Lahore) and Karachi, Manager of Publications, North-Western Railway Press, 1949), 6.

240. 'Effect of Partition on Traffic arrangements, routing and trend of traffic,' *Report on the Railway Division on Pakistan Railways*, 1948–1949 (Moghulpura (Lahore) and Karachi, Manager of Publications, North-Western Railway Press, 1949), 6.
241. 'Plans to Send More Troops to Punjab,' *The Times of India*, 17 August 1947.
242. 'West Bound Refugee Train Passes Amritsar Safely,' *The Bombay Chronicle*, 26 September 1947.
243. D.V. Reddy, *Inside Story of the Indian Railways*, 140–142.
244. 'Security Measures on Railways,' *Report by the Railway Board on Indian Railways for 1947–1948*, 7.
245. 'Effect of Partition,' *Report by the Railway Board on Indian Railways for 1947–1948*, 13–14.
246. *Report on the Railway Division on Pakistan Railways*, 1947–1948, 4.
247. 'Effect of Partition,' *Report by the Railway Board on Indian Railways for 1947–1948*, 13–14.
248. 'Effect of Partition,' *Report by the Railway Board on Indian Railways for 1947–1948*, 7, 22.
249. *Report by the Railway Board on Indian Railways for 1948–1949*, 5.
250. 'Effect of Partition: on Power Position, Rolling Stock, and Workshop Capacity,' *Report by the Railway Board on Indian Railways*, 1947–1948, 12–13.
251. 'Effect of Partition on Power Position, Rolling Stock and Workshop Capacity,' *Report on the Railway Division on Pakistan Railways*, 1947–1948 (Moghulpura (Lahore) and Karachi, Manager of Publications, North-Western Railway Press, 1948), 6.
252. Vinita Belani, 'A 1947 Partition Tale–Thwarting the Ghost Train,' *India Currents*, 12 March 2018, accessed 18 May 2023.https://indiacurrents.com/thwarting-the-ghost-train-a-1947-partition-tale/.
253. 'Casualties in Attacks on Refugee Trains,' *The Bombay Chronicle*, 25 September 1947.
254. D.V. Reddy, *Inside Story of the Indian Railways*, 140–142.
255. 'Three Killed in Train Holdup,' *The Bombay Chronicle*, 25 August 1947.
256. 'Railway Goods Wagons Held Up,' *The Bombay Chronicle*, 28 August 1947.
257. A. Kalam, *Recollections of a Railwayman*, 35–45.
258. Reddy, *Inside Story of the Indian Railways*, 140–142.
259. 'Saboteurs Derail Train Near Shafiabad,' *The Bombay Chronicle*, 4 September 1947.
260. 'Railwaymen's Assurance to Nehru Government,' *The Bombay Chronicle*, 22 September 1947; 'Railwaymen Not to Take Strike Ballot,' *The Bombay Chronicle*, 2 October 1947.

4. 'This Dawn is Not that Dawn'

261. D.V. Reddy, *Inside Story of the Indian Railways*, 142–143.
262. *Report by the Railway Board on Indian Railways for 1948–1949*, 11–12.

263. Ibid, 12.
264. *Report by the Railway Board on Indian Railways for 1947–1948*, 62–65; *Report by the Railway Board on Indian Railways for 1948–1949*, 69–71; *Report by the Railway Board on Indian Railways for 1949–1950*, 72–73.
265. *Report by the Railway Board, 1947–1948*, 12.
266. *Report by the Railway Board on Indian Railways for 1948–1949*, 10–11.
267. J.N. Sahni, *Indian Railways: One Hundred Years, 1853 to 1953*, (New Delhi: Ministry of Railways, Government of India, 1953), 152, 154.
268. *Report on the Railway Division on Pakistan Railways*, 1947–1948, 4.
269. *Report on the Railway Division on Pakistan Railways*, 1948–1949, 1.
270. *Report on the Railway Division on Pakistan Railways*, 1947–1948, 1–2.
271. Ibid., 22–23.
272. *Report on the Railway Division on Pakistan Railways*, 1948–1949, 29.
273. *Report on the Railway Division on Pakistan Railways*, 1947–1948, 6.
274. Kalam, *Recollections of a Railwayman*, 49.
275. *Report by the Railway Division on Pakistan Railways for 1949–1950*, 6.
276. *Report on the Railway Division on Pakistan Railways*, 1947–1948, 6.
277. *Report on the Railway Division on Pakistan Railways*, 1947–1948, 1.
278. *Report on the Railway Division on Pakistan Railways*, 1947–1948, 2.
279. *Report on the Railway Division on Pakistan Railways*, 1948–1949, 2, 3; *Report on the Railway Division on Pakistan Railways*, 1949–1950, 2, 6.
280. *Report on the Railway Division on Pakistan Railways*, 1947-1948, 5; *Report on the Railway Division on Pakistan Railways*, 1948–1949, 6.
281. Op cit, *Indian Railways: One Hundred Years, 1853 to 1953*, 150–152.
282. Op cit, Mathai, 'Speech of Dr. John Mathai Introducing the Railway Budget for 1948–49,' 24.
283. Op cit, *Indian Railways: One Hundred Years, 1853 to 1953*, 150–152.
284. Ibid, 155–156.
285. Ibid, 156.
286. Ibid, 105–110.
287. Ibid, 105–110.
288. *Report on the Railway Division on Pakistan Railways*, 1948–1949, 2.
289. *Report on the Railway Division on Pakistan Railways*, 1949–1950, 2.
290. *Report on the Railway Division on Pakistan Railways*, 1948–1949, 3.
291. *Report on the Railway Division on Pakistan Railways*, 1948–1949, 2.
292. Kalam, *Recollections of a Railwayman*, 48–53.
293. *Report by the Railway Board on Indian Railways for 1947–1948*, 65; *Report by the Railway Board on Indian Railways for 1948–1949*, 72; *Report by the Railway Board on Indian Railways for 1949–1950*, 74.
294. *Report by the Railway Board on Indian Railways for 1947–1948*, 65–66; *Report by the Railway Board on Indian Railways for 1948–1949*, 72; *Report by the Railway Board on Indian Railways for 1949–1950*, 74.
295. *Report by the Railway Board on Indian Railways for 1947–1948*, 69
296. *Report by the Railway Board on Indian Railways for 1948–1949*, 76.
297. *Report by the Railway Board on Indian Railways for 1949–1950*, 78.
298. Ibid, 78.
299. *Report by the Railway Board for 1947–1948*, 67.

300. Op cit, *Indian Railways: One Hundred Years, 1853 to 1953*, 106.
301. Ibid, 124–125.
302. Ibid, 127
303. *Report by the Railway Board on Indian Railways for 1949–1950*, 79.
304. *Indian Railways: One Hundred Years, 1853 to 1953*, 128.
305. Government of Pakistan, Ministry of Communications (Railway Division), *Report by the Railway Division on Pakistan Railways for 1947–1948* (Karachi: Manager of Publications, 1953), 24.
306. *Report by the Railway Division on Pakistan Railways for 1948–1949*, 30.
307. *Report by the Railway Division on Pakistan Railways for 1949–1950*, 29.
308. *Report by the Railway Division on Pakistan Railways for 1947–1948*, 25.
309. *Report by the Railway Division on Pakistan Railways for 1949–1950*, 30.
310. *Report by the Railway Division on Pakistan Railways for 1947–1948*, 24.
311. *Report by the Railway Division on Pakistan Railways for 1948–1949*, 30.
312. *Report by the Railway Division on Pakistan Railways for 1949–1950*, 29.
313. *Report by the Railway Division on Pakistan Railways for 1947–1948*, 24.
314. *Report by the Railway Division on Pakistan Railways for 1948–1949*, 30.
315. *Report by the Railway Division on Pakistan Railways for 1949–1950*, 29.
316. Ibid, 29–30.
317. *Report by the Railway Board on Indian Railways for 1947–1948*, 62–63.
318. *Report by the Railway Board on Indian Railways for1947–1948*, 68.
319. *Report by the Railway Board on Indian Railways for 1948–1949*, 69.
320. *Report by the Railway Board on Indian Railways for 1949–1950*, 72.
321. *Report by the Railway Board on Indian Railways for 1949–1950*, 76–77.
322. *Report by the Railway Division on Pakistan Railways for 1947–1948*, 22.
323. Ibid.
324. *Report by the Railway Division on Pakistan Railways for 1948–1949*, 29.
325. Ibid.
326. *Report by the Railway Division on Pakistan Railways for 1949–1950*, 29.
327. Sahni, *Indian Railways: One Hundred Years, 1853to1953*, 150-154.
328. *Report by the Railway Division on Pakistan Railways for 1949–1950*, 3.

5. The Specter of Class Conflict

329. Bombay Police, 'Annual Police Administration Report of the Province of Bombay, Including the Railways,' (Government Central Press, 1941), British Library, 18.
330. Bombay Police, 'Annual Police Administration Report of the Province of Bombay Including the Railways for the Year 1947, (Government Central Press, 1950), British Library, 21.
331. D.V. Reddy, *Inside Story of the Indian Railways: Startling Revelations of a Retired Executive*, 161.
332. Ibid, 162.
333. Government of India, Railway Department, Railway Board, *Report by the Railway Board on Indian Railways for 1942–1943*, vol. 1 (Delhi: Manager of Publications, 1944), 31–32.
334. Government of India, Railway Department, Railway Board, *Report by the*

Railway Board on Indian Railways for 1943–1944, vol. 1 (Delhi: Manager of Publications, 1945), 34.

335. Government of India, Railway Department, Railway Board, *Report by the Railway Board on Indian Railways for 1944–1945*, vol. 1 (Delhi: Manager of Publications, 1946), 54.
336. Government of India, Railway Department, Railway Board, *Report by the Railway Board on Indian Railways for 1945–1946*, vol. 1 (Delhi: Manager of Publications, 1947), 56.
337. Government of India, Ministry of Railways (Railway Board), *Report by the Railway Board on Indian Railways for 1946–1947*, vol. 1 (Delhi: Manager of Publications, 1948), 51.
338. Government of India, Ministry of Railways (Railway Board), *Report by the Railway Board on Indian Railways for 1947–1948*, vol. 1 (Delhi: Manager of Publications, 1949), 66.
339. Government of India, Ministry of Railways (Railway Board), *Report by the Railway Board on Indian Railways for 1948–1949*, vol. 1 (Delhi: Manager of Publications, 1949), 73.
340. Government of India, Ministry of Railways (Railway Board), *Report by the Railway Board on Indian Railways for 1949–1950*, vol. 1 (Delhi: Manager of Publications, 1951), 75.
341. Government of Pakistan, Ministry of Communications (Railway Division), *Report by the Railway Division on Pakistan Railways for 1947–1948* (Karachi: Manager of Publications, 1953), 24.
342. Government of Pakistan, Ministry of Communications (Railway Division), *Report by the Railway Division on Pakistan Railways for 1948–1949* (Karachi: Manager of Publications, n.d.), 30.
343. Shashi Tharoor, 'But What about the Railways...? "The Myth of Britain's Gifts to India",' *The Guardian*, March 8, 2017, accessed 19 May 2023, https://www.theguardian.com/world/2017/mar/08/india-britain-empire-railways- myths-gifts.
344. Ibid, 160–161.
345. Bombay Police, 'Annual Police Administration Report of the Province of Bombay, Including the Railways,' 44– 45.
346. Government of India, Railway Department, Railway Board, 'Railway Accidents, No. 27'
347. Government of India, Railway Department, Railway Board, 'Railway Accidents, No. 28' (Manager of Publications, 1941), British Library, 4–6.
348. Reddy, *Inside Story of the Indian Railways*, 157–158.
349. Ibid, 158.
350. Ibid, 158–159.
351. Ibid.
352. Ibid, 165.
353. Ibid, 166.
354. Ibid, 161.
355. Ibid, 167–168.
356. Ibid, 169.
357. Ibid, 169, 173.
358. Ibid, 169–170.

359. Ibid, 174.
360. Ibid, 172–178.
361. Indian Railway Board, *Annual Report of the Indian Railway Board*, 1940–1941, 74.
362. 'Stay-in-Strike by G.I.P. Rly. Workshop Men,' *The Bombay Chronicle*, 7 November 1941
363. Ibid.
364. '11,000 men on Stay-in-Strike,' *The Bombay Chronicle*, 12 November 1941
365. 'GIP Railway to Cancel Lock-out,' *The Bombay Chronicle*, 16 November 1941.
366. 'Railway Workers Strike to be Called Off,' *The Bombay Chronicle*, 18 November 1941.
367. Nrisingha Chakrabarty, *History of Railway Trade Union Movement: A Study* (New Delhi: Center of Indian Trade Unions, 1985), 42–43.
368. 'Call off Strike in GIP Workshops,' *The Bombay Chronicle*, 18 November 1941.
369. *Report by the Railway Board on Indian Railways for 1948–1949*, 68–69.
370. Ibid, 68.
371. Ibid, 68.
372. Ibid, 68–69.
373. Ibid, 69.
374. '24-Hour General Strike on S. I. Railway,' *The Bombay Chronicle*, 10 May 1948.
375. 'Train Services in South not Seriously Affected,' *The Bombay Chronicle*, 11 May 1948.
376. 'Calicut Strike,' *The Bombay Chronicle*, 11 May 1948.
377. 'Strike on GIP Railway,' *The Bombay Chronicle*, 12 May 1948; 'GIPR Casual Labor Strike,' *The Bombay Chronicle*, 16 May 1948; 'Strike on GIPR called off,' *The Bombay Chronicle*, 23 May 1948.

Conclusion

378. See US Department of Transportation, 'Rail Passenger Travel: Not Seasonally Adjusted,' accessed 19 May 2023, https://data.bts.gov/Research-and-Statistics/Rail-Passenger-Travel-Not-Seasonally-Adjusted-/x4gw-ya6n; 'US Ton- Miles, Freight,' Bureau of Transportation Statistics, accessed 19 May 2023, https://www.bts.gov/content/us-ton- miles-freight.
379. Michael Sainato, 'US Railroad Workers Prepare for Strike as Rail companies See Record Profits,' *The Guardian,* US Edition, 14 September 2022, accessed 19 May 2023, https://www.theguardian.com/business/2022/sep/14/us-railroad-strike-union-pacific-bnsf.
380. Michael Baudendistel, 'What is Precision Scheduled Railroading,' *Freight Waves*, 9 January 2020, accessed 19 May 2023, https://www.freightwaves.com/news/what-is-precision-scheduled-railroading-psr
381. Timothy Noah, 'Strike Settled: Now Let's Nationalize the Railroads,' *The New Republic*, 16 September 2022, accessed 19 May 2023, https://newrepublic.com/article/167758/nationalize-railroads-biden-train-strike

382. Ibid.
383. 'British Rail Workers Lead Fight Against Cost of Living Crisis and Anti-Worker Policies,' *Peoples Dispatch*, 24 June 2022, accessed 19 May 2023, https://peoplesdispatch.org/2022/06/24/british-rail-workers-lead-fight-against- cost-of-living-crisis-and-anti-worker-policies/
384. Kate Nicholson, 'BBC Question Time Takes a Curious Turn as RMT is Compared to...The Dinosaurs,' *Huffpost*, 24 June 2022, accessed 19 May 2023, https://www.huffingtonpost.co.uk/entry/bbc-question-time-guest-compares-rmt-dinosaurs-mick-lynch_uk_62b58389e4b0cdccbe69d94e
385. 'UK Rail Workers Support US Railroad Struggle,' *World Socialist Website*, 15 September 2022, accessed 19 May 2023, https://www.wsws.org/en/articles/2022/09/15/soli-s15.html
386. 'Ten Thesis on Marxism and Decolonization,' Tricontinental Institute of Social Research, accessed 19 May 2023, https://thetricontinental.org/dossier-ten-theses-on-marxism-and-decolonisation/

Bibliography

'3000 Dead in Indian Train Massacre,' *The Advertiser*, 25 September 1947. Trove, National Library of Australia. https://trove.nla.gov.au/newspaper/article/36001501 (Accessed 19 May 2023)

Aggarwal, Priya. 'The Role of Indian Railways in COVID-19 Crisis Management,' Global Railway Review. https://www.globalrailwayreview.com/article/123127/indian-railways-covid19-crisis-management/ (Accessed 8 December 2021)

Ali, Asaf. 'Speech of the Transport Member introducing the Railway Budget for 1947–48 on 27th February 1947.' Budget Speech 1947-48, Indian Railways. http://www.indianrailways.gov.in/railwayboard/uploads/directorate/finance_budget/Previous%20Budget%20Speeches/1947-48.pdf (Accessed 19 June 2018)

Badigannavar Vidu, John Kelly and Manik Kumar, 'Turning the Tide? Economic Reforms and Union Revival in India,' *Industrial Relations Journal,* vol 52, no. 4 (2021): 364–85.

Baudendistel, Michael. 'What is Precision Scheduled Railroading,' *Freight Waves*, 9 January 2020. https://www.freightwaves.com/news/what-is-precision-scheduled-railroading-psr (Accessed 19 May 2023)

Bear Laura. *Lines of the Nation: Indian Railway Workers, Bureaucracy, and the Intimate Historical Self*. New York: Columbia University Press, 2007.

Behal, Rana and Sabyasachi Bhattacharya. *The Vernacularization of labour Politics*. New Delhi: Tulika Books. 2016.

Bose, Aniruddha. *Class Conflict and Modernization in India: The Raj and the Calcutta Waterfront (1860–1910)*. New York: Routledge, 2018.

Bose, Keka. 'The Role of the Working Class in the Political Upsurges in Undivided India (1945-46),' *Proceedings of the Indian History Congress*, vol 51 (1990): 619–24.

——. 'Post-War Labour Unrest: A Case Study of the South Indian Railway Strike (1946),' *Proceedings of the Indian History Congress*, vol 49 (1988): 505–10.

'British Rail Workers Lead Fight Against Cost of Living Crisis and Anti-Worker Policies,' *Peoples Dispatch*, 24 June 2022. https://peoplesdispatch.

org/2022/06/24/british-rail-workers-lead-fight-against-cost-of-living-crisis-and-anti-worker-policies/ (Accessed 19 May 2023)

Brown, Judith, 'India', *The Oxford Companion to World War II*, eds. I.C.B. Dear and M.R.D. Foot. New York: Oxford University Press, 2003.

Butalia, Urvashi. *The Other Side of Silence: Voices from the Partition of India.* Durham, NC: Duke University Press, 2000.

Census Organization (Pakistan). *Census of Pakistan 1951*. Vol. 1. Karachi: Manager of Publications, Government of Pakistan, 1954.

Chakrabarty, Nrisingha. *History of Railway Trade Union Movement: A Study.* New Delhi: Centre of Indian Trade Unions, 1985.

Chatterjee, Arup. *Purveyors of Destiny: A Cultural Biography of the Indian Railways.* New Delhi: Bloomsbury, 2017.

Debroy, Bibek, Sanjay Chadha, and Vidya Krishnamurthi. *Indian Railways: The Weaving of a National Tapestry*. New Delhi: Penguin Random House India, 2017.

Gidla, Sujata. *Ants Among Elephants: An Untouchable Family and the Making of Modern India.* New York: Farrar, Straus & Giroux, 2017.

Gilmour, David. *The British in India: A Social History of the Raj.* New York: Farrar, Straus and Giroux, 2018.

Gopalaswami, R.A. 'Table B-III Employers, Employees, Independent Workers in Industries and Services by Divisions and Sub-Divisions,' *Census of India, 1951*. v. 1, India, Pt. II-B, Economic Tables (General Population), 1954.

Government of India. *Report of the Indian Railway Inquiry Committee, 1947.* https://archive.org/stream/in.ernet.dli.2015.23128/2015.23128.Report-Of-The-Indian-Railway-Enquiry-Committee-1947_djvu.txt (Accessed 1 February 2018)

Government of India, Railway Department, Railway Board, 'Railway Accidents, No. 27' (Manager of Publications, 1940), The British Library, London.

Hurd, John and Ian J. Kerr. *India's Railway History: A Research Handbook.* Handbook of Oriental Studies, Section 2, South Asia Series. Leiden, NL: Brill, 2012.

Hutchins, Francis G. *India's Revolution: Gandhi and the Quit India Movement.* Cambridge, MA: Harvard University Press, 1973.

India, Census Commissioner, and India, Office of the Registrar General. *Census of India.* Volume 1. Part 2b. New Delhi: Census Commissioner. 1951.

Kalam, Abdul. *Recollections of a Railwayman.* Karachi: Royal Book Company, 1995.

Kaur, Navdip. 'Violence and Migration: A Study of Killing in the Trains During the Partition of Punjab in 1947,' *Proceedings of the Indian History Congress*, vol 72, part 1 (2011): 947–54.

Kaur, Ravinder. 'The Last Journey: Exploring Social Class in the 1947 Partition Migration,' *Economic and Political Weekly*, vol 41, no 22 (2006): 2221-28.

Kerr, Ian J. *27 Down: New Departures in Indian Railway Studies*. New Delhi: Orient Longman. 2005.

——. *Building Railways of the Raj: 1850–1900*. New Delhi: Oxford University Press, 1997.

Khan, Yasmin. *The Raj at War: A People's History of India's Second World War*. London: Penguin Random House. 2015.

——. *India at War: The Subcontinent and the Second World War*. New York: Oxford University Press. 2015.

Khaitan Urvi. 'Women beneath the Surface: Coal and the Colonial State in India during the Second World War,' *War & Society* vol 39, no. 3, (2 July 2020): 171-188. https://doi.org/10.1080/07292473.2020.1790473 (Accessed 17 May 2023)

Malik, M. B. K. *Hundred Years of Pakistan Railways: Pakistan Western Railways* 1861–1961, *Pakistan Western Railway* 1862-1962. Karachi: Ministry of Railways and Communications (Railway Board) Government of Pakistan, 1962.

Mathai, John. 'Speech of Dr. John Mathai Introducing the Railway Budget for 1948–49, on 24 February 1948.' Indian Railways. http://www.indianrailways.gov.in/railwayboard/uploads/directorate/finance_budget/Previous%20Budget%20Speeches/1948-49.pdf (Accessed 20 June 2018)

Ministry of Labour, Government of India. *Annual Report on the Working of the Payment of Wages Act, (IV) of 1936 on Railways including a Note on the Employment of Children Act, 1938*. 1940–1941, 1945–1946, 1946–1947. Manager of Publications, Government of India Press, New Delhi, 1941-1949. India Office Records and Private Papers. British Library, London.

Mishra, Dinesh Kumar. 'The Bihar Flood Story', *Economic and Political Weekly*, vol 32, no. 35 (5 September 1997): 2206–17

Mitra, Asok. 'The Great Calcutta Killings of 1946: What Went Before and After,' *Economic and Political Weekly*, vol. 25, no. 5, (3 February 1990): 273-285.

Mukherjee, Janam. 'Japan Attacks'. *Calcutta: The Stormy Decades*. Tanika Sarkar and Sekhar Bandyopadhyay (eds.) London and New York: Routledge. 2018.

Nicholson, Kate. 'BBC Question Time Takes a Curious Turn as RMT is Compared to...The Dinosaurs,' *Huffpost*, 24 June 2022, https://www.huffingtonpost.co.uk/entry/bbc-question-time-guest-compares-rmt-dinosaurs-mick-lynch_uk_62b58389e4b0cdccbe69d94e (Accessed 19 May 2023).

Noah, Timothy 'Strike Settled: Now Let's Nationalize the Railroads,' *The New Republic*, 16 September 2022. https://newrepublic.com/article/167758/nationalize-railroads-biden-train-strike (Accessed 19 May 2023)

Parthasarathi, Prasannan. 'Indian Labour History,' *International Labour and Working Class History*, vol 82. (2012): 127–135. http://dx.doi.org/10.1017/S0147547912000208 (Accessed 11 September 2018)

Pollack, Ricardo, director. *Partition: The Day India Burned*. British Broadcasting Corporation, 2007.

Railway Board, Government of India. *Report by the Railway Board on Indian Railways*. 1938–1939 to 1949–1950. Manager of Publications, Government of India Press, New Delhi, 1940-1951, India Office Records and Private Papers. The British Library, London.

Railway Board of India, *Full Steam Ahead: The Indian Railways–Their Problems and their Work, and their Future Plans*. New Delhi: Press Information Bureau, Government of India, for the Railway Board, 1945.

Railway Division, Government of Pakistan. *Report on the Railway Division on Pakistan Railways*, 1947–1948 to 1949-1950. Moghulpura (Lahore) and Karachi, Manager of Publications, North Western State Railway Press, 1948-1951. India Office Records and Private Papers. The British Library, London.

Raghavan, Srinath. *India's War: World War II and the Making of Modern South Asia*. New York: Basic Books, 2016.

Reddy, D. Narasimha. 'Unionization in Indian Railways'. *Economic and Political Weekly*, vol 14, no. 39 (29 September 1979): 1651–56.

Reddy, D.V. *Inside Story of the Indian Railways: Startling Revelations of a Retired Executive*. Madras: M. Seshachalam & Co., 1975.

Richardson, William. 'The Mutiny of the Royal Indian Navy at Bombay in February 1946', *The Mariner's Mirror*, vol 79, no. 2 (1 May 1993): 192–201. https://doi.org/10.1080/00253359.1993.10656448 (Accessed 18 May 2023)

Sahni, J. N. *Indian Railways: One Hundred Years 1853–1953* New Delhi: Ministry of Railways (Railway Board), Government of India, 1953.

Sainato, Michael 'US Railroad Workers Prepare for Strike as Rail companies See Record Profits,' *The Guardian*, US Edition, 14 September 2022. https://www.theguardian.com/business/2022/sep/14/us-railroad-strike-union-pacific-bnsf (Accessed 19 May 2023)

Sanchez, Andrew and Christian Strumpell. 'Anthropological and Historical Perspectives on India's Working Classes.' *Modern Asian Studies*, vol 48, no 5 (September 2014): 1233–1241.

Sen, Amartya. 'The Great Bengal Famine,' *Poverty and Famines: An Essay on Entitlement and Deprivation*. Oxford: Oxford University Press, 1983.

Sinha, Nitin. 'The World of Workers' Politics: Some Issues of Railway Workers in Colonial India 1918–1922,' *Modern Asian Studies*, vol 42, no 5, (September 2008): 999–1033.

Taneja, Kabir. 'A Train to Partition: My Grandfather's Narrow Escape from Death was a Small Triumph for Humanity,' *Huffpost* 15 August 2017 https://www.huffpost.com/archive/in/entry/a-train-to-partition-my-grandfather-s-narrow-escape-from-death_in_5c10f2d0e4b085260ba754fc (Accessed 17 May 2023).

Tharoor, Shashi. 'But What about the Railways...? "The Myth of Britain's Gifts to India",' *The Guardian*, 8 March 2017. https://www.theguardian.com/ world/2017/mar/08/india-britain-empire-railways-myths-gifts (Accessed 19 May 2023)

The Bombay Chronicle, 1939–1949. Online Newspaper Collection. Granth

Sanjeevani. Asiatic Society of Mumbai. https://granthsanjeevani.com/jspui/collectionView?id=7&filtername=publisher&filtertype=equals&filterquery=The+Bombay+Chronicle (Accessed 19 May 2023)

The Times of India, 1939–1949. Proquest Historical Newspapers Database, The Pennsylvania State University Libraries. https://libraries.psu.edu/databases/psu01832 (Accessed 19 May 2023).

'Ten Thesis on Marxism and Decolonization,' Tricontinental Institute of Social Research. https://thetricontinental.org/dossier-ten-theses-on-marxism-and-decolonisation/ (Accessed 19 May 2023)

Tripathi, Amales. *Indian National Congress and the Struggle for Freedom: 1885–1947*. New Delhi: Oxford University Press, 2014.

'UK Rail Workers Support US Railroad Struggle,' *World Socialist Website*, 15 September 2022. https://www.wsws.org/en/articles/2022/09/15/soli-s15.html (Accessed 19 May 2023)

Index